FRIEND
AHOLIC

ALSO BY ELIZABETH DAY

FICTION
Scissors, Paper, Stone
Home Fires
Paradise City
The Party
Magpie

NON-FICTION
How to Fail: Everything I've Ever Learned
From Things Going Wrong
Failosophy: A Handbook For When Things
Go Wrong
Failosophy for Teens

FRIEND AHOLIC

CONFESSIONS OF A FRIENDSHIP ADDICT

ELIZABETH DAY

4th ESTATE • London

4th Estate
An imprint of HarperCollins*Publishers*
1 London Bridge Street
London SE1 9GF

www.4thestate.co.uk

HarperCollins*Publishers*
Macken House, 39/40 Mayor Street Upper
Dublin 1, D01 C9W8 Ireland

First published in Great Britain in 2023 by 4th Estate

2

Copyright © Elizabeth Day 2023

ISBN 978-0-00-837489-1 (hardback)
ISBN 978-0-00-837490-7 (trade paperback)

Set in Adobe Garamond Pro
Printed and bound in the UK using 100%
renewable electricity at CPI Group (UK) Ltd

MIX
Paper | Supporting
responsible forestry
FSC™ C007454

For Emma, my best friend.

CONTENTS

INTRODUCTION

I was once told about a man who despised small talk. If he found himself at a party, he would never ask about someone's job or comment on the weather or enquire how long it had taken a guest to get there and what route they had taken and did-they-avoid-the-traffic-on-the-A40. Instead, his opening gambit was always: 'Aside from work and family, what's your passion?'

When I was first told this story, I admired the man's inventiveness. But I couldn't immediately think of how I would answer. What *was* my passion?

As a teenager, I had been taught the importance of having hobbies to put on your CV in order to show you were a well-rounded person. I had struggled to scrape any together. I went to one salsa class and hated it, but I whacked it on my CV to placate the careers adviser. My father had taken me abseiling as a child, so I added that into the mix. I played the trumpet and put that down too. 'Film' I typed because it's true that I did like going to the cinema and ordering a medium bucket of sweet and salty popcorn. The result was that any prospective employer would consider me a well-qualified salsa-dancing, trumpet-playing, cinema-going abseiler. But I couldn't say that I felt *passionate* about any of it (other than the popcorn). Besides, a passion is different from a hobby, isn't it? The former can be a concept, a feeling, a person; the latter involves some form of activity, occasionally with crampons.

Then, two years ago, the answer came to me with sudden clarity. We were living through a pandemic and, like millions of people around the globe, I went from having an active social life to none at all. I missed my friends with startling acuteness. I missed their faces, their hugs, the smell of their particular perfume. I missed our chats. I missed making sense of things by talking to them.

I had discovered my passion: it was friendship.

My friends had seen me through life's unexpected turns. They had been there to support me through break-ups, fertility issues, marriage, divorce, miscarriage, job changes, home moves and more. They had given me support and kindness and good advice. And when things had gone well, they'd celebrated with me. We had laughed and cried and walked hand in hand through both hardship and success.

There wasn't any language I could reach for to describe precisely what they meant to me. Most of the vocabulary around love had been co-opted for romantic relationships. I told my friends I loved them all the time. But of course I wasn't *in* love with them. It was more nuanced than that. I was passionate about them.

Like many passions, it had grown to obsess me. Looking back, I realised that I loved the feeling of connection so much I came to rely on it. I sought out new friendships again and again and again. I would meet a person and instantly want to bond with them in some small way. We would fall into conversation and I knew that if I listened closely enough, I would be able to find something we had in common: a shared sense of humour or a mutual liking for a particular book or song or TV show. I would get a buzz from that moment of exchange; a hit of pure friendship adrenalin. In that moment, I would feel worthwhile and liked and accepted. I wanted more of it. Then I *needed* more of it. Then it became something I relied on for my own self-worth. *I must be OK*, the reasoning went, *I've got so many friends!*

At some point in my late thirties, it started to feel unsustainable. I found myself unable to keep up with all my friendships in the way that I wanted to. There wasn't enough time to be there for everyone and still maintain a functioning life. It meant that I became a conspicuously less good friend because I was spreading myself too thinly. I was trying not to let anyone down, which ensured inevitably that I did. I said yes to invitations and dinners and shopping trips and weddings and birthdays and baby showers because I was worried a friend might be disappointed with me if I didn't. I was indiscriminate in my attentions. The most important thing, it seemed to me, was to keep saying yes in order to keep the friendships afloat. If I didn't manage that, I would be deemed unlikeable. I would be excommunicated from the circle of the sociable. And if I had no friends, I would have to look honestly at myself. I would have to confront the existential loneliness of the unloveable. That felt scary.

It turns out I wasn't just passionate about friendship: I was addicted to it. I had a physical and emotional dependence. I had an urge to pursue it, even when it came at a damaging cost to my own peace of mind. I was, in short, a friendaholic.

You might be reading this and thinking 'well, too many friends hardly seems like a problem'. You might be reaching for your metaphorical tiny violin and your imaginary crocodile to cry the requisite tears. And you'd be partially right: having a wide circle of acquaintances can be a wonderful thing, especially when the alternative is enforced isolation. There are those who suffer from crippling social anxiety, who have communication difficulties or live with an array of mental health conditions. They can struggle to leave the house, let alone make friends. A 2017 report published by the counselling service Relate found that 13 per cent of people have no friends at all.[1] A lack of social interaction can be just as bad for your health as smoking fifteen cigarettes a day, and it can be twice as harmful to your life expectancy as obesity.[2]

But if having no friends decreases the quality – and length – of your life, having too many friends also has a negative impact. Researchers studying adolescent friendships have found that those with either too large or too small a social network both have higher levels of depressive symptoms.[3] People aged fifty or over from across Europe display a similar pattern: depression is minimised when individuals have four to five close relationships and engage in social activities on a weekly basis. Any more than this, and the benefits decline, disappear altogether or become actively disadvantageous. This downward spiral is especially marked in those who have seven or more close relationships. The demands of maintaining those friendships were linked to an upswing in depressive symptoms.[4]

And while there is a widely held assumption that someone with lots of friends must be a person worth being friends *with*, it turns out the opposite is true: people prefer to befriend someone with a relatively small social circle, rightly intuiting that if someone has an overabundance of friends, their ability to reciprocate in any meaningful or reliable way will be severely diminished.[5]

All this time I'd been busily making and maintaining connections and I'd actually undermined the thing that was most important to me. I'd become a worse friend to the few who really counted in my desperation to be accepted by the many I barely knew.

It wasn't, in fact, that I had too many friends, it was that I'd misunderstood the fundamental concept of friendship, which is that it should be stable, reciprocal and attentive. And for the purpose of clarity, my definition of a friend is someone you voluntarily want to spend time with, to whom you are not attached through familial bonds and with whom you don't have a sexual or romantic relationship. A true friendship, to my mind, is founded on mutual respect, support, affection and kindness. You can't be those things to everyone who enters your orbit unless you first work out a way to reconstruct the space–time continuum.

But understanding that you might be addicted to friendship does not mean you know how to cure yourself. I had no idea how to course-correct. I did not know where to look for resources, for understanding or for a lexicon of friendship itself. I didn't really know what friendship *was*. It was a term so diffuse as to be rendered almost meaningless. Yet, for me, it simultaneously encapsulated all that was most meaningful and this also rendered it beyond the grasp of mere words.

So I did what I always do when I try to make sense of the world: I spoke to my friends. This book is the result. It is an attempt to fill in some of the gaps and provide some of the words. It is a journey of discovery, with a starting point of curiosity, and as such it will not have all the answers. It might not have any. But I hope it asks some interesting questions and contains some thoughtful jumping-off points for bigger conversations.

There are so many ways to be a friend that it's impossible to do justice to them all, especially because attitudes to friendship diverge according to background, upbringing, age and geography. Ghanaians are more likely to advocate caution towards making friends and to emphasise the need for practical assistance, for instance. Americans, by contrast, have larger friendship networks and are more likely to emphasise companionship and emotional support.[6] Chinese adolescents are concerned with the moral quality of close friendship whereas their Western counterparts focus predominantly on interaction, intimacy and keeping promises.[7] The British and Australians value friends who are alike in outlook, with whom they can bond over similarities. In India, the Middle East and Southeast Asia, people are more likely to say that 'a large social network' is an essential quality to have in a best friend.[8] In Kazakhstan, the nineteenth-century poet and philosopher Abai Qunanbaiuly had this to say about how to recognise true companionship: 'A false friend is like a shadow: when the sun shines on you, you can't get rid of him, but when clouds gather over you, he is nowhere to be seen.'[9]

Friendship is highly valued in various religious traditions. In Islam, the importance of surrounding ourselves with good company is emphasised as a necessary social and spiritual construct. The Hadith encourages us to 'try to have as many as possible true friends, for they are the supplies in joy and the shelters in misfortunes'.[10] One of the foundational principles of Christianity is to 'do unto others as you would have them do unto you'.[11] In the gospels, Jesus prepares his disciples for his impending arrest and death by saying that 'greater love has no one than this, that someone lay down his life for his friends'.[12]

In Buddhism, a true friend is someone with the compassion and courage to tell us even those things we would rather not hear, with the Buddha quoted as saying that: 'Admirable friendship, admirable companionship, admirable camaraderie is actually the whole of the holy life.'[13]

But if most religions agree on the virtue of friendship, the approach to it differs according to age group. Gen

Zedders (born between 1996 and 2006) and Millennials (born between 1979 and 1995) are more practised in the art of internet friendships: 33 per cent of them feel loved after interacting with a friend online, while only 18 per cent of those born between 1944 and 1964 feel the same.[14]

There is no single work on friendship that could accurately convey this multi-faceted magnitude, which is why this book is, by necessity, a personal take.

This means that my perceptions are informed by my life which, broadly speaking, has been a very fortunate one. I am grateful to live in an era when past injustices and systemic inequalities are beginning to be addressed and I wholeheartedly support the idea that people like me must be aware of privilege and the advantages it has given us. Part of this privilege means acknowledging that I cannot convey every different experience of life with equal authority – and it would be ham-fisted of me to try. Where necessary, I have asked for contributions from individuals who can speak far more eloquently to the things I cannot.

We should all be allowed to tell our stories. And stories, by their nature, are specific. So, yes, this is a personal book, with personal reflections, insights and research. Along the way, I have been lucky enough to interview a great many people with wise and interesting things to say, including five of my dearest friends, each of whom represents some different, integral aspect of what friendship means to me. You'll meet Joan, Sathnam, Sharmaine, Clemmie and Emma. And there are first-person glimpses into what friendship means to others – from a neurodivergent Iraqi woman to a paraplegic film-maker in her thirties and an eighty-year-old living with a terminal illness. They all have their own extraordinary stories of friendship to tell. As do you. Perhaps the following chapters will inspire you to tell them.

All of which is to say: I hope this book is encompassing, inclusive, generous and wholehearted; that it keeps you company and entertains you. I hope you are seen in its pages and that it helps you understand your own passions. I hope, in short, that it feels like the best kind of companion.

And if it doesn't? That's OK too. As I'm learning, we don't *have* to be friends.

1.
PANDEMIC

What Lockdown Taught Me about Friendship

There is a car park in a drive-through Starbucks that will forever hold a special place in my heart. It's located just off the A3, one of those modest roads out of London with pretensions: not quite a motorway but somewhat more chic than a standard dual carriageway. The Starbucks itself is a low-slung, single-storey building painted a slate grey that a posh paint brand would probably call 'Pigeon Breath'. If you google it, which I had to do for directions, you will find that it has a 2.5 star rating on Tripadvisor. The reviews that customers have gone to the trouble of writing are quite disparate in tone. One is entitled 'Shambles of a coffee stop'. Another has criticised the breakfast roll, claiming 'The Smell [capitals, reviewer's own] upon opening was disgusting'. If you keep scrolling down, you'll get to a man who is delighted that there is 'loads of parking even for long vans', so I suppose it all depends on personal proclivities.

I have not left an online review for this Starbucks, but if I did it would be a rave. For it was here, in May 2020, that I saw my best friend Emma for the first time in two and a half months. We had, like so many others, been separated by the Covid-19 pandemic. The first national lockdown had been imposed some weeks previously. The government announced on 16 March that all unnecessary social contact should cease. By 23 March, the then Prime Minister Boris Johnson gave a televised address in which he instructed the British people to 'stay at home'. We were allowed out only for one form of exercise a day, he told us. Gatherings of more than two people from different households were banned. Non-essential shops were told to close. Weddings and funerals were immediately halted. We shut our doors that night on a very different world. The worst part was that no one knew what was to come.

In times of crisis, I have routinely turned to my best friend. But this was a situation where I knew I would be unable to hug her for an unidentified period of time. I couldn't just catch the train to go and visit, safe in the knowledge that she would already have stocked the kitchen cupboards with my favourite foodstuffs (namely crumpets and Marmite). She couldn't come up to see me and spend the night in the spare room which she claimed – quite rightly – as hers and subsequently felt aggrieved any time we had other guests who slept there. We couldn't sit next to each other on the sofa, analysing the finer nuances of *Married at First Sight Australia* as one of us reached out her arm to be lightly stroked by the tips of the other's fingers.

Knowing this wasn't going to be possible for the foreseeable future made us both feel untethered, even a bit panicked.

Emma and I have been best friends since meeting in freshers' week at university. She was funny, smart, half Swedish and popular. I was unsure of myself and had sprained my ankle after the Lacrosse Club fed me one too many vodka jellies and encouraged me to run for the ball while wearing high-heeled boots on the college bar's concrete forecourt (which, if anyone reading this is tempted to try it, is definitely Not A Good Idea).

Emma had long, curly blonde hair. I sported an ill-advised brunette crop – the legacy of an over-enthusiastic Cape Town hairdresser I'd met on my gap year. It took me several years to grow that crop out, by which time I'd burned through approximately 570 hair clips from Claire's Accessories and Emma and I had bonded over our shared talent for recalling word-perfect dialogue from the first *Austin Powers* film.

I still consider it an extraordinary stroke of good fortune that I met Emma, let alone that I somehow bamboozled her into becoming my best friend. What were the chances that the extraordinary randomness of the universe had led us both to that point? What serendipitous magic ensured that her Scandinavian forebears passed down a chain of genetic chromosomes to her mother Ingrid that would mesh so perfectly with the DNA of Keith, her British veterinarian father, and form the foundational structure of this uniquely special human? How was it that despite our different backgrounds and being raised in entirely different parts of the country and wanting to study different A levels and different degree subjects, we still ended up meeting and falling in platonic love?

It was gorgeous happenstance, as it is for anyone who is lucky enough to meet a kindred spirit, and the frequency with which this occurs is in itself a kind of beauty. For while most of us only ever anticipate meeting a tiny handful of romantic partners (and, ideally, one true soulmate, according to Mills & Boon and the legacy of Victorian puritanism), we are expected to fling ourselves into multiple friendships throughout the course of our lives.

We do not have to be monogamous with friendship. In fact, people think it's odd if you are. Imagine someone saying during the course of a conversation 'I only have one friend'. You'd probably think there was something a bit strange about them, wouldn't you? Whereas to say you only have one spouse at any given time is not only socially acceptable but the Westernised default, unless you're a Mormon.

My friendship with Emma has sustained me through some of the toughest periods of my life – miscarriage, divorce, illness – as well as being one of the greatest sources of joy. Before I met my husband, Emma was the person I most wanted to spend my time with. She understands me better than I do myself, partly because she's known me longer than most and partly because she's a psychotherapist, so is professionally qualified to call me out on my bullshit.

Of course, as time has moved on, so have we. When she was twenty-seven, she got married to a lovely man and they are still together. I ricocheted from one relationship to the next, before ending up divorced at the age of thirty-six. After my divorce, I set about putting all I had learned about dysfunctional relationships to good use by ignoring it and falling into a rebound that lasted two years before ending dramatically just before my thirty-ninth birthday. By the time I met Justin, my now-husband, on an app,[15] I had lost so much faith in my own judgement that one of the first things I did after a few weeks of dating was ask him to have dinner with me and Emma. That way, I could get her eyes on him and she could tell me what she thought. I imagined her silently raising or lowering her thumb like a Roman senator as he ordered his starter. She didn't actually do this, but she did send me a thumbs-up emoji the following day which was all I needed to know. Justin didn't realise he was sitting a test (I wasn't going to tell him, are you mad? No, I would just leave it a few years and then write about it in a book), but luckily he passed and I felt able to carry on getting to know him, with full confidence.

If anything, Emma and I have become closer over the years, even though there are things that set us apart. Geography, for one – we don't live in the same city. Then there are family responsibilities: she has two children; I have a ginger cat. She is no longer blonde, having reverted to her natural darker colouring. But the nice thing is that I am still brunette and the older we get, the more people tell us we look like sisters.

Before lockdown, it wasn't that we were seeing each other every single day. Nor were we talking every single day, because neither of us likes a phone call when a lengthy text or voice note will do just as well. But knowing that we *could* see each other if we wanted gave us both a sense of security. When lockdown happened, that safety net was ripped from under us. We couldn't have seen each other even if we'd wanted to. And we did want to. We longed for it. We missed each other with a numb, foggy sadness. We missed each other so much, in fact, that we broke our usual communication rules and began FaceTiming. It wasn't that bad, it turned out. It was actually quite nice.

We even started doing the same live online yoga class together on Saturday mornings, but after a while the pleasure started to pall. It turned out that peering into Zoom squares to see each other's downward dogs and crow poses as Bart, the instructor, gradually became more uptight about our lack of attention to detail, had a finite appeal.

'Rachel, left leg forward,' I would hear him say as I tried to float effortfully into Half Moon. 'No, not the right leg, Rachel. The left leg.' Bart's voice would become tighter and more clipped. As I glanced at him through the screen, I could feel his attempt to project external Zen while his interior organs melted into a lava of inexpressible rage. 'Left one. That's it. Look at me. No, Rachel, not that one. The left leg.' By this stage, both Emma and I would be wanting to scream 'THE LEFT FUCKING LEG, RACHEL' and any hopes of leaving the class refreshed and enlightened would be dashed. I really hope Rachel worked it out in the end.

Emma and I felt a bit silly about missing each other so much because it wasn't *that* different from our usual level of interaction but I suppose, if I look back now, we were scared. We'd never experienced a global pandemic before, with an unknown virus running rampant across the globe and killing millions of people with unexplained ferocity. None of us had. And when you're feeling frightened, even if you can't acknowledge that fear to yourself, you turn to the people you love and trust most in the world.

For me that was Emma. Which brings us, poetically, to the Cobham drive-through Starbucks. After a six-week, near-total lockdown, restrictions were very slightly relaxed. Some cafes opened for collection only. Emma knew how much I'd missed my regular cup of Starbucks jasmine tea[16] and so she started googling to find a place we could meet that was equidistant for us both and that would provide us with refreshments and enable us to hang out in the car park afterwards like a pair of lovesick teenagers. That's why I found myself there on a windy Saturday morning, having driven the best part of an hour to get there with my heartbeat pitter-pattering in anticipation. I felt excited. I felt emotional. I felt, dare I say it, nervous. All those feelings that we're told to expect in romantic love were transposed here to platonic companionship. It was like going for a first date with an old flame you're reuniting with after a prolonged absence, but without any of the bother of working out what to wear to give an impression of nonchalant sexiness and enigmatic availability. It didn't matter what I wore to meet Emma. All that mattered was that I would see her.

Then: there she was. Driving up behind me in the grown-up, family-sized car that always shocked me when I saw her at the wheel because it reminded me we were adults. We got our drinks. We parked up side by side (and that Tripadvisor reviewer was right: there *was* plenty of space for long vans). We sat socially distanced on a concrete breeze block until we tacitly acknowledged that it was a bit too cold and went back to our cars, speaking to each other with the doors open. It was overwhelmingly lovely to be with her, but it was also odd and constrained. I'm used to bowling up and hugging her as soon as I see her. Emma, although far less given to tactile displays than I am ('I just need to not be touched for a bit,' I remember her once saying when she'd had a morning of being pawed over by her two young children), found it strange that I couldn't do my normal thing. So we sat there awkwardly, wanting to touch but not being able to, and there was a moment of emotion when we both had tears in our eyes from the simultaneous joy of being together and the inability to give physical expression to that.

We talked about everything and nothing, as we usually do: how lockdown had affected our families, how wretched and tragic the pandemic was, how lucky we were to be comparatively safe and sheltered, how our self-esteem had taken a nose-dive because all the usual beautifying tactics we used were now beyond our reach and we had to embrace our grey hairs (or at least pretend to embrace our grey hairs) and did we think Bart was all right because he seemed on the brink of a nervous breakdown the last time he had almost screamed at Rachel during side-plank and also, was Rachel OK, and was there maybe a kind of illicit flirtation going on between the two of them? On it went. The joyous, untrammelled flow of conversation and laughter and fellow feeling. We talked long after we'd finished our drinks until finally we realised we couldn't sit in this car park forever, however much we might want to. There were other people driving through and needing parking spots, including an HGV that was even longer than a long van. So we closed our car doors and turned our keys in the ignition, and we smiled at each other through the windscreen (I say 'we' but actually Emma made a comedy sad face) and we drove back to our homes, unsure of what the future held but surer than ever of our friendship.

I kept hold of that takeaway Starbucks cup. I took it home with me and washed it out and set it on the kitchen countertop. Every day for a few weeks after that, I would make myself a cup of tea in that paper cup. When I drank it, I felt closer to Emma. After a while, the cup became soggy and gross and I had to throw it out, but the mental nourishment I'd gained from those couple of hours in the Starbucks car park sustained me for much, much longer.

A few days into the lockdown, long before I'd got my take-away tea cup and discovered online yoga classes, I received a message on Facebook from a friend called Ella. This was a strange way to contact me, given that she also had my phone number and we normally chatted via WhatsApp and honestly, who has time to check their Facebook messages any more? Despite Facebook's stated ambition to connect the world, it has instead become a primordial soup of irritation and misinformation: the online equivalent of one of those wedding receptions held on a boat so there is literally no escape from the groom's cousin, Bob, who believes the mainstream media is lying to him about the efficacy of vaccines.

Anyway, Ella had fallen victim to that haunting online algorithm, the Facebook Memory. A picture of us taken at a party some years previously had popped up on her feed like an overnight mushroom on a moist garden lawn. My friend had sent it to me, accompanied by this message:

'Before you became obsessed with babies and decided you didn't want to have fun with me any more,' she wrote.

I had to read it a couple of times before I realised she wasn't joking. She was being deliberately mean. I was surprised not only by the content, but by the fact she had actually pressed send. I'm sure we all feel annoyed by most of our friends at various points during our life, but to write it out in black and white and then decide that you want the other person to see how angry you are – that seemed like overkill. And to do it on Facebook seemed, well, naff.

But, I reasoned, the pandemic is making everyone feel a bit unhinged. Maybe this was just an error of judgement. And perhaps I would have been able to let it slide, had it not been one of many slights Ella had casually lobbed my way over the time we'd known each other.

We'd met through work when we were both temping at the same recruitment agency over the summer holidays. Ella was fun. She was a party friend. We'd go out and drink too much over dinner and a man at the adjacent restaurant table would hit on her (she is extremely hot) and then we'd go clubbing and more men would hit on her while I danced alone, nursing a tepid vodka tonic in a plastic tumbler, pretending that I was fine with having no attention, pretending I was absolutely, positively having a total riot, pretending that I knew how to dance to Britney Spears' 'Toxic' in a nonchalant way until I finally had to admit I probably wasn't having as much fun as I should have been. I didn't know any better then. I had fallen into the trap of assuming that culturally sanctioned fun – the kind of heteronormative, unimaginative fun enshrined in a million television sitcoms and American frat boy movies – was the sort of fun I should be having. If I didn't enjoy it, then the fault surely lay *with me*?

On and on it went. And then, in our thirties, we both got married and Ella, who had never wanted children, carried on having fun, and I was happy for her, and then she moved to a different country for a while. This was the first sign that our friendship had fissures. She would ask me to come and visit her all the time – and I did, on several occasions. But it never felt as though it was enough. Ella actually said as much, and it began to feel as though I were trying to feed a ravenous beast whose appetite would never be fully sated.

She moved back to London at around the time I was trying to have babies. I wasn't conceiving naturally. Then IVF didn't work for me either. Then, some months later and entirely out of the blue, I did get pregnant and Ella persuaded me to go to Krakow for a weekend because she'd been invited to a hen do she didn't want to attend alone. So I went, not thinking to question whether it would be enjoyable to spend money attending a hen do of a woman I'd never met before, in a foreign city without being able to drink. I went because Ella had asked me and she had made it sound Fun-with-a-capital-F and I desperately wanted to be Fun-with-a-capital-F for her. As it turned out, I spent most of the time feeling ill at ease in a group social setting with lots of impenetrable private jokes. I was generally exhausted by midnight, at which point I would schlep back to our Airbnb, getting lost on the way, only to be woken by Ella as she careened upstairs at 4 a.m. having forgotten her keys. Which was, of course, exactly what she should have been doing at her friend's hen do. It's just that I didn't understand why I was there. On the Sunday, I started bleeding.

'It's probably fine,' Ella said reassuringly.

But, deep down, I knew it wasn't. I got back home that night feeling anxious and drained. By this stage, I'd been through so much fertility treatment that I was already jittery about this natural pregnancy. I told myself I was overreacting. I googled 'pregnancy spotting first trimester' and was told it was common and would pass. The spotting went on for a week. On Friday, I went into the hospital for an emergency scan. The baby's heartbeat had stopped.

As I cried, the sonographer told me she would book me in for a procedure in a few days to remove what was now gruesomely referred to as 'early pregnancy remains'. In the event, I started miscarrying the following day. I spent a lonely, painful weekend in hospital. I was numb with distress. At the time, I thought it took me a few days to recover. Now I realise it was years. Now I understand that part of me is still recovering, and part of me always will be.

In the wake of that miscarriage, my marriage broke down. I got divorced. My life was spiralling. But because I'd made such a habit of putting on a front and because I mistakenly put an inordinate amount of value on the outdated British notions of stiff upper lips and soldiering on, you probably wouldn't have known from the outside. You probably would have thought I was coping really well. You would only have known if you'd made the effort to listen to what I *wasn't* saying or doing; to understand the silences and the absences. That's a difficult ask of a friend.

One of the things I did in the immediate aftermath of my marital breakdown was to go out a lot. It was a distraction technique. I also think there was part of me that wanted my external life to reflect the chaos of an internal sadness I wasn't fully expressing. Ending a marriage, in my limited experience, nearly always feels like a failure. Even if some part of you senses it's the right thing to do, you can never be fully certain. In the place between action and certainty, self-loathing takes root. So going out and falling into bed in the early hours and being tired and not getting enough sleep and not eating regularly and running always just that little bit late for everything was a way, I think, of punishing myself for not having made my marriage work. I didn't deserve to feel good. So I set about actively making myself feel bad.

Because I was going out a lot, it made sense to turn to the friend who was always up for doing exactly that. Ella was readily available for fun. Fun that involved sushi and vodka and dark rooms and random encounters with men and more vodka and throwing up because of too much vodka and solitary moments locked into a toilet cubicle when I'd find myself crying without ever fully acknowledging that I might be sad. The next morning, Ella would leave and I would wait for the hangover to pass. Then I realised the hangover wasn't because of the alcohol. It was because of the friendship.

Over the years, I had gradually noticed that any time Ella and I met up, the conversation would mostly be focused around her. This wasn't a bad thing. I'm sure she was also going through a lot and, besides, she was there for me! We had fun! Or, at least, I *think* we had fun … didn't we? Then it dawned on me: I don't think we did. I think we were both using fun to avoid looking at what was lacking in the rest of our lives, for each of us.

After my first miscarriage and subsequent divorce, I slowly began to realise that I had spent a whole chunk of my life trying to be someone I wasn't. I'd wasted time trying to please others without ever working out who I was underneath that insatiable desire to be liked. I'd allowed my own needs to be silenced by whoever had the more confident voice. In short: I'd sold a lot of people a lie. I was, albeit unconsciously, acting a part in my own life. And I was deeply convincing. I mean, I wasn't as method as Daniel Day-Lewis in *My Left Foot* or Marlon Brando in *Apocalypse Now*, but I was good enough that I even managed to convince myself for the best part of thirty-plus years.

It was Emma who made me confront this duality and who taught me that feeling sad and crying in a locked toilet cubicle can sometimes be a mask for a more difficult emotion you feel scared to show. An emotion like rage. An emotion like grief. It was Emma who made me understand that maybe I could be me – the real me, not the one trying to meet everyone else's projected expectations of me – and that it would be OK. More than OK, in fact. It might be better.

Unsurprisingly, Ella and I grew apart. I was changing. I wasn't the person I had been when we'd first become friends. Neither was she, but although she could acknowledge her own life changes, there didn't seem to be as much space in our friendship for mine.

In their book, *Big Friendship*, the authors Aminatou Sow and Ann Friedman talk about the concept of 'stretching'. They argue that just as our physical muscles require stretching in order to remain supple and resilient, so do friendships.

'There are little stretches that crop up early in a friendship, like getting over the fact that it always takes your friend a full day to text you back or admitting that you don't like the same music,' they write. 'And there are slightly bigger stretches, which often present themselves later. Maybe you used to live in the same neighbourhood, and now that you live farther apart you have to decide whose turf you're going to meet on. Or bigger stretches, like you used to feel like financial equals, then one of you started making a *lot* more money, and suddenly things are tense every time the check comes.

'Then there are huge stretches, like renegotiating the terms of your friendship when one of you moves away, or becomes a parent, or develops a chronic illness. For years a friendship might require only a comfortable, familiar set of stretches, and then one of you starts working a night shift, becomes a primary caregiver, or meets their future spouse, and you have to learn a whole new repertoire.'[17]

A healthy friendship involves reciprocal stretching to accommodate each other's shifting needs. But we don't have to stretch if we don't want to. Some relationships will be worth it and others won't. If there's too much stretching in one direction, the muscles of the friendship become out of whack.

This is what happened with me and Ella. There was already stretching involved because we had lived in different countries and were now at different life stages. And when another stretch was demanded by the fact that I had changed (in her eyes) and become more myself (in my eyes), it proved to be too much. The muscles were already so tightly pulled that they were on the brink of causing ligament strain.

To her credit, Ella sent me a text wondering what had gone wrong. But I, being a conflict-avoidant friendaholic, didn't really know what to say. It was a life-stage thing, I insisted. I was still actively engaged in trying to find a partner and start a family. Ella, who was contentedly childfree, couldn't fully understand my preoccupations. In truth, it was more than that. It was a person-stage thing. I wasn't the same and in not staying the same, I felt I had let her down. In a way, it was like another divorce.

We still saw each other, but mostly in groups and unspoken tension crackled whenever we got together. I noticed that Ella would make comments in front of others that undermined me. I never called them out and I probably should have. Instead, my hurt festered: a dry piece of kindling on a slowly accruing fire.

So when, in the early days of the pandemic, I got that Facebook message, I wasn't entirely surprised. In a way it was a confirmation of what I had long suspected. Besides, perhaps I genuinely wasn't that much fun any more – or at least not in the way Ella wanted me to be. And if this is what Ella really thought of me, why would she want to be my friend? And why would I want to be friends with someone who had such a low opinion of who I was? This was the end, I thought. This was the exit point of our friendship, the slip road where one of us indicated and took the turning, while the other drove on. I could let it go with grace. For a time, we had been on the same byway, travelling to the same destination. Now our destinations were different, and that was all right. That was as it should be.

I felt relief. Relief that I'd no longer have to try. Relief that this was my get-out-of-jail-free card. Relief that there was a clear reason now not to keep on stretching for our

friendship. Fuck stretching, I thought. It's boring and painful even if you're doing it right and I'm not willing to do it
any more for this person.

But it's never as simple as that. For all the tricky moments
of our friendship, there had also been great memories. It
wasn't Ella's fault I no longer sought enjoyment in the same
places she did. It wasn't her fault she had never wanted children. It wasn't her fault that I found myself needing space
from her in order to deal with my own stuff. None of it was
her fault. Maybe none of it was mine either. Maybe there
was no fault. It was simply a question of having grown
apart.

These things happen and yet there is a sense of shame
that attaches itself to a friendship slipping out of reach that
doesn't exist in other spheres. In romantic relationships,
endings are far more common. I've got six serious exes.
Either I broke up with them or they broke up with me and
no one treated us as sociopathic for finishing a relationship
that wasn't working. We might have disagreed with each
other. One of us might have wanted to hang on in there a
bit longer. But ultimately, we made our peace with the decision and it was the right thing to do. As much as I feel
fondly about most of my exes, I wouldn't want to be in any
of those relationships now.

That doesn't make the immediate heartbreak any easier
to deal with, but it does mean that there is a way to express
it. If Ella and I had been a couple and we'd been together
for ten years, during which time we'd had many highs and
some lows, and we'd come to realise that we both wanted

slightly different things from each other and decided to break up, it would be far more socially acceptable. If friendship break-ups were seen as a noble part of the necessary evolution of selfhood, and if it were more widely acknowledged that some friends will be lifelong, while others will walk by your side for a finite, but important, period of time, the whole thing would be a lot easier to deal with. We wouldn't place unrealistic expectations on our friends. We would stretch to accommodate each other's growth. And we would say goodbye with love still in our hearts when it didn't work out.

But when Ella and I broke up, as we eventually did, I felt shame. I didn't reply to the Facebook message. Later, she wrote to me to apologise, and I replied saying I appreciated it. We texted here and there but I realised I didn't really feel safe in the friendship any more. I didn't know the next time she might say something uncharitable. I now understood that I would never know what she truly thought of me.

The lockdown had made me re-evaluate how I wanted to spend my time. On a philosophical level, there's nothing like a global pandemic to remind you that life is vanishingly short. On a practical level, the fact that my diary emptied overnight of social obligation gave me space to understand who I actually wanted to see and compare that to who I was spending most of my time with. There was very little overlap. Generally speaking, my pre-pandemic evenings were given over to the most demanding people in my life – the ones who kept asking to meet, insisting that we *really had to* catch up and guilt-tripping me into believing I was a bad friend because even when I said yes, they still never believed I saw them enough. Well, you might think, what a lucky situation to be in, you ungrateful wretch. And perhaps it was.

I spent much of my adolescence without having that many friends. As I grew older, it was a constant surprise to me to find that someone might quite like me. Having people I randomly met at a work event or in a yoga class suddenly wanting to hang out with me made me feel special. Crucially, it made me feel *likeable*. It shored up my self-esteem. As long as I had lots of friends, my reasoning went, I would never be alone! I would be loved!

In my mid-thirties, my friendship spree reached fever pitch. By then, I was a divorced woman of a certain age who hadn't yet had children and one of my genuine fears was that I would end up abandoned and lonely if I didn't make the effort to spin as large a web of social connections as I could. That way, if some friendships fell by the wayside, I'd have others to take their place. My friends proliferated like socks in a drawer. And I liked them all so much – I honestly did. But as time went on, I realised that a lot of these new friends had different standards for friendship from my own. They wanted regular lunch dates and phone calls and replies to texts within the hour. They were offended if I failed to meet the terms of their imaginary contracts. They would accuse me of being 'too busy' and say things like 'I only know what's going on in your life from Instagram!' (To which I would silently respond: well, isn't that great? We live in a technological era where you can see a bit of what's going on in your friend's life even when you're not together! Hooray!) These were the social obligations that were clogging up the plughole of my iCal like clumps of damp hair. And still I want to emphasise: I liked these people. I liked them a lot. I just didn't have endless time to spend face to face with them with the regularity they desired, and I didn't enjoy the overwhelm of guilt I experienced any time I had to say no to their invitations.

So lockdown made me see how out of sync my diary had become. I was spending all my time trying to satisfy everyone who asked things of me, while almost never seeing the friends I loved the most. These were the friends I craved during lockdown – the ones who nourished, and radiated good energy; the ones you always felt better after speaking to; the ones who never expected anything of me; who appreciated me despite my limitations; who thought of me always with a generous heart. If I was stressed, these were the ones who never took it personally; who knew I would get in touch when I could and who understood my frankly outrageous dislike of phone calls. God, I loved them. And, I realised, maybe I hadn't shown them how much I did love them because I'd been so consumed with appeasing everyone else. Maybe I needed to start. And by maybe, I meant definitely. In order to have space for my loved ones, I had first to create that room. It was quite simple, really. That meant phasing out the things that consistently took from my life rather than adding to it.

So when it came to it, I sent Ella a text saying (truthfully) that I was working through some of my own issues and that meant conserving energy and making choices about how I wanted and needed to feel. I send you nothing but love, I said. I signed off with kisses.

I'm not going to pretend it was easy. It took me months – literally *months* – to get to that point. I felt terrible when I pressed send, nauseous with dread. It seemed so indescribably unnatural for me to end a friendship rather than contort myself in every direction to make it work. And yes, there was shame. A great deal of shame. How could I have been so horrible? What kind of a monster was I to have let Ella down without having had the courage to confront how I was feeling with her head-on? I was a coward. I was a fraud. I had failed to meet my own standards of friendship. These were the thoughts that circled my mind like hyenas.

I let them circle. Eventually they settled down a bit. After a few weeks, they were still there, but at least the hyenas were now sitting on their haunches rather than ripping apart a carcass with their teeth (I might have failed at friendship, but never let it be said that I can't squeeze a metaphor until the pips squeak).

Several months passed. Lockdown lifted. The hyenas slunk off into the shadows. I chose the friends I spent my time with more carefully. I started to feel better. Then, unexpectedly, I started to feel affection. Affection for Ella, in her gloriously perfect imperfection. Affection for the times we'd had, the nights that had ended in fits of hysterical laughter, the meals we'd eaten together. Affection for the cracked, multi-faceted, unexpected friendship we'd shared.

Affection for the flawed people we were and the journey we'd both been on to become the people we are – still flawed, but perhaps with more awareness of those flaws. Perhaps, despite our friendship ending, we had grown because of and not in spite of each other. Perhaps in the letting-go, we had understood something integral about ourselves. Perhaps that was all right. Perhaps that was a kind of love.

None of this is to say that I've stopped making friends. I have not pulled the drawbridge up to my castle of companionship. The moat is still passable; it's simply that I've become more selective. In the past, I would say yes to being friends with anyone who showed even slightly willing, because it was more important for me to be liked by others than to value myself as I was when no one was watching. It was very important to me to be thought of as 'nice'. Or 'good'. Or 'dependable'. Or 'pleasing'. Or 'kind'. And those qualities are admirable, of course. But they should be felt intrinsically, rather than a person relying on extrinsic validation for their continued existence.

In short, I suppose the pandemic made me see that you have to be yourself first, then choose who to be friends with on the basis of still being able to be exactly yourself with them. Not only that, but you should be loved *for* being yourself, with all your neuroses accepted as part of the deal. In effect, the foundational rule for friendship is the same as the phrase often wrongly attributed to the Hippocratic Oath for physicians: 'first, do no harm'. For me, an equitable friendship should be founded on an unspoken commitment to avoid acting maliciously and to always start from a place of generosity when thinking of the other.

It sounds straightforward but it's taken me forty-three years to get it. Still, that's not necessarily a bad thing. As Cicero puts it in his seminal essay, *How to Be a Friend*, written in 44 BC: 'As a general rule we shouldn't commit to friendships until we've reached an age when our character and way of living are established and confirmed.'

In the same essay, which has inspired everyone from Dante to Thomas Jefferson, Cicero also writes of the desirability of having a trial period in friendship: 'The problem is that it's difficult to determine who has the desirable qualities of a friend without trying them out – and the only way to try them out is by being their friend. Thus friendship runs ahead of judgement and removes the possibility of a trial period. Therefore it is prudent to restrain a headlong rush of goodwill just as we would hold back a chariot team. As we always test horses before racing them, so in the same way we should test the character of potential friends.'[18]

The enforced isolation of the pandemic gave me a chance to reassess my approach to friendship, to take a step back and ask myself what I really wanted in a companion and, just as importantly, what I had to offer. It was, I suppose, a reflection period of the kind Cicero suggested, but applied retrospectively. I needed to assess my horses before keeping them hitched to my chariot. I needed, in short, to work out why I was addicted to friendship and what to do about it.

And if I wanted to understand my mania for friendship, I would have to go back to where it all began – to the first friend I ever made.

The Friendship Tapes
LIBBY

Libby Hall, 80, former press photographer,
now largely confined to her house by
a terminal illness

'Regular communication with friends is hugely important to me now at this point in my life with a terminal illness and being housebound. It's a matter of life and death, absolutely.

'Before the days of email, there was a friend who I didn't see for about twenty years, and that was to do with a misunderstanding between us. But it was incredible how within literally five minutes [of being reunited], it felt like it always had been, there was no awkwardness beyond the first couple of minutes.

'Now we're terribly close, very close, and I rely on him and his wife enormously emotionally. And we forget there was that gap. We've known each other since we were twenty-three or twenty-four – we're the same age, we're both eighty now – so I think, in really solid relationships, you can have big long gaps, and it's OK.

THE FRIENDSHIP TAPES

'I'm not scared of losing friends. Actually, at one stage at school I was bullied, so I tend sometimes to be a little bit paranoid in my friendships and think somebody doesn't like me as much as they do. So in that sense I'm scared. [But] I can't be scared of losing them through dying because they just do. You're not scared of it beforehand, but it's very difficult when it happens.

'I'm not in any kind of pain, but I get very tired and breathless and we didn't understand it was going to go on for so long. It's been four years and the prognosis was months. So it's very odd, adjusting to who you want to see in these last stages of your life. I found it quite interesting that there could be friends I was very fond of, and whose company I enjoyed very much, that I didn't want to see – they were the wrong sort of friends, they were too tiring, too emotionally demanding, in a way that when I was able to support people I didn't mind at all. So that was curious to me.

'Then, as time has gone on, and I've got less and less strong, I have wanted to see fewer people, but the people I do want to see, I want to see very much. And it really is a matter of life and death – not just because they have given me practical support, but emotionally, it's essential to me. Life wouldn't be worth living – apart from this creature! [She indicates Pip the dog, curled up on her lap.]

'It isn't good to need to be around people – the wrong people, for the wrong reasons – and not be able to be alone. In the same way you can be in a bad romantic relationship, bad friendships can be just as bad.

'I want to emphasise that I really think it's love that makes the world go round. You know, love is all, love is the absolute essential that makes life bearable. So I think friendship is the most important thing going.

'I'm so aware of how richly my life has been full of friends and love. And thinking, *What would it be like to be looking back on a bleak life with hardly any friends?* And there *are* people who have hardly any friends, and that's awful. We're pack animals. Solitary confinement is the worst possible punishment you can give people. So, yes, I just think it's essential, friendship.'

At the time of writing, Libby is still very much alive and busily confounding the medical prognosis.

2.
MAKING FRIENDS
Why Do We Do It?

The starting point for this particular story is north Surrey. I was born in Epsom, a bustling commuter-belt town whose former residents include an eighteenth-century bone-setter called Sally Mapp, famed for fixing musculoskeletal injuries using manual force and also for wandering the country in a drunken state, shouting obscenities. Under 'other names' Wikipedia recounts that she was also known as 'Crazy Sally'.[19]

By the time I came along in 1978, times had changed and Epsom was an eminently respectable market town with only the occasional shouted drunken obscenity to be heard on the high street on Friday nights.

I made my first friend in nursery school. I was four, an age when most of my coherent memories begin. Before four, I can remember things in flashes. As a baby, I vividly recall the sensation of being put down for my afternoon nap and hating the thought of missing out on whatever would be happening without me. I remember, also, my older sister stretching her arm into my pram to offer me a bite from her apple. I was too young (and too toothless) to eat it, but the simple kindness of that gesture has stayed with me. Another word would be 'friendly'. It was a friendly thing to do. After all, although she was my sister, there had been no guarantee when I was born that she would also be my friend.

Our ability to create memories with any kind of consistent narrative through-line starts at the age of four, which is why I remember making my new friend so vividly. She was the first friend I made outside my immediate family. We had been lined up in rows in the village hall, and I was sitting cross-legged behind a girl with shiny brown hair and a parting that zig-zagged down the back of her head. I was entranced by this parting. My own hair was parted straight to the side and held back with an unglamorous kirby grip. The girl's hair was parted down the centre and divided into pigtails, each one held in place with elastic bands that had shiny red baubles on the end like cherry gobstoppers. My hair had never been in pigtails. It was too short, and would remain so for much of my childhood because my mother (who cut it) was adamant that shorter hair looked better on me. I railed against this for the best part of four decades before eventually realising she had been right all along.

The girl's parting, with its perfectly executed zig-zag, giving way to two equally perfectly executed pigtails seemed to me the epitome of style. Ah, I thought to myself. Now there's someone I want to be friends with. Her name was Emily Carter.

I can remember almost nothing of how the friendship was actually forged, although the fact that our surnames jostled companionably next to each other in the alphabet must have had something to do with it. Then there was the fact that she lived locally, within walking distance of my house, so we were thrown together by geographical ease, too. Our mothers were a similar age and, as any parent with a young child can understand, I imagine they were probably keen to foster any kind of friendship that could result in playdates and shared activities where they could each enjoy a few hours' respite. Sometimes friendships need nothing more than a degree of pragmatism to help them succeed.

Emily and I were not kindred spirits. I remember, after that first flush of hairstyle envy had worn off, finding her rather bossy and a little humourless. But it didn't cross my mind, at that age, to go looking for anything better and I don't think it crossed hers either. We simply accepted that our shared age, our shared interests (hair), our geographical closeness (Epsom, Surrey), the regularity of our contact (weekday mornings) and our mothers' desire for us to be friends was more than enough.

When it comes to understanding why we seek out connection, the academic literature is fairly obsessed with this idea of common interest. In the 1970s, a few years before Emily and I met on that nursery school floor, a whole raft of research papers had sought to identify the stages of human relationships and what made us attracted to other people. Why the sudden academic interest in how we sought each other out? I suspect it might have been because of the seismic impact of the 1960s. After a decade of free love, during which previously restrictive social norms were challenged and sometimes even overturned, the basis of mutual attraction must suddenly have seemed even more exciting and worthwhile to examine with fresh eyes.

So it was that, in 1970, the sociologist Bernard Murstein posited that we select our romantic mates through a three-stage model.[20] The first stage is stimulus: we like what we see of their physical attributes, just as I did with Emily Carter's hair. The second stage is comparing our values to see if they fit. The third and final stage is allotting roles – sharing out activities to build a working relationship.

In 1973, Irwin Altman and Dalmas Taylor came up with a 'Social Penetration Theory' that has five distinct phases.[21] The first is 'orientation' (small talk), the second stage is 'exploratory affective' (we start to reveal ourselves and express personal attitudes), then we graduate to 'affective' (we begin to talk about private and personal matters), before moving onto 'stable' (we plateau in our intimacy and can predict each other's emotional responses) – after which the only way is down. The authors label the final stage 'de-penetration' and write that this is the point when 'costs exceed benefits … there is a withdrawal of disclosure'. In 1976, an academic called George Levinger was still so hung up on stages that he actually coined 'Stage Theory', in which putative companions move from initial attraction right through to longer-term commitments 'such as marriage'.[22]

What's noticeable about all these studies is that although their findings have been applied to platonic friendships over the years, the focus is entirely on romantic attachments. It's also interesting how similarly they are expressed. Although they might be drawing up new theories, the language itself is retrograde. It's all 'penetration' and 'withdrawal' and 'exploratory affection', which sounds more like a series of Pornhub categories than anything else. Unlike Pornhub, however, in most of these studies the outcome of a successful relationship is deemed to be *marriage*, and preferably one that lasts forever.

You might spot another common denominator. Yes, that's right – all of the research quoted was conducted by men. Maybe for these particular men, conventional romantic relationships were their specific area of expertise. But I can't help but feel it reflected a wider consensus in sociology, psychology and beyond at the time: that intimate heterosexual attachment was the only one worthy of academic research because of its reproductive value. Tied to that is the assumption that all other kinds of interpersonal relationships must stem from this singular example, a bit like a sourdough culture replicating itself through the centuries. Of course, that isn't the case.

To me, it seems self-evident that friends perform many extremely important functions that lie outside our family units or our romantic relationships, and although later academic research has examined friendship as a valid topic in its own right, I'm not sure the playing field has been altogether levelled. It takes a long time to uproot assumptions that are so deeply implanted in the soil.

This bias is mirrored in our culture, too. When I was growing up, there were countless romantic comedies to be watched and family soap operas to entertain us in the after-school hours. Endless books, music, plays, paintings and sculptures were devoted to a celebration of heterosexual love. Friends were, for a long time, overlooked. Probably the first time I remember seeing an entire television series devoted to friends was, well, *Friends*, which launched in 1994, when I was fifteen. Even then, a lot of the key storylines were about the quest for a romantic partner. In fact, the six main characters all at some point date or have crushes on someone else within the group: Ross goes out with Rachel; Monica hooks up with Chandler, and they eventually get engaged; Phoebe develops feelings for Joey but he falls instead for Rachel, and then Joey and Rachel end up together for a few episodes. Now that I think about it, it was a missed opportunity that none of the women fell in love with each other. Maybe that's material for a reboot?

I'm sure those 1970s sociologists who were so fixated on marriage as an end goal would be disappointed to learn that Emily Carter and I did not end up either penetrated or de-penetrated (or at least, not by each other). Instead, my father got a job in Derry, Northern Ireland, and we moved a few months before I turned five. I would start primary school many miles away across the Irish Sea from Emily, and, this being the pre-internet age, we didn't keep in touch. I can remember no feelings of sadness about this separation. I don't think I missed Emily once, which makes me sound either callous or self-confident, when in truth I was neither. I was just a four-year-old. I simply accepted that this was part of life and that I had no control over it.

I never saw Emily again, but her parents kept in touch for many years by sending us a Christmas round robin letter that listed their myriad achievements and went into an unanticipated level of detail about their eldest son's interest in philately. But although Emily fell out of my life without leaving much behind, her legacy continued in a different way: for whatever reason, I was left in no doubt of the need to continue making friends. It became a fact of life I never thought to question, in much the same way as I knew two plus two equalled four and accepted the earth was round. It was just how things were. So when I started my new primary school and immediately realised I was the kid with the funny accent who didn't know the words to the Lord's Prayer by heart and would therefore stand out for all the wrong reasons, I wanted very much to be someone's friend. Instinct told me there was safety to be had in numbers. After I tearfully said goodbye to my mother at the door of the classroom on the first day, I was encouraged by the teacher to play in the sandbox and picked up a red pan with square holes in the bottom. When I sieved sand through it, the granules slid and parted into thin, shifting streams in a particularly satisfying way. It was the best toy in the joint, and it soon became clear another girl with dark curly hair also wanted a piece of the action. I offered the toy to her. Her name was Susan Marshall and she became my second friend – a friendship that lasted all the way through primary school and beyond. So this time, although the initial spark for making a friend was definitely common interest (the sand sieve) it was also because of something deeper: an unspoken desire not to be alone.

This is one of the foundational premises for friendship, dating back millennia to the pre-industrial era of hunter-gatherers. According to a widely promulgated thesis, men would form parties to hunt large game, while women would rely on each other's help for raising their children.[23] As a result, the idea that having people around was beneficial to one's own survival took hold. It also meant that in times of need, members of the same ad-hoc network could step in and provide assistance. Men who were injured could receive meat from a fellow hunter; mothers with sick babies could rely on group childcare.

A quick side note here is that in recent years, the gendered assumptions at the heart of much anthropological study have been challenged by modern discoveries, most notably the remains of a teenage female hunter found during 2018 archaeological excavations in Peru. She had lived 9,000 years previously, would have been around seventeen to nineteen at the time of her death, and was buried alongside a 'comprehensive array of hunting and animal processing tools' including 'stone projectile points for felling large animals, a knife and flakes of rock for removing internal organs, and tools for scraping and tanning hides'. What a badass.

The researchers then looked at further archaeological records across the Americas and found that between 30 and 50 per cent of big-game hunters who lived more than 10,000 years ago might have been women.[24] And women would also have had a pivotal role to play in the development of agriculture – some studies have shown that the hunter was responsible for only 10 per cent of the group's food, while the gatherer (alongside raising babies by the campfire) provided a whopping 90 per cent.[25]

What I find particularly appealing about this is the concept of mixed-sex hunter alliances and the idea that some of the earliest friendships in human history might have been between men and women. So much of what we're taught contradicts the notion that this is even possible. The popular belief is that the closest friendships tend to be among people of the same gender, or at least between people who do not want to have sex with each other. But those hunter-gatherers formed social systems across genders in order to co-operate effectively and survive.

And because humans have evolved to live in groups, loneliness can be actively dangerous – that goes for present-day friendships too. A 2010 study conducted by Brigham Young University found a 50 per cent increased likelihood of survival for people with stronger social relationships, even after accounting for disparities in age, sex, health and cause of death.[26] In short: not having friends can kill you.

The alienating feeling of loneliness – that all-encompassing psychic discomfort of not being part of something bigger than you – is also believed to be an evolutionary trigger for a person to go and seek out companionship, thereby increasing their chances of survival.

I wasn't aware of all this when I handed over my red plastic sand sieve to Susan Marshall, but all these complex evolutionary, genetic, anthropological and historic inheritances clearly shaped that unconscious decision. I made a friend because it was safer that way. And also, as it would turn out, nicer, because Susan was fun and kind. She was the first person I knew who owned a shell suit (the last word in style back in 1990) and she liked New Kids on the Block and Philadelphia cream cheese spread on toast – *toast!* – rather than bread. We went to the bowling alley together and Laser Quest and, when we both got our driving licences, our favourite evening's entertainment consisted of pizza followed by a movie at the local cinema, where we once sat through *Independence Day* – a film deemed so revolutionarily long by the projectionist that we were treated to an interlude halfway through when the screen went black. I looked up the running time recently. It's two hours and twenty-five minutes.

Where Susan was cool, I was indubitably not. I was English, wore corduroy trousers without irony and the first album I owned was a *Now That's What I Call Music* compilation given to me by my older sister. Yet despite our differences, we got along. Susan never judged me for what I wasn't and therefore gave me more confidence to be what I was. I think we also shared a sense of humour, which for me is possibly the most important characteristic for any successful friendship.

In secondary school, I wasn't so lucky. At the age of ten, having been moved up a year, I became a weekly boarder at a co-ed school in Belfast. I went from being one in a class of six at primary school and going home every evening, to being a single pupil in a sea of over 1,000 navy blazers. I was let out on day release every Saturday morning, when I would schlep to the local bus station, walking past the Europa Hotel (which once bore the indignity of being the most bombed hotel in Europe), and sit on a crammed coach for the one-and-a-half-hour journey home. These were the days when you were still allowed to smoke on public transport (you were still allowed to smoke anywhere, really) and I would frequently emerge coated in a fragrant patina of nicotine. I was expected to return by 6 p.m. the following evening in time for a dreary religious service in the school chapel, so I'd get back on the coach, laden down with home-cooked treats packed in a surprisingly practical toolbox my parents had bought specifically for the purpose. At the other end, I'd walk the twenty minutes from the bus station to school with a leaden feeling in my stomach.

I must have made for a curious sight as I trailed the streets of Belfast in my anorak, laden down with bags. Once, when I was carrying the toolbox, a man stopped and shouted 'Been fishing?' which I can now appreciate was pretty funny, although at the time, I was mortified.

During the weeks, I slept in a long Dickensian-style dormitory with several other girls. Our beds were metal-framed and creaky. It genuinely looked like a Victorian tuberculosis ward. At night, I would fall asleep to the sounds of shuffles and coughs and the odd shout from someone else's bad dream. I clutched my teddy bear tighter to me and tried not to miss home.

I know it sounds as though I'm talking about something plucked from the pages of a nineteenth-century novel, but I promise I'm not exaggerating. Years later, I would watch the Netflix adaptation of *The Queen's Gambit* and during the early episodes, set in a mythically awful orphanage, I'd think, 'Yes, that's *exactly* what our dorms were like.' The school was primarily for day pupils, and the boarding department was a relic from a bygone era which no one was quite sure what to do with. The food was appalling and served in a gothic wood-panelled dining hall. I've never forgotten that they used to give better meals to the boys' boarding department because there were 'more of them' – a logic that seemed irrefutable in its absurdity. My classmates and I once discovered a box of groceries intended for the boys which had been wrongly delivered to the girls' kitchen. It was filled with all sorts of treats like marshmallows and chocolate biscuits. We girls counted ourselves lucky if the cabbage hadn't been boiled to the point of extinction.

Astonishingly, we were allowed only one bath a week. I can't remember there being any showers. I took my bath on Wednesdays. When I slid the lock on that bathroom door, turned on the taps and watched the steam creep across the mirror, I remember the utter relief of unaccustomed privacy, followed swiftly by the sinking knowledge that this moment would soon be over. For a long time, I didn't tell my parents I hated it, partly because I wanted them to be proud of me and partly because I had actively wanted to be a boarder, fuelled by one too many *Malory Towers* books.[27] It all would have been a lot easier if I'd had friends, but I struggled to forge any meaningful connections.

If my primary school contemporaries had been tolerant of my differences, secondary school proved more brutal. I was ostracised for my strangeness, for being the youngest in my year and for my desperate inability to be in any way trendy. Looking back, I can understand why. I still slept with a teddy bear. I had no sense of fashion. My mother cut my hair. I had bad teeth. I played the trumpet. I had ripped-out magazine images of female Calvin Klein models on my wall because I found them beautiful, where others had Chesney Hawkes and Bros by their bedsides. All of this was pointed out, mocked and laughed at. My accent was mimicked to the point where I got quieter and quieter and realised it was safer not to say much at all.

In my third year, I became friends with another girl who suffered the same fate – although she was Irish, she had red hair and freckles, which in our school meant you were a borderline pariah. We were both so miserable that we attempted to hatch a plan where I would stay with her family during the week, but it never came to anything.

One lunchtime, I felt a thwack in the back of my head and then the sound of boys cheering and scuffling as they ran away. When I touched my hair, I realised it now contained a ball of warm chewing gum, which embedded itself in my hair with the permanence of superglue. The more I tried to extract it, the tighter its putty-like grip became. I went to the school nurse who tried to freeze it off by applying an ice-pack. When that failed, she cut it out, along with a chunk of hair. I was late to my next class and for the rest of the day, I was trailed by the sickly smell of sweetened mint.

That was one example of the kind of thing that happened. I was never physically assaulted, and for many years I thought this meant that I wasn't bullied. I was used to watching *Grange Hill* and seeing school bullies punch their victims to the ground and steal their schoolbags. Now, with the benefit of hindsight, I realise that bullying can take many forms and I feel that the word accurately describes what happened to me. As an adult, I remember once talking to a comedian who told me about his secret hunch that most stand-ups had been bullied at school and had discovered cracking jokes as the first line of defence. A class clown can become popular through humour and is therefore less easy to pick on. For me, being bullied made me determined in later life to prove my worth. Becoming successful, having my name in print, being blessed with a wide circle of endless friends: these became inviolable markers of my sense of identity. It was a way of being seen and it was a way of proving those bullies wrong.

It wasn't the school's fault, in that I never told anyone or did anything about it. I simply thought this was what happened and that it was an ordeal to get through. And since then, I've met many lovely people who went to the same school and had a more positive memory of it. But the north of Ireland in the late 1980s and early 90s could be unforgiving and mistrusting of the people they deemed to be 'outsiders', for a host of understandable reasons connected to a traumatic past of invasion and conquest. It was 1982 when we moved to Derry, and the province was in the midst of a civil conflict fuelled by nationalism, sectarianism and politics. There were those who wanted a united Ireland and saw the English as unwelcome occupiers, and there were those who wished to remain part of the United Kingdom despite the ignoble history of colonial settlement. This had its roots in the early seventeenth century, when English and Scottish settlers assumed ownership of plots of land in Ulster, and was followed by a 1649 invasion by Oliver Cromwell and his New Model Army. To this day, Cromwell is reviled in parts of Ireland for the terrible violence he wreaked.

The civil conflict that raged across the north of Ireland in the 60s, 70s and 80s was known, somewhat dismissively, as 'the Troubles'. Military checkpoints, manned by helmeted British soldiers wearing camouflage, with rifles slung across their chests, were part of my daily life. One August, Susan Marshall and I went to watch as men holding Unionist flags and disguised in balaclavas marched in the streets to commemorate the lifting of the siege of Derry – an event that took place in 1689.

We were caught up in regular bomb scares, when shopping centres would have to be evacuated rapidly because of an anonymous phone call tipping off the authorities. When bombs went off, we often heard the shattering explosion and watched details of the victims on the evening news.

The next day, the roads would be strewn with broken glass and mangled steelwork. My father, a surgeon at Altnagelvin Hospital, was one of the first on the scene in the aftermath of the Omagh bombing in 1998, which killed twenty-nine people and injured 220 others. Earlier that year, the Good Friday Agreement had been signed, which eventually ended most of the paramilitary violence. But it was a long time coming.[28]

My peers wouldn't necessarily have known all the historic ins and outs of anti-English sentiment, but their view of the world was indelibly shaped by it, unconsciously or otherwise.

I recently talked about my childhood with a new therapist.

'But you weren't just treated as an outsider,' she said. 'You were treated as the enemy.'

I had never thought of it in those terms and it was an epiphany. No wonder I had felt the need to make friends, to forge alliances in order to be safe. No wonder I constantly still feel, as an adult, that I have done something wrong, that I am the one at fault, the shameful one who is guilty of unspecified crimes.

When I went home at weekends, I never fully relaxed because I knew I'd have to go back to school the following day. The dread would slink heavily into my body the moment I walked through the door. It would skulk there for the whole weekend, crouching in the corner like a shadow as we watched *Antiques Roadshow* and ate roast chicken. I could feel myself becoming slowly constricted by my school self as every minute passed.

My experience was by no means exceptional, and in many respects it was privileged. But privilege doesn't insulate from feeling, even if it cushions the fallout. Many of us will be able to tell similar stories. When we are on the brink of adolescence, we are trying out our identity to see how it fits for size. We are often confused and fearful and hormonal. At secondary school, our teachers expect more of us than they did before. We start sitting serious exams that might shape our future life choices. We are growing apart from our parents as part of our necessary progress towards independence. And yet we don't have sufficient control over our own existence because we're still too young to be trusted with true independence. So we spend a lot of time feeling annoyed and enraged that no one understands us. We try to connect with our peers, just like our hunter-gatherer antecedents before us, because we're primally aware that there is safety and power in tribal alliance. When we're cast out by our peers it can be frightening and make us feel insecure.

But school can also be a crucible in which important friendships are made. My friend Sharmaine had a difficult relationship with her mother and left home at sixteen, and for a year, she lived with a friend from school and her family. After that, it was a shared flat in Balham, south London. Then it was hostels in Soho. Then she slept rough behind bins in Leicester Square. Every single day, she made it to school, where she found refuge in the books she read in the library – each one a portal to a different, imagined life. She is now the most senior Black woman in British publishing.

When I asked her about this period in her childhood, Sharmaine told me that the reason she made friends back then was 'to understand that you can be loved in a different way outside of your family. Where there wasn't that unconditional love with my family, there has been an unconditional love with my oldest friends.'

I thought that was such a beautiful way of putting it: that the intentional act of making friends can be a way of understanding oneself away from the family unit and that school is often the first place we can do that. It's not that our friends become our family, exactly; it's that they accept us outside the roles we perform with our close relatives and in doing so, they allow us to be a version of ourselves we might not previously have inhabited.

But because I had no friends and was separated from my family, school was a lonely place. Halfway through my third year, I suddenly told my mother that I had to leave. She couldn't understand why, and I couldn't fully explain it to her. At twelve, I didn't think 'I don't have any friends' was enough of a reason, so I talked more generally about not liking the atmosphere and not feeling that I fitted in and I was unrelenting in my insistence that I had to go. My grades were spiralling. I felt angry a lot of the time. I realised I had to leave or risk losing myself entirely.

My parents ended up taking me out halfway through the term and I won a scholarship to a full-time boarding school in England. I was put back into my rightful year so that when I arrived, I was the same age as everyone else. And, ironically, because I spoke with an English accent, I was immediately accepted in a way I hadn't been before. This time, I was aware that making friends was key to survival. I quickly identified the most popular girl in my year and made it my mission to befriend her. It worked. By the end of the year, I had a lot of friends. More than that: I had friends who also seemed to like me. It was a culturally diverse year group with many students from different countries, which I think helped because I was no longer deemed the sole outsider.

But that feeling of not having any friends at my Belfast secondary school would stay with me for a long time. It was such an acute level of isolation that it shaped how I approached friendship for years to come. I was absolutely determined that I would never feel that way again. And so I became almost manic in my pursuit of friends. Everyone I met was a potential ally, to be won over and charmed so that they would like me and I could be safe. The more friends I had, my reasoning went, the safer I was, especially when my life hit various speed bumps. Someone would always be available to take my call or answer my text or go to the cinema with me. Someone who made me feel worthwhile. Someone with whom to share this complicated thing called life.

In my twenties, I discovered I was good at friendship. That formative sense of not belonging in my early teenage years had left me with an empathetic instinct for when others were feeling excluded or less than and my brush with outsidership had given me an ability to relate to lots of different kinds of people. I basked in the glow of successful connection, whether it was a stranger I met at dinner who was wearing the same top as I was, a work colleague with whom I bitched about unreasonable bosses, or a longstanding friend who called me first after a fight with her boyfriend. I felt I was succeeding at friendship and being a Good Friend became an integral part of my identity. If someone else liked me, my logic went, then I didn't have to go to all that bother of trying to like myself. In place of self-worth, I stitched together a patchwork of other people's opinions of me. It became disproportionately important to me that I ensured these good opinions were never lost, because I was relying on them to prop up my self-esteem. So I would spend a lot of time adding to the patchwork, or re-stitching the pieces that were already in place in order to bind them more firmly together. I couldn't run the risk of it tearing or of one of the patches falling off. I kept stitching frantically. I tried to keep everyone in my life happy, feeding them tokens of my love like amusement arcade machines.

Whatever a friend asked of me, I would try and accommodate. When they asked, I would give up free evenings and weekends. I would say yes even if I didn't want to. In fact, during this time in my life, I didn't even question what my own desires were. It was far more important for me to be seen as the reliable one, the consistent one, the *loveable* one. My problem was I didn't, back then, distinguish between who I actually wanted to spend time with and who was simply asking me stuff that I felt I couldn't say no to.

I wondered how many other people might also have felt like this at some point in their lives. In search of an answer,

I came across a 2020 study of 1,316 participants conducted by the University of Nicosia in Cyprus.[29] The participants were interviewed about their views on friendship, and given a questionnaire to complete (sample: 'Please indicate as many reasons as you could think [sic] that have led you in the past or could lead you in the future to make friends', which is quite the humdinger). Overall, the researchers identified forty-one perceived reasons, including 'to have someone support me' and 'the need for socialisation'. No one said, 'Because my inner critic needs to be sated with an Excel spreadsheet of Good Friend Deeds', which I suppose isn't altogether surprising. The most frequent reason cited, however, was 'common interests with someone'.

Common interest, again! I find this fascinating because I can think of only one occasion when I started a friendship with someone in adulthood by bonding over a shared interest and that was because we both watched *Real Housewives* (if you're reading this, Dom, I love you, and your Dawn Ward impression is without parallel). Perhaps it's that, as previously mentioned, I don't actually have that many hobbies. Maybe if I'd stuck with salsa dancing or went to a weekly Zumba class it would be a different story. Perhaps it's that I haven't yet had my own children so I don't have the 'common interest' of being at the same life phase. Most of my lasting friendships have been sparked not by a shared hobby but by an initial frisson of kindred feeling. It's intangible. It's not predicated on whether they like the same things as me or even have the same opinions or worldview as I do. Admittedly, I probably wouldn't be friends with someone who was rabidly fascist or violently opposed to female suffrage, but I am friends with lots of people who vote differently from me and have different passions.

The second most popular reason for making friends in the University of Nicosia study was 'so that I do not feel lonely', which makes perfect sense given what we know about the evolutionary basis of friendship and my own salutary experience at school. The third was 'someone's character' – that is, liking a person for who they are and wanting to spend time with them. Again, that tracks. A few participants replied that they wanted to make a connection in order to pursue a friend's relative romantically, or to advance their career or social status. Call me sexist but I'm hazarding a guess that all of them were men (don't @ me).

The caveat to all this is that the methodology required participants to give their opinions, so the stated reasons are inevitably founded on their biased perceptions of their own actions. There's no way of analysing the data to work out if that is what was really going on or not. Still, I like the idea that even when we take into account the flawed nature of our self-awareness, two of the top three reasons for friendship were the same as my own and all three were supported by the evolutionary science, dating back millennia.

So if I were to ask myself the same questions as the University of Nicosia asked their participants, what are the reasons I have been led in the past or could lead me in the future to make friends? I think, for me, the overriding impulse is a need to connect as the antidote to loneliness. As much as I might once have had a deep-seated evolutionary need to be part of a pack, I believe that nowadays it's more that I want other people around me who can share experiences and, in doing so, make them meaningful. That, and the fact I want to shag their uncle (just kidding).

When I was mulling this over, a memory came back to me of winning a journalism award when I was a twenty-six-year-old Sunday newspaper reporter. The prize came with a generous travel bursary and I took a month off to go on a trip through South Africa, Kenya, Tanzania and Zanzibar. My then boyfriend came with me for the first week, but after that I was left to my own devices. None of my other friends could afford the flights or take the time off work to join me, so I saw the mosques of Stone Town and the foot-hills of Kilimanjaro and the mists of the Great Rift Valley on my own. In the Ngorongoro Crater, the landscape was memorably stunning: tumbling slopes of dense green trees like miniature broccoli crowns, giving way to red-brown impasto sweeps of earth. I saw rhinoceros and lions and wildebeest. I took photos frenetically, but my film ran out (hey, it was 2004) and then I had nothing to do and no one else to share my excitement with. At the end of each day, I would force myself to go out for a solo dinner, taking a book with me to ward off unwanted attention, and it would feel strange that there was no one to talk with about what we'd seen together. There was no one who had witnessed the same things as I had, who could laugh or enthuse, and there would be no one in years to come with whom I could recall this specific trip; no one who would sit on the sofa with me and drink wine and be able to say, 'Do you remember that time when …?' It felt like a loss. It felt like the experience itself had been diminished.

So perhaps the true reason I make friends has always been this: to have someone to walk through life with, who can share, challenge and deepen my understanding of it. We make friends not simply because we have the same hobby or because we live nearby or because we need to build up our self-worth or ensure safety in numbers when we're hunting big game with stone projectile points, but because we long for someone to make sense of what we're doing and what we're feeling and thinking and seeing. I make friends so as not to be alone. I think this is why, at one of the loneliest points in my life, I met a woman who would become like a sister to me.

Her name is Joan.

Joan would teach me about boundaries and self-respect. We found each other when she was in her fifties and I was in my mid-thirties. It was at a specific time in my life when I was reaching a tipping point in my friendships. Although I hadn't yet put words to the thought, I had accumulated too many friends because of my mania for co-dependency, and I needed someone to show me how to redress the balance. Joan, at twenty years older, did that for me. I was interested in asking her about her own reflections on friendship – the one we had when we first met, and the one we now enjoy, having the benefit of a few years' wisdom under our belt. So I decided to ask, and she would be my first friendship interview.

First, let me tell you the tale of how our paths crossed.

The Friendship Tapes
PAULA

Paula Akpan, 30, historian, freelance journalist and director of the Black Queer Travel Guide website

'I don't think there is a purpose to friendship, and maybe that's what makes it so beautiful.

'If you go into any kind of relationship with a purpose, you're undermining the connection that can take place. The purpose of friendship, for me, is that there *is* no purpose. There shouldn't be any agenda or any goals that you're trying to reach through that kind of relationship. And I think it gives so much space for friendship to take so many different forms.

'A lot of my close friends are Black women because we reflect one another, we can understand each other on a level that you can't see with a white friend. When I think about how beautiful those other relationships are, not through their Blackness, but aided through that connection of Blackness, I can't understand why I would settle for someone taking me for granted or making me feel that they didn't respect me.

'I think that, for my friends who aren't Black and queer and women etcetera, there has to be a lot of work done on their part in order to still give me the support that I need, when I am existing as all of those things. It's the same thing for my friends who are neurodivergent, for example: there are certain things that I have to do as someone who's neurotypical to ensure that I'm providing them with as much support [as I can] and acknowledging that difference and how much that difference shapes their life in a way that it doesn't shape mine.

'So I think it's possible, you just have to work hard. You have to acknowledge your position and how your position affects that person and their friend and your friendship together. I think that's crucial.

'Friendships aren't recognised by the state in any kind of formal way as something that you have to do, so you're choosing *how* you love one another, and everything that you do within a friendship is through pure choice.

'I was super depressed for a couple of months earlier this year, and one of my best friends came and stayed with me for a week. And there were so many facets to that, that were pure love. It was my partner who suggested for her to come and stay. And for me it was my partner saying: "You need me, but you also need your best friend" – taking herself out of it – because I think there are a lot of partners who might be threatened by the idea of someone else also providing you with some love and comfort. It was loving in that she knew that ... The two of them together is what I needed at that time. My best friend, she was living in north London, and she came all the way down to South Norwood for a week to sleep on the sofa, look after me, talk things through with me. And all of that was her choice, there's no duty on her part where she has to be my person in this way. She has entirely chosen to do that. It's the choice without any historical duty that really makes friend-ships beautiful because you are committing to that relationship again and again.'

3.
JOAN

Age Difference Friendships

I have been to Las Vegas twice in my life. The first time, Emma and I went in our mid-twenties to visit our friend who was studying at Stanford. He had invited us to stay with him on campus in Palo Alto, a forty-minute drive from San Francisco, and dangled before us the lure of endless Californian sunshine. As it turned out, Emma and I arrived in a freak thunderstorm.

'This is weird,' the taxi driver told us. 'It doesn't normally rain at this time of year.'

The wet, overcast weather lasted for days.

'This is weird,' every subsequent American we met would say. 'It doesn't normally rain at this time of year.'

Emma and I, who had envisioned ourselves sunbathing by the pool and drinking holiday beer straight from the bottle, fell into a slough of despond. So our friend made an executive decision that we should all go to Vegas.

'It's in the middle of the desert,' he said. 'It never rains there.'

He knew a fraternity who were organising a 1970s-themed trip and said we could tag along. So that's how we found ourselves on a flight to Nevada dressed in bell-bottoms and rose-tinted shades surrounded by inebriated men shouting, 'What happens in Vegas stays in Vegas, bro!' It wasn't ideal, but at least there'd be guaranteed sunshine. I mean, Vegas was in the middle of a desert. Shortly before landing, the captain came on the intercom.

'Just an update on the weather, folks,' he said. 'Tonight, Las Vegas is experiencing its first significant rain in twenty years.'

The following weekend passed in a blur of pouring rain, pinging slot machines and twenty-four-hour steak restaurants. I can dimly remember dancing to the Bee Gees' 'Stayin' Alive' with a handsome frat boy in an air-conditioned casino nightclub, and being astonished that one of the hotels had a convincing painted rendition of sky on its vast ceilings so that you never once felt the need to go outside. Other than that, I was not enamoured of the city.

I didn't think I ever wanted to return to Vegas. But then an unexpected opportunity presented itself. In 2014, I was approached to join the British American Project – a transatlantic fellowship of interesting people who annually gather for a four-day conference to network and foster what is nebulously referred to as 'the special relationship'. If that sounds confusing, it's because it is. No one who belongs to BAP really knows what it does or who funds it. But once I'd got through the selection process, I was offered a free trip to Vegas, so it could have been the CIA for all I cared.

Despite my earlier distaste for the city, I was at a difficult place in my personal life. It was late 2014 and earlier in the year, I had undergone two gruelling cycles of IVF. Neither of them had been successful. Then, out of the blue, I had got pregnant naturally, only to lose the baby at three months. I was numb and sad and tired. My marriage was hanging by a thread. Suddenly, jetting off to Vegas with a bunch of strangers in November seemed like an amazing idea.

This time, the sun shone as advertised. The delegates were put up in a hotel so vast it had a cinema in its foyer. My social anxiety kicked in almost as soon as the plane took off, but because of my learned coping mechanism of pursuing safety in groups, I quickly made friends. My favourites were Phoebe, Duncan and Adam, the three other Brits who also seemed to find the whole thing mildly absurd (if we had a common interest, our common interest was very much Not Taking Anything Too Seriously).

Over the following days, I went to one conference talk, then opted out of anything that didn't include free booze. What can I say? I was in a slow-motion emotional break-down and I knew that sitting through yet another earnest panel discussion about gambling laws wasn't going to make me feel better. Double measures of vodka, however? That was a different story.

On the third night in Vegas, it was my birthday. The four of us worked out that, because of the time difference, I should probably start celebrating several hours in advance in order to be aligned with my friends and family back home. That was just common sense.

There was a themed ball that night, which required us all to dress up as gangsters and molls. I began downing vodka tonics, taking care not to let my feathered flapper's headband get in the way. The party passed in a bit of a blur, and then a charity auction was announced. All the lots, we were told, had been donated by previous conference attendees.

At this stage, I had drunk (at a conservative estimate) approximately seventy-eight vodka tonics, and because it was my birthday, Duncan kept going to the bar to buy me drinks.

'And now we're approaching our final lots of the night,' the auctioneer was saying over a crackling speaker system. 'Next up: a week's stay in Los Angeles, donated by BAP fellow Joan Harrison.'

I'd only ever been to LA for work. As a Sunday newspaper journalist, I had sometimes flown in for forty-eight hours in order to interview a celebrity through a blur of jet lag. I'd always liked the city during those brief forays, partly because my cousin Andrea lived there and showed me all the nicest restaurants and shopping malls. But I'd never thought of LA as a holiday destination until this auction lot was announced. And because I was reeling from all that had happened that year, and because I felt inexpressibly sad at the thought of going home, and because, let's be frank, I was pretty tipsy, I found myself bidding for the lot. I wasn't entirely sure I had the money in my bank account, but somehow I kept raising my arm until I was told that I'd won it for $700.

'What have I done?' I asked Duncan as the auctioneer banged his gavel.

'Made a sound investment,' he reassured me. 'That's actually really good value for seven nights in LA.'

'Yes,' I said, slurring slightly as I polished off the last dregs of my drink. 'I'm sure you're right.'

I put it on my credit card and delayed worrying about where I was going to find the money until the conference was over and we had all limped, ashen-faced and hung-over, back to the UK.

I didn't book my trip immediately. There were other things to deal with first. I rowed with my husband over Christmas because he couldn't understand how upset I had been over the miscarriage and I couldn't understand why this seemed beyond his comprehension. The weeks passed. Nothing changed. By February, I had made the difficult decision to leave. I walked out with two bags of clothes.

My ex was disbelieving. He put pressure on me to come home. And there was a warped part of me that still loved him, so it was difficult to navigate, to convince myself that it made sense. As someone who, historically, had possessed so little faith in her own judgement and who avoided conflict at all costs, this was a notable shift in behaviour. It seemed uncharacteristic even to me. I was confused, exhausted and unsure of what to do next. And yet some long-buried but irrefutable instinct was pushing me forwards. It was the same way I had felt when I knew I needed to leave my school in Belfast. Either I stayed and disappeared, or I went and saved myself.

Then I remembered my LA auction lot. They'd given me the contact details of the woman who had donated it, so I emailed her.

'Dear Joan,' I typed. 'I'm sorry it has taken me so long to get in touch …'

She replied almost immediately. When I tell you that her return email was warm, that doesn't quite convey the measure of it. It was so thoughtful that I had to read it several times over. Not only was she saying I could come any time that was convenient, but that when I did make it to LA, she and her husband Michael would like to throw a small gathering in my honour so that I could meet their friends and, oh, also, please could she treat me to a blow-dry and brunch when I arrived?

Blow-dry, brunch and sunshine far away from the wreckage of my marriage? Yes please. I booked my ticket the next day. I turned up on Joan and Michael's doorstep in West Hollywood in March 2014, thirty-five years old and trailing a single wheeled suitcase and substantially more emotional baggage in my wake. They welcomed me in and poured me a glass of red wine. And that is how three of my most important platonic love affairs started – with Joan, with LA and with Californian Pinot Noir.

What I remember of Joan from that first meeting was her composure. I was someone trying to make sense of both the world and herself, so I admired this quality straight away. Joan seemed to know herself and what she thought about life, and I wished almost immediately that I was more like her. She was shorter than I was, with shoulder-length brown hair, brown eyes and a ballerina's poise. She held herself with elegance and a kind of strength. When she spoke, it was considered and thought through. She asked questions and really listened to the answers. I would later discover that she was also funny, and would occasionally swear with a force that always appeared slightly shocking coming from her.

Over the ensuing week, Joan and I became close. But it wasn't the friendaholic quick-hit kind of close I was used to. I didn't feel I was befriending her to avoid looking at myself. Quite the opposite: I felt that being her friend would help me understand what kind of woman I was.

I confided in her about my fears of not becoming a mother. She took me for that brunch and over scrambled eggs she looked me in the eyes – this pale, lost, Englishwoman she had only just met – and said, 'But Elizabeth, you will be a mother because you *want* to be a mother. There are so many ways to do it.'

She explained how many celebrities in Hollywood in their late forties and even early fifties had babies through egg donation and surrogacy; how LA was at the forefront of fertility medicine and how, not so long ago, she and Michael had tried to have children but it hadn't worked out for them and that, at a certain point, it had felt right to stop trying, and that she was at peace with that decision. She had stopped wanting it, and the two of them now had a great, full life, with successful careers and a gorgeous home.

Joan provided me with a hopeful vision of a different kind of life, where you could write your own story rather than dutifully living out someone else's version of what a conventional woman should do or be. It helped that she was twenty years older. I found enormous solace in befriending a woman who had been through so much of what I was experiencing, and who was willing to impart her non-judgemental wisdom to me from the other side.

Joan made me feel better about my own indecision. My head was a tangle of conflicting impulses and I was caught between the desire to return to the comparative safety of my marriage and live with a degree of familiar unhappiness, or to take the greater risk and gamble on the prospect of fulfilment. In the face of this distress, Joan was calm. She didn't pry. But slowly, over the course of several more conversations, I told her more. Where I was unclear, she was clear on my behalf. She didn't think I should go back to my ex. She thought I was worth more than that.

When I arranged a Zoom call with Joan to talk about our friendship, I asked what her first memory had been of our meeting. She mentioned Michael opening the door on that dark March night to find me on the other side, but a more distinct recollection was of a few days later, when the two of us sat in the hot tub in their backyard, drinking mimosas and confiding in each other about our lives.

JOAN: I guess that was our breakthrough conversation, when you shared your heartbreak over the divorce and the miscarriage. And I really felt your overwhelming pain. I mean, I still feel that moment. It was so clear to me that if you want to build a family you *will* have a family, absolutely. And as painful as that has been, it's a passage to get you to a place that you deserve. I very much remember that conversation because it often takes years to build up to that kind of forthrightness – and with you it was just so easy.

And it went on from there. That you took that chance with me, not knowing me, meant a lot. And I just wanted – as any good friend would – to make you feel better and give you a sense of hope. But also take the burden, help you shoulder your pain, I guess is all I mean to say.

In the hot tub, Joan went on to talk to me about her life. Her childhood had been dysfunctional and poor. She was one of six siblings ('Third from the top, fourth from the bottom: title of my memoir,' she joked), raised by a mother with bipolar disorder in a blue-collar town in Long Island. Relations with her siblings were strained and they made her feel as though she was the 'weakling child and the stupid child. And then I went out into the world and came to realise that the family narrative was far from accurate.'

For Joan, friendship became something that helped adjust that narrative so that it more accurately reflected the reality of who she was.

JOAN: If you're a deeply feeling person and your family isn't, you craft your own tribe to fill in where your family couldn't: to meet your emotional needs. And I think that's a key component of friendship. We particularly see that in bigger cities to which people migrate. Here in Los Angeles, it's the city of reinvention; it's not a place where people are easily defined. You're rarely asked, 'Where did you go to school?' I mean, people don't care. So it's a place where people create their own stories and their own families.

ELIZABETH: So is the purpose of friendship, for you, to fill the gaps left by family dysfunction?

JOAN: I think that's a big part of it. And, look, I think that's part of friendship for everyone. Every family has its gaps, whether it's a withholding or overbearing parent or, in my case, a bipolar mother and some very difficult sibling relationships. I had an ugly break-up with my only sister. Filling that void with other relationships was critical. So I did. But even if you have a happy family, friendships add a different dimension to life.

The week in Los Angeles I spent with Joan back in 2014 allowed me to redefine myself as a woman independent of her marriage and her desperate need to be liked. In the city of self-discovery, Joan had taught me that alternative paths were open and that I was not defined by the difficulties of my past. Instead, what lay ahead was boundless possibility – if I chose it.

Within weeks, I had pitched the idea of being an LA-based feature writer to my newspaper editor. He agreed.

In August that year, I moved there for three months. I saw Joan regularly, and since then, I see her every time I go back. Speaking to Joan is like having a regular emotional MOT, and our closeness is such that I have started referring to her as my 'sister from another mister'.

An integral part of our friendship is the twenty years between us. I have learned from her *because* we're not the same age, so there's a perspective we get from each other as a result of our different starting points. She gives me wisdom and a template of how to be. I give her an emotional openness that wasn't part of her childhood and an endless stream of book recommendations. (Actually, to be fair, those book recommendations go both ways.) When I spoke to Joan about age difference friendship, she saw it this way too.

ELIZABETH: I remember the conversation we had in the hot tub so vividly because it was a seminal conversation for me. I was like, 'Oh, there's a different way of doing life.' And it felt like you gave me back hope.

JOAN: Well, and you did that for me too because reliving my painful experience with whether or not to build a family was healing and reassuring. So there's reciprocity, always. It's never just giving or receiving. If there's not reciprocity in a friendship it's not really a friendship.

I went through many years of pain and disappointment. Pain and disappointment deepens our empathy and understanding and I don't regret that for a second. Now one thing I can do is to give back to our younger [feminist] sisters. And I get so much back from them. I get their optimism, and I get their vulnerability, which I would never show when I was younger. They're just an open book! They talk about their depressions and their breakdowns, their bad sexual experiences, they'll talk about anything, and I love that. And yeah, I get so much from that, so much from that openness and that 'just say yes' attitude. I derive so much joy and wisdom from much younger friends.

I also get a lot from older friends. I have a dear friend, Max, who is ninety-two. Whenever I'm deeply troubled, mostly about the goings-on in the world and our country, I call him. This is a man who has been a top journalist, he escaped the Holocaust … I mean, he has lived a big life. His son married a 9/11 widow. You know, he's seen it all. I called him the morning after Trump was elected. At these hinges of history, I always seek Max's counsel. And he gives me great comfort. So having both older and younger friends is always a plus – there are gifts from every end of the spectrum.

I loved that phrase 'the hinges of history' and the more I thought about it, the more I realised it applied to friendship too. My connection with Joan was itself a hinge between different life stages, and like all hinges it was an attachment that gave us both movement and safety; that made two discrete elements greater together than they might have been on their own.

JOAN

ELIZABETH: Do you fear your friends dying?

JOAN: I've had friends die. I first lost a close friend in his early forties. Then I lost – this is really painful – a very close girlfriend to early onset dementia and that was horrific. And there was another girlfriend, also fabulous, who died in her early fifties. More than anything, I embrace loss as an opportunity to live my best life in their honour. I think about them all the time. I speak their names, especially when I'm doing something that I think they would enjoy.

My husband is older than I am. So, of course we've talked about loss. And I have made him promise that should I pre-decease him, he will live a rich, full life. I hope he finds love again and he wants the same for me. And does it scare me? Not so much. Weirdly. Because I have faith that my friends will help me through that period. I will stick close to them and they to me and I'll be OK. I don't need to get married again, that's for sure. But I do need to always have intimacy in my life, psychological intimacy.

Joan's sense of perspective has, again and again, enabled me to find my own. She taught me the value of a well-placed boundary at a time when I was incapable of introducing them to either my friendships or my marriage. She reassures me it's something she's learned how to do over time, rather than a skill we're gifted with at birth, so there's hope for me yet. It's been helpful for me to witness how she handles social situations with clear-sighted polite-ness.

In the early days of our friendship, I noticed that where I would fall into people-pleasing, Joan was always able to state clearly what she needed and what she was willing to do for someone and what she wouldn't be able to invest her emotional energy in. In part, this was because for years, she was a successful and high-powered television executive in Hollywood. She worked at the highest echelons in a profes-sional world that relied on back-scratching and schmoozing and telling everyone how fabulous they were, while also being asked for favours on a daily basis from writers want-ing their scripts made or pushy agents or actors desperate for a part. In short: she got used to dealing with the demands of narcissists. This, combined with an upbringing in which her mother's behaviour was often unpredictable has made her into someone who values consistency and honesty. Joan would not be my only friend in Los Angeles, but she would be one of the most influential because of how she *did* friendship.

A few years ago, when I was staying once again in Joan and Michael's guest room, I got a Facebook message from an acquaintance in London who had seen that I was in Los Angeles.

'I am too!' she wrote. 'Let's meet up.'

This was a woman I had met a couple of times through journalism colleagues. she was a publicist who wanted to get newspaper coverage for various beauty brands she worked for, which I'm sure is why she was courting me. I groaned.

'What is it, sweetie?' Joan asked.

I explained that there was this woman and she'd seen I was here and I didn't want to meet her but now I was going to have to, wasn't I? I was going to have to be *friendly*. I absolutely must do the right thing.

Joan put her coffee mug down on the counter and looked at me. She didn't ask me why on earth I felt I had to accommodate someone I barely knew, nor did she dismiss my issue as inconsequential. She somehow knew that the thought of letting this woman down was painful to me.

'Just say, "Lovely to hear from you. I've only just arrived and am still finding my feet. I'll let you know when I resurface."'

Imagine, for a moment, that scene in the television police procedural where the sleep-deprived, rumpled detective stands by a whiteboard and suddenly the penny drops and she figures everything out and starts energetically drawing lines in heavy black marker, connecting all the disparate pieces of evidence. That was me when Joan uttered those words.

It was a magically elegant solution to my quandary. First of all: it was true. I didn't have to deploy a white lie to get out of an unwanted social obligation. Secondly: it gave me the opportunity to get back in touch or *not* as I desired. Thirdly: it was nice. I wouldn't offend anyone. I had set a boundary, but I had not been rude in doing so.

It might seem a trivial exchange to anyone who doesn't understand the friendaholic's perpetual desire to keep gathering people close and their mortal fear of being disliked, but for me it was pivotal. Joan gave me permission to say no. Not only that, she provided me with the words to do so. I've lost count of the number of times I've used that particular phrase to let people down gently. I'm sure the individual in question probably couldn't have cared less whether I was going to see them or not, but the point is that saying no in this way made me feel better, rather than living under a cloud of guilt for hours afterwards that I hadn't said yes. Or, worse, that I *had* said yes and would then want to cancel at the last minute. Or that I had said yes and would force myself to go, with a reluctance that left me drained by social obligation. No, I could just say, 'I'll let you know when I resurface'!

Slowly but surely I was edging towards having a friendship backbone. And when I looked at Joan, I saw a fulfilled, vibrant woman with a full circle of friends. Clearly, her straightforward communication skills had not done her a disservice. Quite the contrary, in fact. By being able to say no, it meant that when she said yes, her friends knew she meant it. She was actively choosing that friendship, and in order to give her all to those relationships, she also, by necessity, had to be selective.

ELIZABETH: Have you ever ended friendships?

JOAN: Yes. When they [the friend] show a very clear pattern of not owning their self-defeating behaviours, or even admitting to them … In fact, thinking about this conversation I realise I barely speak to four of my oldest girlfriends. There's been a ghosting of each one for different specifics, but I realise that the common ground is that I can no longer live with the fictions they've created.

Joan's most meaningful relationships have existed outside her blood relations, so naturally she mistrusts dishonesty in her friends. For Joan, if a friend is unable to project that same honesty inwards, and be truthful about who *they* are, then she can no longer feel safe in their company. She has to trust in their integrity in order to believe in who she really is. Interestingly, given that much of Joan's identity relies on this honesty, when it comes to breaking up with friends, it feels scary to her to state the facts.

JOAN: It's tough to say to someone, you know, 'Your life is built on a series of delusions.' So plenty of women, in particular, ghost relationships, or change their behaviour so the relationship becomes untenable. We don't break up with people particularly well … I'm no paragon of the art of the break-up, that's for sure. Actually, I have a very fragile friendship right now that is teetering on a break-up and I think when it comes – because I think it's inevitable – I think this time I will be specific and forthright.

ELIZABETH: Should we feel guilty when we ghost a friend?

JOAN: Yes and no. I have felt guilt. Maybe I would feel less guilt had I been more explicit about the ending. But we don't want to hurt anyone … I ran into one of those old friends I don't talk to any more. She was very cold to me and I understood – I hurt her. So yeah, there was guilt.

Yet for Joan, simply because she experienced guilt did not mean the friendship itself deserved resurrecting. Her ghosting was the most honest thing she could do in the circumstances. Yes, she could have told them to their faces what the issue was, but that would have been cruel and Joan still wanted to be as compassionate as she could.

Was it OK to experience guilt and not to act on it? Was it true that sometimes, the easiest or kindest way to end a difficult friendship could be falling silently out of each other's lives? As I ended the Zoom call with Joan, waving and blowing kisses at the screen, I shut my laptop and sat back on the sofa. A painful memory edged into the corner of my mind. I didn't want to write about it. But if I was examining friendship in all its multifarious contexts, I knew I would have to.

The Friendship Tapes
KYLA

Kyla Harris, 37, film-maker,
writer and activist

'When I first had my accident, I was fifteen years old. I had my accident on a school trip and went from that school trip, at the beginning of the year, straight into rehab [Kyla is now a C5–6 tetraplegic and requires round-the-clock care].[30] The way that that affected my friendships was life-changing. It was a life-changing thing in any case, but there was a stark before and after of my friendships – after my accident, 90 per cent of my friends left; stopped being my friends.

'That's for a variety of reasons. Obviously, ableism was paramount. [Before the accident] I was in a group of four and we were super tight. I finally felt that I had found this supportive female friendship group, I was coming into my own in terms of independence, understanding who I was, what I loved speaking about.

'After I had my accident, one of my best friends in that foursome stopped talking to me for years. We both ended up running to be head girl at our school, and she didn't get through the next round, and I did, and I remember seeing her crying in one of the classrooms and I went up to her and I said, "Listen, I know it's been a few years and we haven't talked but I'm still here for you, and I still love you and I wish the best for you, and if ever you want to talk about what we've been through, what happened to you all those years ago, I'm here," and she never took me up on it. She has kids now and is married and I think, "Are you passing that fear onto your children?"

'When I had my accident I lived a five-hour journey from where all of my friends lived – it was a ferry ride and it was very expensive to come back and forth. In the first month and a half, it seemed like the entire school was so supportive, and everyone was crying to my mum who worked at the school, and my dad wrote blog posts about all of my progress and what was happening. And then everything stopped. As soon as I started living back at home, when I was out of rehab eight months later and was going back to school, nobody talked to me. I was a complete outcast, [a] total outsider. And everything that had previously happened felt like lip service.

'The closest equivalent I can think of is when there's bereavement and people flood in, show support, then forget two months later, when you're only starting to fathom it. It was so real. It was so isolating. And it felt like such a slap in the face. It felt like everyone was my cheerleader and that it had happened to them, and that they were going through this awful trauma. And then when that trauma came back to school, it was like "Let's all ignore it, it's not here, it's not happening. I don't know how to engage, I don't know if I should."

'I had one friend – she was my best friend out of those four people that stuck with me – and she would piggyback me upstairs at parties and help me pee. She became my absolute rock; she was the only person that stayed friends with me.

'I think the person that they knew, the Kyla that they knew, had died. I felt like I'd come back and I was a ghost in my school, going down hallways. Before I met other disabled people that I connected with, I felt like my existence was as a ghost, and it took friendships with disabled people to really ground me in the present and to make me feel like I was living again, living without isolation.

'I had to shed so much internalised ableism, and still am shedding because you don't realise how deep it goes. It's so ingrained in all of us.

'My disability acts as an invisible security guard. There's a lot of people who would not talk to me or initiate conversation or friendship because of my disability. And to me, they're clearly not people I want to spend time with anyway. So what I [look for in a friend] is empathy, fun, a sense of humour, flexibility, because I think for me to, for people to really engage with me as a friend, you have to be quite flexible in terms of understanding crip time.'[31]

4.
GHOSTING

When Friends Disappear

About a year after returning to London from LA, I was walking home from the tube one night when one of my closest friends blanked me in the street. It was as I waited at the traffic lights, thinking about what I'd buy from the Co-op for dinner, that I saw her. Becca was coming down the street towards me, on the other side of the road. She was dressed in her trademark leather jacket, white vest-top, ripped jeans and Doc Marten boots. She had dyed a streak of her fringe bright pink. I felt the pang of not knowing she'd decided to change her hair; it's the kind of thing we would have talked about. But that was before.

We hadn't seen each other for a while. I wasn't sure why but Becca had started ignoring my texts and emails. At first, she'd reply with a few non-committal words when I suggested meeting for coffee. A birthday message I'd sent had been curtly received. It was weird. It wasn't like her. It wasn't *like us*. But, I reasoned, maybe she needed space. There had always been something unknowable about Becca, an unreachable quality that meant when she bestowed on you the gift of her attention, you felt special. When it was removed, it was as if the seasons had changed and you were left outside without a coat in the windy chill of autumn. I told myself it was nothing to worry about, that Becca just needed some time. I didn't want to annoy her by pestering her endlessly.

Then something even weirder happened: Becca stopped answering altogether.

Seeing her in the street that day made me oddly nervous. And yet, I reasoned as we approached each other, Becca was one of my dearest friends. There was no need to be anxious, I told myself, grabbing more tightly to the straps of my bag. We'd say hello and the strangeness that had been festering between us over the last few months would dissipate and we'd hug and chat and I'd feel much better about it all. I'd probably been inventing the distance, I thought. I had a tendency to do that: to imagine the worst when I hadn't heard from someone, when in truth they had simply been busy or preoccupied or on a work deadline.

We got closer and closer. Although we were on different sides of the road, I could quite clearly see her turn her head and clock me. There was a flicker of recognition in the way she tilted her face. She didn't smile. I caught myself in the act of raising my hand to wave: an automatic reflex. Embarrassed, I brought my arm back down by my side. Becca carried on walking.

I was so shocked, I actually laughed. Her blanking of me had been so nakedly deliberate and I wasn't sure how to react. I failed to say anything in the moment. I couldn't reach for the right words. In place of where there should have been the shared vocabulary of our friendship, there was instead an all-encompassing shame. I felt humiliated. My internal logic decreed that I must have committed some terrible error. What had I done or said or not done or not said to make her act in this way?

I never got an answer from Becca, because it turned out that blanking me in the street was the start of a comprehensive ghosting. I would never hear directly from her again. No more calls or emails or texts or cups of coffee. No more nights out, laughing riotously over one too many vodka tonics. No more long conversations where we would talk about everything from casual sexism and politics to the best romantic comedies of all time and the optimal ingredients for a sandwich filling (me: cheese and tomato; Becca: tuna mayonnaise). No more of Becca's eight-year-old daughter giving me unsolicited style advice.

'Elizabeth, that top is ugly,' the daughter had told me when I turned up in a knitted yellow sweater one day. Becca had laughed and although I wanted to ignore it – because honestly, who was going to take sartorial guidance from an eight-year-old wearing a Hello Kitty onesie? – I chose not to wear that jumper again.

I ended up giving it to a charity shop at around the same time as I finally admitted to myself that my friendship with Becca was over. Like the jumper, I would never again feel its consoling warmth. Worse, I would have to live with the fact that I would never know what her reasons were. Sometimes a friendship ends and the only explanation you're given is silence.

I first met Becca at a spin class. For most of my twenties, I had actively avoided exercise as if it intended me harm. I was always the person during weekends away with friends who refused to go on a hearty Sunday afternoon walk if the *EastEnders* omnibus was on. It was because I had bad memories of school games lessons during which we were forced to wear the scratchy regulation maroon knickers under too-short skirts while we attempted to hit a ball with a wooden stick in the freezing winter months. In the summer, I would so often claim to have my period in order to skip swimming class that the teachers must have genuinely worried about the frequency of my menstrual cycle. In short: I believed I was bad at sport. As I grew older, this belief translated to all forms of exercise.

But in my thirties, this changed. It was partly because I was going through fertility treatment and wanted to give it the best chance of success by being as healthy as I could, but it was also because I needed to reclaim my own body. It was a body that was being injected and scanned and prodded and probed and examined. It was a body that was trying to have a baby and yet kept failing to do so. In this, it was a body that had been found wanting. It was my body, but it felt disconnected from my own desires. I began to yearn for wholeness. I wanted to inhabit my physical self; I wanted to love it even if I was being made to feel by medical professionals that it was failing in this supposedly simple biological task. I wanted to feel good about it again.

I had an urge to make myself powerful. I was so sick of being buffeted around by the crashing waves of self-administered hormones that I needed to build up my own strength. I needed to be able to stand and withstand, to cope with whatever came next. And I needed to show myself that sometimes, if I put in the effort, my body responded in the way it was meant to.

Someone I knew suggested I try a spin class. She explained spinning to me as a cross between a nightclub and a religious experience.

'Basically,' she said, 'there's this fit instructor at the front telling you you're amazing to pumping music and it's so dark you don't have to worry about anyone seeing you look shit.'

I was sold. Soon, it became a borderline obsession. Any time I was disappointed by a failed IVF round or angered by the hopelessness of infertility or had had an argument with my husband, I would pound it out on the bike. I would sweat and cry and whoop with joy when the instructor swung their towel around their head at the end of class. Afterwards, as I washed my hair in the shower, I felt better. I felt empowered. I had done something good with my day. I noticed that, over time, I started finding it easier to ride to the beat of whatever frenetic remixed pop track was playing. Inch by inch, pedal by pedal, I was getting stronger.

When she walked into one of those classes, I noticed Becca immediately because unlike me, who liked to skulk in the back where no one could see my face grimacing in agony, Becca had booked a bike in the front row, directly in the instructor's line of sight. She was wearing leopard-print leggings and a gold sports bra. Her hair was tied up in bunches. Her nails were long purple talons. I watched as she adjusted the height of her seat and nonchalantly swung one leg onto the handlebars as a warm-up stretch, reaching for her toes with a dancer's poise. This particular spin studio was situated in Oxford Circus, central London, and apparently it was a regular occurrence to see someone a bit famous there. Rumour had it that Harry Styles came all the time, although I only ever saw John Torode, the *MasterChef* judge. No shade, John, but I wish it had been Harry.

There was something about Becca – her swagger, her indifference to what other people were thinking of her – that made me think she must be a celebrity. She was like the love child of Kim Kardashian and David Bowie. During the class, she effortlessly kept pace with the instructor and was able to do all the difficult, choreographed dance moves.

After the class was over, I unclipped from my bike and rushed to the shower, hoping to beat the inevitable queue. But when I got to the changing room, there were already three people ahead of me, each one wrapped tightly in the gym-issued towels, rosy-cheeked from the forty-five-minute ride. I stood in line and the woman in front turned to me and smiled. It was *her*. The lady in the leopard-print leggings. She caught my eye and smiled and when she did, her whole face crinkled sweetly. She seemed instantly more approachable than she had been in the studio.

'I like your tattoo,' I blurted out, searching for something to say that would compensate for my earlier silent dislike. But it was true: I did like her tattoo. In fact I'd never seen one like it. It was a York rose on her forearm, drawn in grey ink.

'Oh thanks,' she said. 'I'm obsessed with Richard III. It's pretty niche.'

Well, I mean, how can you resist a person who wears gold sports bras and tattoos themselves with the insignia of long-gone monarchs? I certainly couldn't.

Over the following weeks, I would spot Becca again and again in class. She always wore mismatched leggings and tops in an array of fabulous colours. Her hair would be styled in plaits or plumped-up ponytails and once she left it down the whole ride, and it shook like a lioness's mane every time she tapped back. I loved the fact that her body wasn't skinny. She had curves and looked stronger for it. She rejoiced in the way her tummy jiggled over the waistband of her leggings. She didn't try to hide herself. We'd exchange smiles and a few words about the weather and gradually we worked our way up to having a post-ride smoothie.

Those post-ride smoothies became a regular part of our weekly routine. I began to get excited about the prospect of going to class not just because of the physical benefit but because chatting to Becca made me feel better emotionally too. We both worked in male-dominated industries – she was in music and was constantly frustrated by the misogyny and late-night culture, while I was a writer for a Sunday newspaper where almost all the important roles were occupied by men. Becca was one of the first people I had proper, engaged, hilarious and energising conversations with about feminism. I would leave our chats high on the fumes of our shared ideas about the world. She was a few years older than me, already in her forties and had been with her university girlfriend for twenty years. She had so much experience of life that her practical wisdom made me feel safe confiding in her. And I did: far more quickly and easily than I might have done otherwise.

Becca wasn't connected to anyone in my life. She didn't know my husband. She didn't know my friends. She hadn't known me at school or university, so she had no preconceptions of how I should be or how I might have been expected to behave. She took me at face value. So if I told her – as I did – that I was having marital issues, she would have a calm, objective perspective. She told me that I deserved to be happy and that if I wasn't, it was OK to make a change. It wasn't my fault, she insisted. A marriage required two people to make it work, she continued. I couldn't do all the work of two people myself. It had to be a dialogue, not a monologue.

The smoothies turned into cocktails and the cocktails turned into evening meals in cosy restaurants with corner booths. Soon Becca was in my closest circle of friendship. The confidences went both ways. She told me she was frustrated and bored in her relationship, and was guiltily nurturing a workplace crush on a younger colleague. She worried that if she and her girlfriend split up, it would have a negative impact on their daughter. And she worried that if she stayed, her daughter would grow up in a household with two bickering, resentful parents. She told me that I was one of only two people she had admitted any of this to and I felt a swollen-headed pride that I was deemed special enough to be the recipient of her secrets.

Rapidly Becca began to occupy the role of a loving elder sibling. She took me under her wing. We went clothes shopping at her suggestion and she told me to buy a pair of boots I would previously have thought too edgy for me. She encouraged me to try on tight skirts and leather jackets and decided that my workout gear wasn't anywhere near stylish enough. Soon, I was turning up to spin classes in leopard-print leggings and gold sports bras too. And because I looked up to her, because I trusted her and most of all because I wanted to be close to her, I went along with it all. I was a willing accomplice in my own re-shaping. Whatever Becca said carried extra weight.

'You're getting very close to this person,' Emma said once when I kept dropping Becca's name into a phone conversation. I laughed, thinking that Emma was pretending to be jealous, that she was striking the pose of the possessive best friend.

'You don't need to worry,' I replied. 'She's not you!'

We moved on, but Emma was right to have sounded a note of caution. I was getting very close to Becca, very quickly. I had never felt such a passionate whirlwind of affection with a friend before. It was akin to falling in love, in that we finished each other's thoughts and sentences.

Being friends with Becca didn't seem like a choice. It seemed a necessity.

I suppose, in a way, it was. My marriage was breaking down, and when I needed to talk to someone with total honesty about what was going on, I turned to Becca because she readily accepted me as I was. The mistakes I had made in my relationship, the lies I might have told to protect myself, the wrong-headed decision to have been with this person in the first place – Becca understood it all because she had done the same. We found mutual understanding in the wreckage of our emotional lives and clung to each other like pieces of driftwood in the current.

After six months, she had quickly become one of the most important people in my life. When, a year into our friendship, I finally found the courage to leave my husband, it was Becca who helped me pack. It was Becca who told me she believed in me; that even if I had no confidence in myself, she had it for me. It was Becca who helped me to navigate the first wobbly moments of newly single life. Looking back now, I realise that Becca was my rebound relationship. There was nothing romantic between us, and yet the excitement I felt each time I saw her and the way that I relied on her acceptance of me, carried with it the same disproportion as the fevered first months of a love affair. It sounds stupid to say it, but I think the respect I thought I felt for her was something more dangerous. I think I idolised her. I wanted her to teach me how to be more confident, more stylish, more assertive, more wise. And she, in turn, seemed to want to be my guide through life. She gave me the details of her therapist, her hair-dresser, her chiropractor. She would press their phone numbers on me with enthusiasm, insisting I call them because they'd helped her and they'd make everything better in ways I couldn't even imagine in my post-marital fog.

'Are you sure you don't mind?' I asked again and again. I was astonished by her generosity and didn't want to exploit it.

'Of course not,' she said.

She made it seem as though this was knowledge she had accumulated over years of trial and error and she wanted to save me the bother. So I took her up on it. I started seeing her therapist, her hairdresser and her chiropractor. I told her repeatedly how grateful I was and then I got the sense that I was annoying her by saying thank you so much, so I stopped. But then she'd suggest something else we could do together or another way of making my life better. She took me to get my ear cartilage pierced at the place she'd had hers done, and she gifted me a tiny, sparkle-studded hoop to wear – just like hers. The piercing was painful, but I loved it. Every time I caught the hoop while washing my hair or pulling a jumper over my head I would wince, but then I'd be reminded of one of the most important friend-ships in my life. It made me feel even closer to Becca. It made me feel that she wanted that closeness too.

After my marriage ended, Becca suggested that I rent a flat close to where she lived. I barely thought about it in the rush to say yes.

'You need your friends around you,' she said. 'You need to be within walking distance. And this is such a lovely area.'

It didn't matter to me that it was a completely new neighbourhood. It would be great to live somewhere with no unhappy memories attached to it, I reasoned. It was the perfect opportunity to get to know a different part of my city! I'd be able to meet Becca for coffee whenever the mood took us! We could order takeout and have sleepovers!

I found a tiny, light-filled one-bedroom flat with a bay window in which I placed my desk as a statement of intent. The previous tenants had put a small dining table there with two chairs. But my focus was going to be my single life and my work. I unpacked my books and the few clothes I had taken out of the Croydon storage unit in which most of my possessions now festered. I felt a quiet sense of pride that here it was at last: a room of my own.

I was extremely happy in that flat and Becca was right: it was a great part of town. But all those promised coffees and sleepovers never really materialised. I discovered that the more geographical proximity there was between us, the less we saw or spoke to each other. It was as if I was allowed to get close, but not too close. Whereas I shared everything with Becca, she was capable of more restraint.

In the flurry to be intimate up to that point, I hadn't noticed the imbalance at the core of our friendship. Perhaps sharing so much of my own experience crowded out the space for Becca's own thoughts and feelings. I realised that while I confided in her, Becca never fully reciprocated.

Although she gave the impression of emotional honesty, I began to realise that there were certain topics that were out of bounds. She kept her daughter very private, almost as if she didn't want to admit she was a mother, and we barely spoke about what must have been a defining part of her life. I would never proffer advice on her relationship unless she invited it. I sensed, without explicitly being told, that it was a no-go area. As much as she complained about her partner, she also made it clear that I couldn't fully understand their dynamic. I wanted to be there for her and yet, at the same time, I felt it was important to respect her boundaries. Perhaps this meant I failed to understand the depths of what she was actually going through behind closed doors.

At the beginning of our intimacy, it had seemed as though we were simultaneously stumbling through the gradual disintegration of our respective romantic relationships, reaching for each other's hands in the darkness. Our solidarity was forged because we were both unhappy. But although I was encouraged by Becca to make the changes I needed, she never applied the same logic to her own life. I began to wonder if she wasn't telling me everything. Maybe, I thought, things weren't as bad as she made them seem and she simply needed to offload her negative feelings onto me as a means of letting off steam. It was hard to know one way or the other because I only met her partner a couple of times over the course of our four-year friendship.

'She never wants to come out,' Becca explained. 'She'd rather be at home watching TV.'

When her girlfriend did appear, it was as a solid, quiet presence in the background of some social event to which we had both been invited. She seemed content to let Becca shine while she propped up the bar with a pint. I would try and engage her in conversation and she would smile but never give much of herself in return. It wasn't my place to question what happened behind closed doors, I told myself, and so I left them to it.

Becca's family was another *verboten* subject. She alluded a few times to the fact that she had a difficult older brother. According to Becca, he treated her badly and only ever got in touch when he wanted to ask her for money. She had deliberately distanced herself from him and described herself as 'estranged'. Occasionally, she made jokes about this and referred to the subject flippantly. I wasn't sure whether to join in with the humour or suggest gently that there was a deeper pain lying beneath the laughter. Any time I tried to ask her how she truly felt about her brother, she batted away the question.

'Oh, I don't want to talk about that,' she would say. Or 'I don't need to work anything out. He's a dick so I don't see him. I'm fine with it.'

I stopped asking for fear of losing Becca or annoying her further and because I became fearful of asking too much, it's perfectly possible I didn't ask enough.

When, shortly after I'd moved into my flat, she told me in passing one day that her brother had been diagnosed with prostate cancer, I told her how sorry I was.

'That's awful. How are you feeling?'

'I'm fine,' Becca said lightly. 'I made my peace with him not being in my life a long time ago.'

'Do you want to meet up?'

'No thank you, darling. Like I say, I'm fine.'

'OK, if you're sure, but I'm here if you want to talk.'

'Thanks. So, are you going to Fox's spin class on Wednesday?'

(The spin studio employed instructors called after an array of fruits and animals. I can recall both a Wolf and a Lemon putting me through my paces.)

'Um. I wasn't going to but yes, if you are, yes I will.'

And just like that the subject was dispatched. I think now I should have pressed her. I should have made more of an effort to show that I cared – because I did; I really, truly did. But, in truth, my way of showing I cared was to demonstrate that I had heard her. That I supported her however she wanted to live her life, just as she had supported me wholesale. If she didn't want to talk about something, I accepted it. I wanted to be the friend *she* wanted me to be and so I melted down some of my own identity to pour into the mould that Becca had created for me.

This included nurturing the same grudges as Becca had. She expected me to feel as enraged as she did when someone at her work passed her over for promotion because, she claimed, the woman appointed had been sleeping with their boss. I didn't doubt her version of events. She was one of my dearest friends, so it didn't make sense that she'd lie to me or skew the facts to suit her own narrative – especially when I actually knew some of the people involved through the music interviews I'd done over the years. I once made the mistake of mentioning that I'd run into one of the people Becca disliked at an industry awards ceremony.

'I hope you didn't talk to her,' Becca said, putting down her coffee and fixing me with a cool gaze.

'I mean, we chatted a bit,' I said. Becca's face grew stony with disapproval. 'But not for long,' I added quickly.

'You know she was the one who …' and Becca would embark on a convoluted story about how this particular woman (it was always a woman) had dissed her in some way, many years before I came on the scene. Even if I had never had anything other than pleasant interactions with said woman, it was my duty as Becca's friend to carry the weight of this person's perceived betrayal and blank her at every available opportunity. This, for Becca, was loyalty. It extended to not liking the funny Tweet of someone who had once written a negative review of one of her artists' gigs.

'I can't believe you did that!' Becca messaged me seconds after I'd naively pressed the 'like' button. 'You know how I feel about her.'

Heart thumping, I immediately apologised and unliked the offending joke. But in truth, it was hard to keep track of all the ways in which Becca felt disrespected or betrayed. The stories all followed a similar arc, in that Becca had previously been friends with the person who then did something unforgivable that necessitated the ending of the friendship. I didn't connect the dots back then, but I should have done. The experience taught me that it's highly suspect if a person you are close to repeatedly mentions a graveyard of past friendships, all of which have supposedly ended because of something the other person did. It's the friendship equivalent of a boyfriend constantly categorising all his exes as 'crazy'. After a while you begin to think: they can't all have been crazy, can they? Isn't the common denominator, well, you?

But of course the starting point for all the grudges was insecurity, which I understood. And I loved Becca, so I didn't think anything of it. The more I tried to be Becca's perfect friend – the person who bore her grudges, who never challenged the things she said, who swallowed whole the stories she told about her life, who pierced her ears the same way, who moved to live near her, the person who, in short, thought she was amazing and could do no wrong – the more she began to distance herself from me.

At first, I didn't notice. It was New Year, and Becca was on a health kick. She'd given up alcohol so didn't want to meet for cocktails. She was going to sleep earlier so that she could get up for early-morning runs, so late-night dinners didn't appeal either. We started catching up over daytime coffees but then these too became more and more infrequent.

My life was starting to turn a corner. The immediate devastation of the breakdown of my marriage had passed. A divorce settlement was being agreed through lawyers. I had gone freelance as a journalist and was starting to get interesting commissions. I had my flat, my friends, and a sense of selfhood was slowly returning. I met a younger man who was handsome and charming and funny and we started dating. Things were pretty good.

On the increasingly rare occasions that we did meet for a rushed catch-up, Becca asked fewer and fewer questions about what was going on for me. When I enquired about her life, she answered in bland platitudes. It was difficult to scratch beneath the surface of her 'fine's and 'yeah, good's. I was overly attuned to Becca's shifts in mood, so I thought the best thing to do was to give her space. I stopped texting her as much. I withdrew. And although I convinced myself I was being thoughtful, there was also part of me that wanted to protect myself. I was hurt by Becca's unexplained neutrality. I wasn't going to keep asking someone who didn't want to answer. It was like prodding a sleeping bear. I was worried that if I continued to do it, I'd be thwacked away with a large paw, and I didn't want to risk that kind of rejection. So if I just ignored the weirdness, I thought, then maybe she'd come back to me in her own time and maybe I could kid myself there was nothing awry.

But of course I see now that Becca was in pain. My life was moving in a different direction from hers, and perhaps this made her feel abandoned or sad or lost or any number of thorny emotions that were difficult to put into words, especially to the person who has triggered them.

Becca never did come back to me. Weeks turned into months and I realised I knew nothing of her life other than what I occasionally saw on social media, where she posted pictures of herself in workout gear sipping on oat milk lattes accompanied by Pinterest-worthy quotes referencing gratitude and blessings. The old Becca, with her sarcastic wisecracks and healthy sense of the absurd seemed to have disappeared. She had always hated Instagram, claiming it was vain and overly self-referential. Now, she was trying to reinvent herself as an influencer.

I wanted her to be as happy as she claimed in her picture captions but I wasn't sure she could be. If you're truly happy, the chances are you won't need to keep vociferously insisting you are in an online public forum. I wondered what was really going on behind the filtered smiles and glossy outfits of the day but I was still too nervous to ask. I should have done. I should have reached out. I attempted to mask my anxiety with an argument stitched together from an alternative logic. *She could reach out to me*, I would say to myself silently as I cooked dinner for one in my flat. *I'm busy and I have things going on, and what does she know about my life? Nothing.* The internal discussion would carry on like this for hours but it never made me feel any better. It made me upset.

I thought I would run into her one day at the spin studio and our old, easy familiarity would be restored. It never happened. I saw from Instagram that Becca had given up spin classes in favour of training for a triathlon. There was a picture of her in a wetsuit after an open-water swim next to her partner and daughter doing peace signs at the camera with the caption #myteam #familyfirst. People I knew – people I had introduced Becca to – had festooned the comments with heart emojis. I tapped a dutiful like. Becca hadn't liked any of my posts for ages. When I checked her name in my follower list, I realised she had unfollowed me. I gasped. To unfollow someone, rather than simply muting them, is an active statement of intent. It wasn't simply that we were going through a phase of distance. It was that Becca wanted to stop being my friend. It seemed so outrageously final. Tears pricked my eyes. I couldn't understand what I had done that was so wrong. What had merited this punishment?

Six months passed. And then, one day, there she was in the front row of Wolf's spin class. My stomach lurched when I saw her walk in and clip into the pedals. When the class was over, I wondered if there was any way of avoiding her, of slipping out before the lights went up but she caught my eye on the way to the changing room and we smiled at each other.

'So lovely to see you,' she said as she hugged me briefly.

'You too,' I said, baffled as to why she was acting normally again. Maybe I'd imagined it all? I found myself automatically asking if she wanted to go for a smoothie after we'd showered and she nodded.

'Sure,' she said, without much enthusiasm.

I met her at our usual table. I'd showered and changed too quickly because I didn't want to keep her waiting and as a result, I was still sweating when she sat down opposite.

'Hi,' I said, surreptitiously wiping my cheeks with the cuff of my sweater. 'How have you been?'

'Great,' she replied. 'You?'

'Good.'

The conversation was almost immediately unsatisfying. It was as though Becca was actively trying to avoid any kind of connection or depth. She wanted to keep our interaction at surface level, as if our words were trapped in the impenetrable lacquer of an Instagram filter. They remained stuck there, suspended in the static air between us. I asked after her girlfriend and daughter. She said her daughter had been having a tough time at school and was struggling with anxiety.

'Oh,' I said. 'I'm so sorry. That must have been really difficult.'

Becca waved away my concern.

'It's fine. She's over it now.'

Was it my imagination or was there an implied criticism there? Was she upset I hadn't been there for her? Was the underlying accusation that I would have known all this if I'd been a good enough friend?

'I'm sorry if I haven't been there for you,' I blurted out.

She smiled at me – that same, stuck-on smile that never quite reached the rest of her face. She didn't say anything. Somehow the banal chit-chat moved on with no further acknowledgement of this exchange. We sat there for about twenty minutes and then went our separate ways after a half-hearted hug. When I got to the tube station, I exhaled. I hadn't realised I'd been holding my breath.

That was the last time I spoke to Becca. A few weeks later, she would blank me in the street. Some time after that, I was writing in a local cafe when I felt the prickle of another person's gaze on the back of my neck. I turned around. It was Becca. She was staring at me. Our eyes met. Instead of smiling in recognition, this time she looked straight through me and then turned back to the friends she was with. I shivered. I understood, for the first time, what that well-worn phrase 'to cut someone dead' really meant. I had witnessed my total excision from someone's awareness. I had been sliced out of her life.

Cutting has a long and ignoble history. In the nineteenth century, the act of 'cutting' was deemed by *Cassell's Household Guide* as 'the most ill-mannered act possible to commit in society.'[32] By 1898, E. Cobham Brewer had gone to the trouble of identifying different kinds of 'cut' in his *Dictionary of Phrase and Fable*.

The 'cut direct', he wrote, was 'to stare an acquaintance in the face and pretend not to know him'. The 'cut indirect', 'to look another way, and pretend not to see him'. The 'cut sublime' was 'to admire the top of some small edifice or the clouds of heaven till the person cut has passed by'. And finally, 'the cut infernal' was 'to stop and adjust your boots till the party has gone past'.[33]

In 1922, Emily Post, the doyenne of modern manners, described the cut as 'a direct stare of blank refusal, and is not only insulting to its victim but embarrassing to every witness. Happily,' Post stated confidently, 'it is practically unknown in polite society.'[34]

Although I bow to Emily Post's superior knowledge in the area of cutlery use and thank-you notes, I'm afraid she got this wrong. Cutting is alive and well, partly because our society of twenty-four-hour communication offers many more ways in which to do it. The street is now not the only place to cut people. We can do it online by unfollowing. We can do it via text, by allowing the double WhatsApp tick to turn blue without response. We can leave voicemails unlistened to and phone calls unreturned. We can end relationships by disappearing. We can become ghosts of our own making.

This is what happened to me: I was ghosted by one of my most valued friends. Becca erased herself from my life. All that was left of our closeness was my ear piercing. There were times in the years that followed when I wondered if I'd invented it. Had it all been a fever dream – the adult equivalent of one of those secondary school crushes you have on girls a few years above you? But then I'd scroll back and find the evidence in old Instagram photos. Or I'd wear the boots she'd made me buy. Or I'd remember one of her pithy bon mots and find myself quoting it in a conversation with someone else. Every time this happened, I would feel a deep discomfort, a dull pain as if the cutting had been physical, as if the wound still ached. Gradually the scar healed over, so that a remembrance of Becca would only cause the slightest twinge, but it took a really long time. It was a slow-motion grief, unlike any other I had ever experienced. To begin with, I think I kidded myself that our friendship wasn't lost forever. I was subconsciously sure that it would come good again, even though we were no longer speaking. Then the denial segued seamlessly into anger – at Becca for never telling me what I'd done wrong; at myself for being so scared of finding out that I never asked – before slowly morphing into acceptance.

'Well,' Emma said when I told her, 'I didn't trust her from the start.'

'Really?'

'Really. She wanted you to stay stuck being sad and trapped and small. Now that you're not, she doesn't like it.'

I mulled this over. I wasn't sure it was true. I didn't think Becca would have consciously felt this way. I was convinced she didn't deliberately befriend me because I was depressed and needed guidance, only to drop me when I started standing on my own two feet. At the same time, I did come to believe that when a person is sad in their life, but can't fully acknowledge that sadness for fear of having to act on it, then they can often be drawn to someone else who appears to mirror their own emotional claustrophobia. In that context, it was perfectly possible that one person moving on with their life could highlight all that hadn't changed in their friend's. But I couldn't help but think it all seemed so unnecessary. Naively, I believed that being such a close friend mitigated any jealousy. But it didn't mean you wouldn't feel it. Women have been conditioned for centuries to believe in the lie of scarcity. We are forced to compete for jobs, attention and romantic partners because the patriarchy has convinced us there is only so much success to go round, and sometimes this terrible lie pollutes even the closest friendship. And to be fair, this doesn't just affect those who identify as women: it was Gore Vidal, a bisexual man, who famously said that 'Whenever a friend succeeds, a little something in me dies.'

Could it really have been that? My reluctance to believe jealousy might have been the root cause of our break-up was partly because it seemed so revoltingly self-aggrandising. But it was also partly a lack of what I term negative empathy. While many of us can empathetically transplant ourselves into the shoes of another person when they are acting in ways that we might also act, it's more difficult to imagine and understand the actions of someone who is behaving in a way you believe you wouldn't.

Although I never did ask Becca what happened, I finally got an explanation of sorts from a mutual acquaintance. This friend, Candice, had also experienced Becca freezing her out.

'It's happened to me too, Elizabeth!' she texted me one day. We met up shortly afterwards for coffee in a park to lick our wounds and compare notes.

Candice had been ghosted by Becca after they had gone for the same job at work. Candice had been promoted. Becca had not. Now, when they passed each other in the office corridor, Becca would look the other way. The simi-larities to my situation seemed striking.

'I don't think she can handle it when her friends are successful in the way she would like to be,' Candice said.

'I feel sorry for her,' I replied. 'Imagine being that unsure of your own worth.'

Candice told me that Becca had never once alluded to our friendship ending. In fact, Becca barely mentioned me at all. If my name was brought up in conversation, she didn't acknowledge it. Only once, Candice said, had Becca ever proffered an insight into what might have been behind it.

'She said you suffocated her.'

'What?!'

'She thought you copied her by doing all the things she did – getting the same ear piercing and stuff like that.'

I was stunned. All that time, I had thought our joint experiences were evidence of our closeness. I had believed they were markers of our love for each other. I had thought she wanted me to act on her advice and her recommendations. I had thought they were willingly shared. I had never understood that Becca felt *suffocated* by it. That, despite her apparent encouragement, she had hated every second of it. To her, our friendship had been pillaged by my attempt to conquer and copy rather than connect. I felt sick.

Afterwards, I found I was grateful to Candice. At least I now had an explanation and, even if I didn't agree with that interpretation of events, it made a kind of sense to me. I understood how all those moments of shared history could be seen in that way, if you chose to apply a retrospective narrative that put you in the position of an exploited saviour whose endless generosity is their undoing. It was ironic that I had been worried about not being close enough to Becca, when she had ended up finding that closeness stifling. Or she wanted closeness but not the kind I offered. She wanted closeness that she could manage and remain in control of and for me, that wasn't really closeness at all.

Still, Becca's ghosting had a profound impact on me. For a while, it made me even more fearful of losing friends or putting a foot wrong. The knowledge that you could accidentally make a friend think so badly of you that their only recourse was to vanish from your life with no explanation was shattering. There was no certainty in any of it, I realised. I could try to be the best possible ally to someone else and they might have a totally different experience of the friendship. Once I took that idea to its logical conclusion, there was an unexpected revelation: I had no control over anyone else's perception of me. So all of this trying to be a 'perfect' friend was a fool's errand. I might as well be my imperfect, flawed, not-always-communicative, no-I-don't-want-to-FaceTime, actually-I-think-walks-are-boring self and take the risk. Because there was going to be risk whatever way you played it, and in a weird sort of way, wasn't it better to be rejected as yourself than as the person you'd exhausted yourself trying to be?

We ghost people because we're too afraid to say what we think or we lack language to do so. A 2018 study of 1,300 respondents found that those who had a fixed mindset about the future, who believed in the concept of fate and destiny, were more likely to ghost in romantic relationships.[35] These are the people who cling to the binary idea of there being one true soulmate hidden in a mass of disappointing pretenders. If they're not convinced they are dating 'the one', they are 60 per cent more likely to see ghosting as an acceptable way to draw proceedings to a close, moving on without explanation. Those of us with a growth mindset – that is, a belief that relationships are not born perfect but need to be worked at – are 40 per cent less likely to see ghosting as acceptable.

The same study found that about a quarter of respondents had been ghosted by a romantic partner. One fifth had done so themselves. Fascinatingly, the researchers discovered that ghosting in friendships was even more common: more than a third reported either that they had ghosted a friend or been ghosted by one – and these are only the ones who would admit to it when questioned by scientists writing a paper on the phenomenon. I found that disparity interesting because although there's a lot written about ghosting in the dating world, there is very little literature on friendship ghosting.

I suspect this is because there is so much shame attached to it. I spent years – literally years – thinking I must have done something unforgivable to Becca in order to merit such an extreme punishment. I felt embarrassed talking about it. The ghosted friendship is dropped like a stone into a lake and the circles of silence keep overlapping and widening until they reach the water's edge, and then the surface is calm again and it's as if nothing has happened.

But if I were to fish that stone out from the bottom of the lake, what would I find? What secrets would it tell me? I think we ghost because the relationship in question doesn't make us feel safe enough to test it. Good parenting is about making your child feel unconditional love, so that when your child needs to express an uncomfortable feeling or admit to bad behaviour, they are able to do so in the full knowledge that while their parent might be disappointed or angry, they will never reject us as unloveable. Although it's not pleasant when a teenager drowning in adolescent hormones says 'I hate you' to a harassed mother, it's generally a storm that can be weathered. Testing these boundaries is integral to making a parent–child relationship stronger.

Some long-term romantic relationships embody the same sort of attitude: a partner will often show their worst side to the person they're closest to because they know there is a sufficient foundation of love to support the occasional bit of bad behaviour.

The majority of friendships are not like this, even though we often expect them to last just as long as a marriage. In my friendships I would never dream of arguing or fighting or acting up in any way that could threaten the delicate ecosystem of platonic love. I suppose that can, in certain incidences, lead to a difficult silence where there should, in an ideal world, be explanation and honesty. But honesty or vulnerability, for me, is safest when I'm reassured that the person I'm confiding in thinks the best of me. I need to know they will start from a position of generosity. When that goes, there is no real friendship.

Becca's ghosting left me with questions that I had to answer myself, groping in the darkness for the most likely explanation. As with any unexpected ending, there is a period of time where it feels senseless and unjust, and you wish you could know *why*. But with a ghosting, you're never given a why. There is just the fact of it.

It was a concept made explicit by a brilliant TV drama which aired in 2022. *Chloe*, which was written and directed by Alice Seabright, aired on the BBC and told the story of a woman called Becky (played by Erin Doherty) who becomes obsessed with the seemingly Instagram-perfect life of a former best friend who ghosted her. The opening episode reveals that her former best friend – the Chloe of the title – has died by suicide. The ensuing narrative is anchored by these two deaths – one literal, one metaphorical – and Becky becomes fixated on the need to investigate both, as if by finding the reason for Chloe's suicide, she will also find the explanation for their friendship ending. Throughout, the character of Chloe who once ghosted Becky appears as an actual ghost in Becky's dreams, making the parallel clear.

Although Becky acts in an increasingly unhinged manner – taking on multiple personae, stalking Chloe's friends through social media and, in one scene, pouring a vial of her own urine into a wine bottle after her boss annoys her – I also found I had sympathy for her. Not only that, but I was rooting for her. She was a transgressive heroine who could also act as an avenging angel for anyone who had ever been ghosted and, as such, I found watching *Chloe* oddly therapeutic. I might have been hurt, I reasoned, but at least I wasn't pissing into wine bottles.

There is an urban myth, oft repeated in popular culture, that it takes half the length of a romantic relationship to get over someone. So if you were dating for two years, it'll take twelve months to feel fully recovered from the heartbreak.

My experience with Becca was different. We were close friends for three years, and I think it's taken me almost double that to find my peace with it. It was a gradual process made up of small actions that ended up having a cumulative effect. I unfollowed her on Instagram. I no longer sought out opportunities to talk about what might have happened with the people who knew her. Eventually, I met the man who would become my husband and we moved to a different part of the city. At times, I would wonder what it might be like to reach out and ask to meet up. Would Becca say yes? Could we rekindle our friendship? Would I ever feel safe enough to ask what had happened? Was the fact I hadn't asked a terrible indictment of my ability to be loyal and loving?

Then, one day, I was talking to my friend Sathnam about it and he said something that stuck with me.

'I'd think less of you if you took her back,' he said. We were walking through Green Park and he was doing his usual thing of pointing out all the interesting historical trivia he'd amassed over the years. In between the factual anecdotes, we'd started chatting about friendships and I'd been drawn, ineluctably, to the topic of Becca.

'What do you mean?' I asked.

'Well, it shows you've got no standards,' he said, not unkindly. 'Like, if you're friends with her again, what does that mean about our friendship? It means you'll be friends with anyone who'll have you, no matter how badly they treat you.'

'Wow,' I said. I fell silent for a moment.

'I'm more tyrannical,' Sathnam continued. 'For me, she's dead to me for life, just because of the way she's treated you. And yet – you're friends with her. This is the way I am. If your friend tells you someone's fucked them off, I hate that person for life. It's not going to change. I would never, ever let her back in my life. Character is action. You've got to judge people by what they do, and she was horrible to you.'

We walked some more, and then he took me to a tiny courtyard notable both for being the smallest square in London and one of the final places in the city that a duel was fought (Pickering Place off St James's, if you're interested). We stopped and looked up, admiring the Georgian brickwork and the flash of clear sky above the rooftops.

'This is why you thinking about letting Becca back into your life worries me,' he said. 'That's a clear case where something should end. You're setting parameters for your other friends. You're saying to your friends, "I really value friendship. It's a rare and beautiful thing for me," but if you're going to be friends with Becca it makes me think, "Oh my God, she'll literally be friends with anyone."'

'OK,' I said.

'It's going to make me think that subconsciously.' He was really warming to his theme now. 'So I'm thinking, "I can't trust what Liz says about our friendship because maybe she thinks I'm awful too. I don't know what she thinks." If she's friends with someone who's fucked her over in the most dramatic way possible, obviously I'm going to be like, "Oh, she could think anything about me." You know what I mean? You're sending a very clear signal there.'

I'd never thought of it that way before. I mulled over what Sathnam had said to me; it made sense, and I think the reason it reached me in a way that nothing else had was that it appealed to that deeply held personal value he'd identified in me: the belief that being a good friend is one of the most important, truest things you can be. If I let Becca back into my life, I wouldn't be as good a friend to Sathnam. I would have less time for him, yes, but it was more than that. Emotional resources can be finite too. My relationship with him would carry less weight because how could you trust me if, in my desperation to accumulate friends and never let them go, I spread my love so thinly and allowed myself to be treated so badly, with so few boundaries, that the act of my friendship itself carried no meaning? What was I offering a true friend if I acted with no discernment in allowing the false ones back into my heart?

'You're right,' I said, and I looked around that small square where one of the last duels had been fought and knew it was time to end my own. It was over. Becca belonged to my past. I was grateful for the love we had shared and I still wanted her to be happy. If that meant she couldn't be my friend, then so be it. I didn't want to cause her pain. I walked with Sathnam back out into the street and I left her there with the other ghosts, encircled by the grey brick buildings.

Afterwards, I felt clearer. If being ghosted had taught me what friendship was not, it had also helped get me closer to understanding what it should be. This, I was grateful for.

The Friendship Tapes
RAY

Ray Winder, 68, chairman of the North Walsham's Men's Shed in North Norfolk, a community-based project that aims to bring individuals and communities together

'Men tend to get in this situation – especially if you're on your own and you've been with a partner, and you've lost them – that you get up every morning, you do some pieces around the house that you might have to do – that's if you can be bothered, which some people can't – and then the next thing, you're looking at your four walls again on your own. And before you know where you are, you pick up the remote control, on goes the TV, and you sit there, then a few hours later you've had a wasted day because you haven't seen anybody. The Men's Shed gives you the ability to say: "I can go out to the shed, I can gain new friendships, speak to individuals."

'There've been studies over the years, that you ladies can go out and meet your own groups and you talk about problems, no problem! One of my sayings is that men, unfortunately, we all think we're James Bond and that we can do everything, but when it comes to the crunch, we can't.

'The purpose of friendship is, in your lowest moments, when you need somebody who you trust, and you want to talk to, you can come out and discuss your problems with them – and vice versa, you talk to them about theirs. The more you talk about your problems, it eases that burden that little bit – it does help you to talk to a friend.

'My real good friend who lives down in Stevenage was up here when I was told that I've got prostate cancer. That was fantastic: to have him around to support me. He was going home that day, back to Stevenage, but he got straight on the phone to his wife and they came up and they stayed up here a week with me to support me. And that's what friendship's about.'

Ray is now in remission for prostate cancer.

———————————

5.
SATHNAM

Male Friendships, Does Gender Matter and the *When Harry Met Sally* Conundrum

I first met Sathnam when we were set up on a date.

In fact, that's not technically true. We had met vanishingly briefly several years previously at a party and over the years that followed, I thought of Sathnam with affection, partly because I admired his writing and partly because we had friends in common who always spoke highly of him. It was odd that our paths didn't cross again, but they didn't – almost as if the universe had a plan for our friendship and knew that the timing wasn't quite right.

When I moved to my single-woman flat, I discovered that I not only lived closer to Becca but also to a whole host of other people who had apparently all decided by some secret masonic handshake that this was the best part of town to gravitate towards. It was astonishing how many people now lived within walking distance of me.

Francesca was one of them. Over the years, she had followed my romantic travails with close interest. For a long time, she had been insistent that Sathnam and I should go on a date.

'He's so *kind*,' she would squeal over our customary meal of chicken, chips and butter lettuce salad at our favourite nearby restaurant. 'And so funny. He's honestly the most eligible man I know.'

If you're wondering why Francesca didn't go out with him herself, that's because she's already married to a lovely man who is so successful that he has a desk attached to a treadmill.

It took months of Francesca trying to persuade me. I didn't want to date another journalist. Later I would discover that Sathnam had been similarly reluctant. We had both been bruised by love, and we were both exhausted by the peaks and troughs (mostly troughs) of online dating. I was thirty-nine, he was forty-one. We had no time to waste on unnecessary vulnerability. We were both hedgehogs, curled tightly up into spiky balls of defensiveness, and we weren't in the mood for yet another disappointment.

But Francesca is extremely persistent. And in the end, it was easier for both of us to submit to her cunning master-plan. I suppose you could say the two hedgehogs caved in the face of her badgering. We exchanged numbers. Sathnam texted. We made a plan to meet at a pub in Hampstead that weekend.

'I feel very strongly that you need to have sex with him that night,' Francesca said to me sternly during a phone pep talk. 'Because otherwise it'll become *a thing*. You need to get really drunk and do it so that it's out of the way.' She paused. 'And if you get pregnant, then so be it!'

(It was also part of Francesca's masterplan that I would irrefutably become a mother, because it was absolutely the only way the world could make sense to her. This is one of a million reasons why I love her.)

I turned up to the Hampstead pub five minutes past the allotted time because I didn't want to be the first to arrive. Sathnam wasn't there yet. *Hmph*, I thought, *not even punctual*.

When he finally arrived, we ordered food and a bottle of red. During one particularly expressive anecdote, he swept his arm across the table and knocked a pint of water over me. My jeans were soaked through. Sathnam was mortified and I found his mortification hilarious. I went to the toilet to dry myself off. When I returned, he proceeded to compare me to a horse because I was tall and said that my face reminded him of a female journalist who actively loathes me. The comments seemed to spill from him without filter.

'You know Francesca thinks we should get absolutely hammered and have sex?' he asked.

'Yes. It makes it a bit awkward, doesn't it?'

He nodded.

'Let's just both agree we're not going to do that,' I said, 'and then we don't have the pressure of it hanging over us.'

Sathnam looked relieved.

'OK, yes, good idea.'

At closing time, he insisted on paying for the meal and then invited me back to his for a cup of tea. We walked the twenty minutes to his flat, and he treated me to an impromptu history lecture as we went, pointing out the modernist house of 1930s architect Erno Goldfinger. When Goldfinger submitted planning applications for the daringly concrete structure, many of his neighbours objected. The controversy was discussed at the local golf club, where another Hampstead resident, the novelist Ian Fleming, heard Goldfinger's name and latched on to it, later using it for the arch-villain in a James Bond novel.

This is nice, I thought. Here's a man who is funny and knows interesting facts and is companionable and yes, kind. I didn't mind about my wet jeans or the horse comparison. We went back to his flat. We drank tea. And … nothing happened. Not one thing. No one made a move. We talked some more. Then I got a cab home. Although I didn't know it then, I had just made one of my dearest friends.

Can straight men and women ever truly be friends? It's the *When Harry Met Sally* conundrum – the age-old debate propounded in Nora Ephron's legendary 1989 movie, in which cynical Harry Burns (played by Billy Crystal) insists that: 'men and women can't be friends because the sex part always gets in the way'. Sally Albright (played by Meg Ryan) disagrees. But the duo *do* go on to become friends, before eventually falling in love – proving, in a sense, that they're both right.

I'm fortunate enough to live in an era when men are more encouraged to talk about their feelings and where some of the historic barriers between the genders have either been torn down or are in the process of becoming more diffuse. Harry Burns, existing as he did in a decade of capitalist greed and rampant testosterone, would have had a far more difficult time escaping from the cliche of what a straight white man 'should' be, just as Sally Albright struggled to see beyond the happy ending of a heteronormative marriage.

When Rebecca Adams, a sociology professor at the University of North Carolina at Greensboro, first started researching cross-gender friendships in the late 1970s, she found that the general assumption in the first half of the twentieth century was that men and women *only* hung out with each other in order to date, marry and procreate. That was largely because of institutionalised and historic sexism. Men and women existed in separate spheres. Women were far less likely to meet men in an office environment, for instance, because in 1950 only 30 per cent of American employees were female. By 1990, women accounted for nearly half the workforce.[36] As more women entered workspaces, higher education and public life, so there were increased opportunities for the genders to socialise together. And perhaps the advent of easily accessible birth control meant that there was, on some psychological level, less anxiety about *any* kind of male–female relationship, not just a sexual one. The reproductive possibility, which so obsessed those 1970s academics, could now be removed from the equation.

I have three close male friends – Sathnam, Ross and Simon. The question of attraction has never once got in the way. Simon is gay. Ross is married to a woman I adore (to be honest, I have way more of a crush on her than on him). And Sathnam – well, we've already covered that. Plus, I tend to believe that all human relationships possess an intrinsic nature. The key to a fulfilling connection is to enable that intrinsic nature to reach its fullest potential, rather than trying to make it into something it isn't. Ross, Simon and Sathnam were only ever destined to be my friends.

So yes, I do think men and women can be friends without sex getting in the way. Of course, I realise that there are some very cheering examples of friends who evolve into romantic partners, but that has never been my experience. I also think it's a slightly retrograde way of looking at things. What I get from my friendship with Sathnam – humour, kindness, an almost encyclopaedic knowledge of historical trivia – is not predicated on his being a man, but on his being a nice person who I want to spend time with. I have never, to my knowledge, asked him how he views a certain topic 'as a bloke', or to explain the straight male perspective to me. He's interesting to me because of his multi-faceted personhood, not because of his gender, and that's the same with all my friends.

I asked Sathnam recently about how he viewed our friendship and its unexpected starting point. He replied without hesitation that 'there was no sexual chemistry'.

We were chatting over Zoom, and although this entire chapter is based on the fact that there was absolutely no frisson between us, I couldn't help but feel offended that he'd stated it so baldly. It was ridiculous of me, but there you have it.

So, I said, just to get this straight: you didn't fancy me *at all*?

'I guess … the fancying thing …' I could see him squirming in his seat. 'I haven't properly thought about it,' he said. 'Maybe it's just something I told myself. I don't know. I also had the sense then that you were dating quite a few people.'

Well. How can I put this? I was.

'And,' he continued, 'I thought, "I don't want to be in a competition." I maybe just partly thought, "I can't compare", you know? You were in a dating frenzy then, weren't you?'

'Dating frenzy' was an exaggeration. I interrupted.

ELIZABETH: I went on one date with another person in that two-week period [when we first met]. But I also remember my mindset at the time: my self-esteem was on the floor and I needed someone to be so fucking focused and directive and to say, 'This is what I want. This is how I feel.' Almost from the off.

SATHNAM: Yeah, you didn't need another vague writer.

ELIZABETH: No. And also, we were destined to be great friends, so I'm glad you weren't like that.

SATHNAM: Yeah. I'm glad we did it, got it out of the way and … Well, we didn't do it, I guess.

ELIZABETH: I'm *really* glad we didn't do it.

SATHNAM: I'm glad we didn't do it. I'm really glad. I don't think we would have been friends afterwards.

ELIZABETH: Also, you told me I looked like a horse.

SATHNAM: I was thinking: not a horse, it's more a llama. Llamas can be quite pretty.

ELIZABETH: Oh, that's so much worse. No, they can't!

SATHNAM: Llamas have really pretty faces.

ELIZABETH: No, they don't. They just have long eyelashes.

Helpfully for me, Sathnam had carried out an effective control experiment on the sex thing some years previously when he'd slept with someone who later became a very good friend. His conclusion was that, one way or the other, a straight man and a straight woman who want a lasting friendship first have to ensure that they don't have any 'unfinished business' in a sexual sense.

SATHNAM: I think there cannot be any sexual tension to be proper friends. So you've got to have it sorted out. Either – you and I, we met through a set-up, it's been sorted. Or you've actually tried to have sex. Or you have had sex and it's been disastrous. You know what I mean? Or you've had a relationship and neither of you have got any unfinished business – then you can be friends.

This was an interesting statement because the question of whether you can ever truly be friends with your ex is almost as hotly contested as the *When Harry Met Sally* dilemma.

Research conducted by the University of Kansas in 2017 found that there are four main reasons exes feel compelled to maintain a friendship or suggest doing so. These four areas break down into: civility (*I want to be polite and moral and to ensure this break-up is as painless as possible*); unresolved romantic desire (*I want to keep you close just in case I change my mind*); practicality (*we share social or family groups*) and security (*I trust you and want you to remain in my life as a confidant and supportive presence*).[37]

But I would add a fifth group, which is: category error (*we were only ever meant to be friends and got a bit confused*). Before Sathnam, I had found myself in the position of being friends with quite a few exes who at first I'd wrongly categorised as 'romantic' rather than 'platonic'. These were people who I'd gone on a few dates with, who I might have slept with over the course of a few weeks or months, but who ultimately proved to be enjoyable company rather than anything more. We'd mistaken the intrinsic nature of our connection. To me, it seemed illogical to lose them from my life because I often really liked them. I just wasn't ever going to fall in love with them. Plus, having got 'the sex part' out of the way, as Harry Burns would say, our friendship was even less encumbered than it might otherwise have been.

I have four male friends who fall into this group. Two of them I would actually categorise as good friends but I know that all of them would pick up a phone in a crisis. I don't fancy any of them. I don't want to have sex with any of them. But I do appreciate the closeness we once shared, because it feels like a shortcut to a level of emotional honesty that can be rare in cross-gender friendships. And because our friendship started in an unconventional way, there is no expectation on either side of the form it will take. I never feel guilty for not having texted or called or met up with them and, almost uniquely among my friendships, there's no pressure for either of us to stay in each other's lives. We can just pick up as and when we want to, sometimes after several months or years have passed. For a friendaholic with an innate fear of abandonment and loneliness, it's rewarding to feel that relationships can evolve into something else without having to lose the person who once brought you joy.

Having said that, it's worth noting that the four cases I mention were not long-term exes. It is much, much harder to remain friends with someone to whom you've been married or co-habited with or dated exclusively for years rather than weeks, and it is only possible with the enormous goodwill and effort of both parties. I am not friends with any of my serious exes. I feel neutrally affectionately towards a couple, but mostly I now realise I wouldn't be able to set aside the sense of betrayal or anger or sadness or frustration that accompanies most big break-ups.

I used to try. I would keep in touch with exes because I told myself it was too painful to go from talking to each other every day to absolutely nothing overnight. Unless the relationship was emotionally or physically abusive, it had always seemed to me to be irrational and unnecessary to lose that foundational friendship, even if you were no longer romantically involved.

This is what I used to tell myself. But honestly? I think this was an excuse. The real reason I tried to stay in touch was probably because I wanted them still to like me, either because I'd broken up with them and needed to assuage my guilt or because they had broken up with me and I needed, on some level, to prove them wrong. I was trying so hard to be perfect that I couldn't assimilate the idea that they had found me, or the relationship, lacking. The irony, of course, was that it was probably my attempts to be perfect, rather than real, that had caused the relationship to falter in the first place.

It wasn't that I ever wanted to get back with these exes. No, it was something far more twisted. I wanted them to want *me* back. I'd meet up with them over disappointing vodka tonics in some hastily chosen pub, and discover that they were happy without me and I would pretend to be happy back. It felt like picking a scab. It took me a long time to understand that the feeling you get when you see someone you used to be intimate with – that sad, restless, queasy feeling at the end of the evening when you hug each other goodbye and smell familiar laundry detergent – is nothing at all to do with loving someone else, and everything to do with how much you refuse to love yourself.

There was a deeper aspect to it too, which was that a former, beloved boyfriend of mine died six months after we broke up. His name was Rich. We had been together for two years in our early twenties, during the final year of university and the first year out of it. I was ready to take our relationship to the next level; he wasn't quite, although he said he still wanted to be with me. I called it off.

We saw each other once after we split, for an evening of tears and promises that things could be different, but I thought it was too late. The last time I saw him was outside Balham tube station in the darkness. A few months after that, I was invited to his leaving party. He was flying himself out to Iraq as a freelance journalist to cover the aftermath of the defeat of Saddam Hussein. I didn't go to the party because I thought it would make things awkward. Two weeks later, he was dead; shot in the head by an unidentified sniper. We never did find out why Rich had been the target.

It was a traumatic time for his parents and sisters. The grief I felt was acute but different, because I didn't know if I had a right to claim it. I couldn't believe I hadn't said goodbye or made things right in some way.

As a result of losing Rich, I became near-maniacal in my attempt to keep exes in my life because, put simply, I didn't want them to die without having smoothed everything over. My next two exes would experience this, and I feel bad now for the mixed signals I must have been transmitting. With one of them, I insisted we go to a Justin Timberlake concert together a fortnight after we'd broken up because I'd booked the tickets for us as a couple (disclaimer: this was the early 2000s and the *Justified* album was huge and we hadn't yet reappraised Timberlake's legacy as it pertained to key women in his life including Britney Spears and Janet Jackson). I finally stopped trying to be friends with exes after my divorce. I decided I would have to accept the risk of someone dying at the same time as I also had to accept that everyone had their own truth about what had happened in a failed relationship and there was no way I could control either the narrative or life itself.

So maybe the conclusion I've come to is that it's difficult to be friends with someone you were once in love with – and still have unresolved issues with – but it's perfectly possible (for me, at least) to be friends with someone you once had sex with. When I asked, Sathnam agreed with me.

SATHNAM: I was routinely friends with all my exes. I remember when I turned thirty I invited about three of them to my birthday party and I remember my friend saying, 'This is why you're fucked up.' He thought it was really absurd. And I was like, 'No, it's great. They know me and isn't it great?' But actually I've come to his view. I think if someone has broken your heart or if you've broken their heart, you cannot be friends. It's healthy not to be friends with your exes, I think. But if there is genuinely no unfinished business on both sides, you can be friends.

So how had Sathnam managed the process of befriending the woman he had once been intimate with? He answered with typical matter-of-factness.

SATHNAM: We went out and it was terrible. It just wasn't there. If it's not there, it's not there, and then it's fine. You can get on with life. It's quite a relief.

ELIZABETH: And having sex never crosses your mind again?

SATHNAM: No. And actually I feel really awkward talking about it. It's like talking about something very cringey, you know what I mean?

ELIZABETH: Yeah, it's more like a brother–sister affection.

SATHNAM: The test again is, 'Are you happy for them?' So I've set her up with people. She's set me up with people. Quite often, I've liked her boyfriends more than she's liked them. If I ever feel jealous or envious about her being in a relationship, it's purely about the fact I'm going to see her less. That's what pisses me off. But almost always I end up liking her partners. *Almost* always …

I think the standard thing is to say it's impossible to be friends with women for heterosexual men, full stop. Which would make my life very sad and empty because I've only got two very close male friends. Most of my friends are women.

I think men are very bad – are terrible at – friendship in every possible way. They don't know how to maintain a friendship. Once they get married and have kids, friendship is a thing they give up on. Along with music. Also it's one of the most common regrets on your deathbed, that you didn't maintain your friendships. And men give up on them and I know they regret it. It's awful.

It seemed that, anecdotally speaking, Sathnam was right. Almost every straight man I spoke to in my age bracket had haemorrhaged friends without ever fully intending to. They had been distracted by work, by marriage, by children and in becoming over-scheduled, they had sacrificed what seemed to be the easiest thing to give up. The American journalist Billy Baker wittily identified this problem in his 2021 memoir, *We Need to Hang Out*, in which he went on a quest, at the age of forty, to re-discover his friendships.

'Yes I had friends at work,' he writes, 'but those were accidents of proximity. I rarely saw those people anywhere outside of the office.

'Most of everything else revolved around my children. I spent a lot of time asking them where their shoes were, and they spent a lot of time asking me when they could have some "Dada time".'

Baker went on to ask whether straight men are less likely than women to have the skillset to maintain friendships through different phases of life – he had simply taken it for granted that friendships made in boyhood would last, whether or not he tended to them. But by middle age, he came to the realisation that his childhood best mates 'had gone down a different path, to a different place and we were no longer a central part of one another's ecosystem. And that was okay. That was life … They were the definition of friends for life. But I needed friends for my daily life.'[38]

It was something I saw reflected closer to home. By which I mean my husband. Fairly early on in our relationship, Justin told me bluntly that he had no friends. He was driving at the time, and I was sitting in the passenger seat and could barely contain my indignant spluttering.

'What … wait … how … what do you mean you have no friends?'

'I have no friends,' he said, calmly indicating right and changing lanes.

'You must do.'

'No, not really. I've got time in my life for you, my kids and my work. Those are the things I prioritise. Well, maybe I have one,' he conceded.

There was a brutal kind of logic to it. As the founder and CEO of his own thriving business, Justin spends a lot of time at work. He has three children, and he had them relatively young with his ex-wife. At a time I was out socialising every night and frantically gathering friends as a bulwark against future loneliness, Justin was changing nappies, coaching rugby to toddlers, attending parent–teacher evenings, keeping his marriage on track and working hard to establish himself as an entrepreneur. As he saw it, he had vanishingly little energetic currency left over to spend on friendship.

Any friends that he did have during that time were circumstantial. They were the other rugby dads or the neighbours on the street where he lived or the people he and his ex-wife would hang out with as a couple. When he got divorced, he lost the latter two categories, and then his focus segued into establishing an amicable, functional relationship with his ex and co-parenting his children in two separate homes. Later, he also wanted to devote time to finding a life partner, so he added dating into the mix. There was still no time for friendship. There were people in the office he got on with, but as the boss it was never a good idea to blur the lines between a work colleague and a mate. Then he met me, and I became someone he wanted to spend time with and he put effort into building the foundations for a lasting relationship.

So: my husband hardly had any friends. Whereas I was addicted to friends and had so many that I sometimes felt overwhelmed with the pressure of keeping them all happy. I found it almost impossible to comprehend his attitude, especially because Justin claimed that he didn't feel the lack.

'You don't fear loneliness?'

'Not particularly, no,' he said.

In fact, what Justin does fear is unasked-for reciprocity – the idea that he owes a friend if they have done something nice for him, even if he didn't want their kindness in the first place. It's why, if we have people round for dinner, Justin will almost always insist on doing all the cooking. He is so grateful that our guests have made the time to join us that he wants to provide them with a reward, almost as if he's paying off a notional debt before it has time to accrue extra value. His idea of hell is someone arranging a surprise party for him (whereas it's my idea of unadulterated bliss: a roomful of people I love gathered there without my having had to do any of the admin? Yes please).

I would find this very hard to wrap my head around were it not for the fact that the other most important person in my life, my best friend Emma, has the same attitude. She explains it slightly differently, in that she is guarded about who she lets into her life and even more guarded about who reaches her inner sanctum (at this stage, that consists of her husband, her two children and me) because she does not want to make herself vulnerable to disappointment. She doesn't want to expose herself to the horrible feeling of being let down, so she'd rather have fewer people in her life who are capable of doing that.

Leaving aside Justin and Emma (the loveable weirdos), I wondered whether it was actually true that women, broadly speaking, were more likely than men to be socially conditioned to think of others, to communicate and connect, to carry out the emotional labour required for sustaining friendship?

It's probably impossible to say one way or the other, and in attempting any kind of conclusion I'm aware that we fall into generalised and imprecise notions of sex and gender. This kind of theorising automatically excludes those with trans, queer, non-binary or gender-fluid identities and marginalises the experience of how they might see the world or feel in it. For what it's worth, from a purely empirical perspective, I would say that friends of mine with fluid gender identities seem to be better at friendship than straight men. This is partly because they (and by 'they' I'm talking specifically about my friends) are well practised at seeing different ways of being, so they don't fall unquestioningly in line with convention. Their friendships have an intentionality to them. It's also partly because they have often had to strive for acknowledgement of who they are and fight for acceptance, so they understand the fundamental need for allies.

I went looking for someone who could give me a bit of perspective on this. Most of my friends are a similar kind of age to me, but I wanted to know if, say, a gay older man could tell me about whether their friendships had stood the test of time. I came across Andrew Lumsden, a gay rights pioneer who was instrumental in the creation of Pride and who also founded the fortnightly publication *Gay News*. Andrew, a spritely eighty-year-old, now gives Queer Tours of London on foot (subtitled 'A Mince Through Time'). Anyway, it turns out Andrew still has loads of friends.

What, I asked him, has kept them together?

'I think the deepest ones probably rely on a shared background,' he replied. 'Usually, in my case, it will be shared politics, because if you've been an activist and are an activist, then you do things together that bond you in a way that nothing else except activism can do … and of course you can fall out, but then you're more likely to be falling out over politics than over personal issues.'

Activism, he said happily, 'is the best way in the world for finding friends.'

He also claimed that the notion of a 'best mate' for him carried specific resonance.

'In the gay male world, we're called sisters. It's a very common usage for two men who are both gay, and they are probably not having any physical or sexual involvement with each other but they see things alike and they do exactly the same for each other as a best mate does. They have got your back. So if you're two queens going out for the evening and liable to physical attack in the street, you are there for each other and you will not abandon the other in any circumstances, at all. If they are attacked, you'll go to their help. If they're arrested by police, you will go to the police station and so on.'

I found this an important and moving point: that if you belong to a minority, friendship can be both a political act *and* a deep personal bond. And if a person's identity is under constant threat of erasure, then a friendship that sees you, protects you and helps you embrace your fullest self must become as crucial to life as breathing.

Historically speaking, straight (and, it must be said, white) men have not lived under this threat, which might be one of the reasons they view their friendships differently: as something that can be allowed to fall by the wayside without any kind of existential anxiety until it's too late. But what if the cliche that women are good at making friends and men are … well, not, is making it harder for men to maintain healthy social networks? Because I suspect men are just as likely as women to crave platonic emotional intimacy, but perhaps they feel unable to say so in a culture that expects them not to express it. Why else would we have developed a distinct terminology to define modern, straight male friendship; a word that pretends to be affectionate but is actually pretty trivialising when you think about it; a word that is dashed off without much thought and – here's what really bothers me about it – is also a terrible pun. I'm talking, of course, of 'bromance'.

The term was coined in the 1990s by a skateboarding magazine called *Big Brother* to describe skaters who spent a lot of time together[39] but, as Billy Baker puts it in *We Should Hang Out*, 'it has morphed into a gentle insult for any guys who dare get too close … the bromance lived in the category of the oh-aren't-you-cute pat on the head … What's saddest to me is that the reason we need a term for bromance is because it's so rare it must be pointed at.'[40]

It wasn't always like this. In the Ancient world, close friendships between men were so routine as to be unexceptional and almost unmentioned. When Cicero wrote his essay on friendship in 44 BC, he did so partly as a corrective because 'in the whole course of history only three or four pairs of true friends are recorded.' He decided to focus on one such friendship – between the Roman General Gaius

Laelius and his loyal second-in-command, Scipio Africanus.[41] It was an alliance forged through war – and perhaps war and military campaigns did provide a culturally acceptable arena for adult male closeness. We can be thankful for living in more peaceful times. But now that national conscription has passed, many men living in the twenty-first century will not have had the same experience. It's not that the military is the only way men can make friends or that it's a wholly positive space – far from it – but I would argue it is still one of the only forums where the physical proximity and close bonds forged by men are not questioned or ridiculed. I mean, there's a reason why The Sealed Knot and its full costume re-enactments of major historic battles has several thousand members.

In the UK, a 2019 YouGov poll showed that almost one in five men admitted to having no close friends, with 32 per cent stating they did not have a best friend.[42] It is a global problem. In May 2021, the Survey Centre on American Life released a similar poll showing that the number of men who view themselves as having 'no close friends' has quintupled over the last thirty years, increasing from 3 per cent in 1990 to 15 per cent in 2021. Just 15 per cent of men considered themselves to have ten or more close friends.[43]

In Australia, men began to tackle the issue by repurposing backyard sheds as community spaces for those beset by loneliness or isolation. The Men's Shed movement has spread globally (there are 600 sheds in the UK alone) with each shed providing an opportunity for men to connect, converse and create without having to feel any embarrassment about doing so.

But if there is a crisis in male friendship, Sathnam is an outlier. At the time of writing, he is (thank goodness) in a long-term relationship with – as he puts it – 'a sane and beautiful woman', but he has never got married or had children, which might account for why he has time to spend nurturing friendships. He also has a different attitude to friends from mine.

'You collect them like a private equity fund building an investment portfolio,' he said.

'No I don't,' I insisted, hurt.

'It's just a basic need to be loved, isn't it?' Sathnam asked.

He was right. And maybe that's why I struggle with serious break-ups and want to maintain friendships with people I've had flings with – I associate them with the possibility of love.

ELIZABETH: Why don't you have that basic need to be loved?

SATHNAM: I was thinking about this today. One of the things I've realised about myself is that throughout my life I've been un-clubbable. I've got a fear of groups. I've never been in a group of friends ever in my life. My idea of a nightmare is a stag do: a) it's men b) it's a group of friends and even at school, from the youngest age, I've never had more than two or three friends. I think it's probably personality, but also if you've ever been slightly bullied you have a fear of groups.

ELIZABETH: But [being bullied and a fear of groups] this is all me! I wonder if the one thing you never doubted in your family was that you were loved.

SATHNAM: Yeah. Maybe that's what it is. Everything comes back to your parents. Yeah, I've always been adored in my family and maybe I've never felt a massive gap I need to fill … I've got enough family. I feel very entrenched and safe with my family. It's also a personality. I'm very lucky. I think you win the lottery of life if you grow up and you're loved. Then you've won.

ELIZABETH: What is the Sikh attitude to friendship?

SATHNAM: One of the defining things about Sikhism is that it's a religion that sees itself in the world. It has a lot in common with Buddhism, philosophically. But a lot of Buddhist monks want to withdraw from the world whereas Sikhism is very much involved in the world, you know? It's all about feeding people literally every day in the temple. It's about working, doing jobs, fighting for injustice in the real world. So I guess it's a very sociable religion and culture, you know? I have fifty-four first cousins. There's just so many people. It's not just your family. Like, every step you take in Wolverhampton there's someone there.

ELIZABETH: So you don't feel that fear of alienation or ending up alone?

SATHNAM: No, I don't at all. If I've got more than three or four close friends, I need to get rid of one.

He wasn't even joking. He went on to tell me that he had no issue ending friendships that weren't working for him. Unlike me, Sathnam is not conflict avoidant so his strategy for ending friendships goes something like this: a period of ignoring their calls. Then, if they ring, stating frankly what the problem is.

Wow, I said, that sounds really emotionally healthy.

SATHNAM: I did it with one of my best friends a couple of years ago and it saved the friendship. It hurt him but he recognised some of what I was saying and changed his behaviour.

ELIZABETH: So what, for you, is the purpose of real friendship?

SATHNAM: I guess it's to feel less alone. Amusement. Gossip. Anecdotes. But mainly it's to give your life experience meaning. You know what I mean? If you just experience things in a vacuum, it's like they didn't happen.

He quoted a line from the U2 song 'The Fly' and said that his test for what constitutes a friendship is whether that person would help if he needed it or if they would ask Sathnam for help if they needed it.

A few months after Sathnam and I had decided we were better friends than [shudder] lovers, I ran into an ex of mine at a party. This was a serious ex, and we had a two-year relationship behind us. My ex had been perfectly polite, but the conversation had lacked any depth. It had been like speaking to a hologram. Any shared experience or love we once had seemed to have disappeared into thin air. I felt as though I meant nothing to him. Most likely, I no longer did.

The next morning, I felt sad about it. Worse than sad, in fact: I felt betrayed. This was an ex who had firmly promised that we would stay friends because he 'couldn't imagine' his life without me. Yet he never made the effort and because he was the one who had broken up with me, I was waiting for him to initiate it. So we didn't stay friends. And because of everything I was coming to realise about myself, this hit me hard. I might not have been the right girlfriend for him, but surely – *surely* – I was a good friend?

I was starting to realise that coming to terms with my addiction to friendship also meant coming to terms with the fact that I wanted to stay friends with this ex for the wrong reasons. It was to keep him close, in spite of the closeness being painful. But too much had been said and shared and lost. The intensity of our initial feelings for each other would not easily translate into another state of being.

And actually, I didn't need to navigate the tricky transition from romantic to platonic just because I was frightened of what might happen if I didn't. I had enough friends already: men and women and people who identified as neither.

So I put on my most comfortable hoodie, made myself a slice of toast and I called one of them. I called Sathnam. I told him what had happened.

'Do you want me to come over?' he said.

'Yes please.'

He arrived twenty minutes later, with a postcard bearing George Michael's face. Sathnam loves George Michael with a passion, so I knew this was a big deal. On the back he'd written: 'Don't let the bastards get you down.'

I propped the postcard up on the kitchen counter and put the kettle on.

I already felt much better. Sometimes it really is this simple: a friend is someone who lets you help.

The Friendship Tapes
ANDREW

*Andrew Lumsden, 80, artist, tour guide
and founder of* Gay News

'Long, long ago before modern social media, the Post Office had a monopoly on telephones in Britain. And so they dictated strange rules like, you could only have a 6-foot cord from your house phone, which required a cord fitting in the wall, where it received whatever electronic stuff it receives. And so more than once, moving from one place to another, I flattered some Post Office engineer into letting me have 20 feet of cord because if your main way of talking to your friends is on a landline, you really do want to be able to lie on your bed and talk to them or go to cook something while you're talking to them for an hour. And you couldn't do it with the Post Office's arrangements.

'That was a wonderful aspect of friendship because I know people snuggle up with their mobile phones, but there's something particularly pleasant about snuggling up with one of those old-fashioned phones with the cradle resting on your tummy and the receiver in your ear – it was very intimate. Of course, you had terrible shocks from time to time, but that was all to do with lovers. They didn't ring! They didn't answer! [So then you'd have to] leave the building and go around to where they live!'

6.

CONTRACTS

Compiling Your Friendship CV, With Help from *The Real Housewives*

I Blu Tacked the George Michael postcard to the cupboard door in my tiny galley kitchen. Every morning, when I reached for the teabags, I would see it there, and the sultry face of one of the 80s' most iconic pop stars would make me smile. As I drank my tea and got ready to leave my flat (dressing, as always, with careful awareness of the remote possibility that I might run into my ex)[44] I'd be cheered by the certain knowledge that I had Sathnam's friendship silently supporting me, willing me on throughout the day, encouraging me not to let the bastards get me down.

George Michael stayed there for months, staring soulfully out at me with soft, light brown eyes and a single crucifix earring dangling from his left ear. The steam from the kettle would gradually curl the postcard's edges over time, and the dirty blond of George's volumised hair would lose some of its lustre in the direct sunlight that streamed in through the bay window. He looked out for me as I went on dates and brought the wrong men back to my flat before eventually meeting Justin. Then, one day, I took George down and placed him in a packing box to take with me to the new home I'd bought with Justin on the other side of the city.

As I left that rented flat, I felt grateful for its consistent shelter during a time in my life where I had lived through a lot of change. Part of me was relieved I would no longer run the risk of watching Becca blanking me on the street. Another part of me was sad that I was saying goodbye to a place that had been so symbolic of my hard-won independence. But mostly I was excited by the prospect of moving in with the man I loved and having considerably more wardrobe space.

Before you start thinking that I was completely sorted and balanced in my outlook on life, rest assured that, along with George, I had also brought with me some of my previous personality traits. As much as I might have begun to learn the value of true friendship and to realise that I didn't need to befriend absolutely everyone I encountered (including my exes), I wasn't quite rid of the all-encompassing desire to be liked. And so, when I moved into my new area, I endeavoured to be neighbourly.

I started by introducing myself to the people who lived on the same street, all of whom were lovely and extremely patient with the absurd number of packages that had started turning up for us and which they kindly took in when we weren't at home (mostly cushions and lightbulbs). But then I ventured further afield. I joined a local WhatsApp group. I eagerly signed up for alerts on bin collections and urban foxes. I had a mental image of myself as a pillar of the community, the kind of woman who organised jumble sales and organised rotas to help refurbish the village hall. Except I didn't live in a village and I wasn't a character from *The Archers*.

No matter. When the woman who ran the group suggested that the two of us meet for a coffee 'to get to know each other' I could not have been more positive.

'Sure thing,' I typed, and my fingers struggled to keep up with the pace of my enthusiasm.

We went for coffee. The woman was called Maggie. She was a bit older than I was and she had divorced her husband some years previously after he'd had an affair. She now co-parented their two teenage children. When she told me, I said how sorry I was and how difficult that must have been. Her eyes filled with tears and I reached across the table and gave her hand a squeeze. We spoke about divorce and the trickiness of mourning the end of something that might not have been all that great in the first place. We moved on to how her parents had remained unhappily married for much of her childhood and how she was grateful, in a way, that at least she wasn't making the same mistake, and I agreed with her that it was healthier this way.

In short, we bonded. Then she told me how her oldest son wanted to get into media but it was so competitive and she wasn't sure how to help.

'Oh, well I'm in that world myself,' I said.

'Are you?' Her face lit up.

There was a pause. Maggie looked at me expectantly.

'Yes. I mean, if your son ever wanted an introduction or work experience, I'd be happy to help.'

'That's so kind. That would be really helpful, actually. Can I take your email for him?'

'Of course.'

I wrote out my email address in the Notes app of her phone. As I was doing so, I deliberately ignored the quiet voice at the very back of my head attempting to make itself heard over the general noise and clamour of my determination to make a new friend. It was the quiet voice that said, 'You know what's going to happen here, don't you? You're going to overpromise and then feel awkward about it and get yourself more involved than you want to be in this woman's life. In fact, Elizabeth, you absolute numpty, you've already done it.'

But the little voice was entirely drowned out by the rest of my head, which had just thrown itself a ticker-tape parade, complete with twenty-four-piece brass band and a float filled with lip-syncing drag queens, in celebration of the fact that I was just, like, *so amazing* at making friends. 'Go you!' the imaginary drag queens were screaming. 'You've got another friend! Woohoo! That'll show the school bullies! That'll show every ex you've ever had that you're someone special that they really missed out on!' And so on. I love those imaginary drag queens. They really are the best hype women. But they don't always tell the truth.

I walked back home feeling puffed up with the satisfaction of having connected. I was on a friendaholic high. I was buzzing. I was energised. I was *alive*.

CONTRACTS

'I met one of our neighbours,' I told Justin excitedly when he got back from work. 'She's so nice. She's been through such a lot, poor thing. Her husband had an affair and they got divorced and she worries about the effect it's going to have on their children and ...'

I launched into an impassioned monologue that could reasonably have been entitled 'Maggie: A Life' and used as a set text for GCSE drama exams. When I got to the end, instead of rewarding me with a round of applause, Justin frowned.

'Are you sure ...'

'No, I know what you're going to say, but Maggie's lovely and I think it'll just be good to have a friend in the neighbourhood.'

Justin was unconvinced.

'Don't do what you normally do which is to feel you have to become someone's best friend.'

I rolled my eyes.

'As if!'

Within days, I was arranging Maggie's son's work experience. I'd never met the boy. I had no idea what he was like. But that didn't stop me from insisting a valued work colleague took him under her wing for a week. Maggie sent a grateful text to thank me. Then she suggested we go for lunch the following Monday. As far as I knew, Maggie was a full-time mother and didn't seem to have a job beyond that, so her downtime tended to be when her kids were at school. But I worked conventional hours and on the Monday she'd suggested, I had a busy day, with work meetings and a podcast recording to do. Although I'd actually only met this woman once, I started to feel guilty about saying no and *letting Maggie down*. Clearly she wanted a friend, and I had willingly offered myself as one. I couldn't back out now, could I? It would seem rude. Worse, it would seem unfriendly.

So I rearranged my diary and I went to lunch, half running there as I only had an hour to spare. Lunch over-ran. Maggie told me more about how challenging her relationship with her ex and his new partner was.

'I feel like such a failure,' she told me over the starters I hadn't wanted to order.

'Oh, Maggie,' I said, trying to speed-eat the guacamole and chips. 'You're not at all. A marriage isn't a failure just because it ends!'

I spent a while trying to make her feel better and after a bit more sympathy and hand-squeezing, Maggie began to rally, but by then it felt too awful to ask for the bill because I had to get back for a work call, so I went to the toilet where I emailed the relevant people and said I'd have to cancel.

Why didn't I just tell Maggie I had a certain amount of time for lunch? Better still, why didn't I say Monday wasn't going to work for me? I think it's because I believed that if someone offered friendship I absolutely had to take it. I was arrogant enough to think that I was good at friendship, so I convinced myself the other person would get what they needed from it. In truth, they would get what I myself needed: a sense of self-worth.

Weeks passed. Maggie texted me most days. I replied when I could but gradually the length and regularity of my answers dwindled. I just didn't have the capacity to take on another friend, but I hadn't realised this when I'd rushed to befriend her. Or at least, I had realised it but I hadn't wanted to acknowledge it because it seemed mean-spirited. And, to be fair to my past self, I had not gone in search of a close friend. I had simply wanted to be a cordial neighbour and strike up a functional, amicable outer-circle relationship with someone I could wave to as I walked past their house. But the problem was that I lacked the skillset to ensure this happened. I only knew one route to friendship, which was the full-throttle, absolutely-no-boundaries, tell-me-your-life-story kind. In my urge for connection, I had trampled over the necessary stages of getting to know a stranger, which was to proceed with caution. I had forgotten Cicero's advice to test horses before racing them, in my rush to sprint the chariot over the finishing line myself.

So now Maggie thought she was a far closer friend to me than she actually was. The disparity was uncomfortable. I didn't know how to extricate myself from the ceaseless demands for cups of coffee (which I didn't drink) and Sunday night dinners (which I never want because only sociopaths want to go out on a Sunday evening). I now felt a sense of dread when I walked near her house, worried that if she saw me, she would invite me in and subject me to several more hours of confessional conversation. At one point, she texted to say she had workmen coming to complete a back-garden extension and the kids were at her ex's so would I mind if she invited herself to stay for a few nights? I read the text and immediately panicked. It says something about my warped state of mind that I thought the only way to respond was in the affirmative, even though I didn't particularly want a woman I had only just met sleeping in our spare room, especially given that I worked at home most days.

'What do I do?' I asked Justin in a frenzy.

'She's absolutely not coming to stay,' he said. 'Just say we can't because I've got my kids over.'

'OK, yes.' I nodded. 'Yes, that works.'

He was kind enough not to follow up with any version of 'I told you so' or 'Why do you keep getting yourself into these pickles?' but later, he did sit me down at our kitchen table and give me a gentle talking-to about my strengths (making connections) and my weaknesses (setting boundaries) and suggested taking some time to work out how I could best protect myself from the same thing happening again.

I told Maggie she couldn't stay, and I decided, when I sent the text, that I would experiment with not being responsible for her reaction. It was perfectly rational to think she might be upset or inconvenienced, but I wasn't obliged to sort those feelings out for her. Ultimately, I asked myself, 'Would I be OK if I lost Maggie as a friend and she thought badly of me?' and I came to the conclusion that I would. If she no longer wanted to be my friend because of something so minor, that wasn't any kind of friend I needed. And besides, if she willingly removed herself from my life, wasn't that ... well, sort of a result? Hadn't I been stressed out for weeks trying to meet her needs? I pressed send.

Within minutes, Maggie responded. 'Sure, no problem! I'll find somewhere else.'

The relief was intense and instantaneous. Maggie was fine about it. I had set a boundary, and she was clear where I stood. If anything, the interaction made me feel more fondly towards her for responding with such maturity. I realised then that perhaps Maggie didn't expect me to say yes to everything; perhaps she was simply testing what kind of friend I might turn out to be. Perhaps she had read her Cicero and was trying out the horse (or llama, as Sathnam would have it) before attaching it to her chariot. And I had given entirely the wrong impression until then of what kind of a horse I could be to her. The fault was mine.

A couple of centuries before Cicero wrote his essay on friendship, the philosopher Aristotle shared his views on '*philia*' – a Greek word that translates broadly as 'brotherly love'. For Aristotle, *philia* could be broken down into three categories. Friendship could be based on mutual advantage (love for what is useful), mutual enjoyment (love for what is pleasant) or mutual admiration (love for each other's character and moral integrity, which Aristotle defined as 'virtue'). The three categories could overlap, but there is a clear delineation here between what we, in modern times, might describe as a best friend in the inner circle and the acquaintances of convenience existing in the outer ones. Maggie should have been a mutual advantage friend – I could arrange work experience for her son; she could cat-sit for me (although obviously I never asked because I was too worried about the imposition). Certain friends, for Aristotle, will always stay in that category. Or, if you discover you enjoy each other's company, then you can move into the second phase. But only the realest kindred spirits will be able to fall in platonic love with someone's nature, without caring how useful they are to you. Aristotle argues that *philia* of the third kind is therefore the most virtuous because it's a friendship in which we find 'another oneself'. Although there was a widely held contemporaneous belief that a happy life was a self-fulfilled one, Aristotle argues that self-fulfilment relies on *this* kind of friendship as a way of understanding who we are. We get to know our true selves through our truest friends.

'Thus, being a wholly virtuous and fulfilled person necessarily involves having others for whom one is concerned – without them, one's life is incomplete,' he writes in *Nicomachean Ethics*. And: 'Anyone who is to be happy, then, must have excellent friends.'[45]

In this context, the truest friendships are the ones that have been freely chosen beyond concerns of mutual advantage. C. S. Lewis put it somewhat more baldly in his 1960 book, *The Four Loves*, in which he devotes an entire section to *philia*. He writes that *philia* is 'the least biological, organic, instinctive, gregarious and necessary … the least *natural* of loves.' Anyone who has experienced the soul-level companionship of a deep friendship might take exception to being thought of as 'unnatural', but what

Lewis was getting at was the scientific fact that humanity doesn't need friendship in order to reproduce and advance itself as an evolutionary species. In fact, as we've seen, scientists have routinely overlooked the study of friendship because it has no reproductive value – this in spite of the fact that a 2016 study showed even zebrafish have decreased levels of fear if they can smell the presence of familiar fish nearby, thought to be the first proof of 'social buffering' beyond humans or mammals.[46] But if friendship has no survival value, it certainly adds value to survival. We *choose* friendship – and this, in Aristotle's view, makes it a higher-level love because of the freedom of intention that lies behind it.

Still, we can't make a truly free choice if we are shackled by obligation or feel resentful that the boundaries we forgot to put in place are being ignored. This was the case with Maggie. She was never going to be a deeper friend because I'd polluted the waters from the beginning. It would have been so much easier to navigate if we had both been clearer about what we wanted from the other at the outset. It would have been easier, quite frankly, if we were zebrafish. But, as has been said with such historic frequency it's now almost a cliche: there are no socially sanctioned rituals for friendship. Romantic couples can choose to date exclusively, to move in together, to get engaged and get married (if they so desire). Each stage symbolises to the outside world a different phase and progression of their relationship. The parent–child dynamic is packed with similar staging posts: first day of school, exam results, eighteenth birthday parties and so on. Friendship is unique in not having anything – no birthdays, no anniversaries, no ceremonies – to mark it. This means it's also uniquely difficult to manage the development of a friendship in a careful and caring fashion. If you're like me, you jump headfirst off the cliff, unaware of whether the waters below are shallow or deep or laced with jellyfish. If you're like Emma, you start with the assumption that every ocean contains sharks and flesh-eating parasites and work backwards from that. Emma is far more mistrustful than I am (a characteristic she puts down to the Scandinavian propensity towards self-reliance and burying any overt shows of emotion deep in the Nordic forest … I'm paraphrasing, but this is more or less what she says). Emma applies considerably more discretion and judgement to these situations than I do. Aristotle would bloody love Emma.

I was struck again by the truth of this when Emma and her family recently moved house. They settled in a new city and she found herself wishing at the school gates where she dropped off her children that she could wear a sign around her neck outlining the contractual basis for her friendship.

'I'd like it to say: this is what I can offer, and this is what I can't. I can be this kind of friend, but if you're in the market for anything more, I'm not the one for you.'

The image of Emma wearing a sign like a St Bernard heading into the snowdrifts with a barrel of whisky strapped around her neck made me laugh. But the more I thought about it, the more I realised she had a point. What if I had worn a sign like that on my first meeting with Maggie?

What might it have said? What would my friendship CV look like?

ELIZABETH DAY
Good friend of over 40 years' experience.

SKILLS: Ability to connect and display empathy. Some people even say I'm funny.

WEAKNESSES: Lack of boundaries, conflict avoidance, difficulty in saying no, a hatred of phone calls and low self-esteem leading to an addiction to collecting friends.

WHAT I'M LOOKING FOR: A neighbourly friend who does not mistake my initial warmth and enthusiasm for a guarantee of closeness, expects nothing of me, and will not overstay any welcome either literal or metaphorical. Available for very occasional cups of tea. Willing to carry out low-maintenance household chores, for instance pet-sitting and/or plant-watering for each other when necessary. Possibility of promotion into closer friend circles after a twelve-month trial period. Absolutely no time-wasters please.

It looks so clinical written down in black and white, doesn't it? It looks demanding, a bit whiney. It looks, well, *unfriendly*. And I think that this is where my problem lies: although, at the age of forty-three, I know what I do and don't want in a friend, I am not good at instigating the non-verbal clues that would make this clear from the outset to any potential acquaintance. Putting boundaries in place has always struck me – wrongly – as being the opposite of a good friend. Shouldn't a good friend drop everything to be there for someone else? Shouldn't a good friend put themselves last, after meeting the needs of those they love? Wasn't that the definition of *philia*?

Yes and no. What I was coming to realise, post-Maggie, was that there would only ever be a certain amount of space in my life for these kinds of friendships. The kindred spirits you drop everything for, whose calls you answer at four in the morning, who you know will be there for you in times of crisis, simply don't come along very often. And friendship lived with that kind of loyal intensity can only extend to a handful of people. As Cicero stated, it can only come after the passage of a certain amount of time, so that the friendship has been tested and grown and evolved to accommodate the shifting needs and desires of the other. Sathnam's point was that in choosing who those cornerstone individuals are, there is a necessary application of discretion that not only makes your closest friends feel safe, but also ensures it's clearer for everyone else what your parameters are.

My mistake had been in treating every potential friend as a kindred spirit, partly because I liked the feeling of enthralled possibility but partly because that was the only way I knew how to do friendship. In many respects, this was a nice problem to have. There might be people reading this who struggle to make any friends at all because their lack of confidence manifests itself in a different way – in shyness, in social anxiety, in a fear of existing in anything other than controlled isolation. But a friendship CV would benefit them as well. If they could, like Emma had suggested, hand over a brief (possibly laminated) summary of what their friendship skillset was, then they too would be spared the indignity and inconvenience of being misunderstood.

Of course no one is actually going to write a friendship CV and hand it out at the school gates. And yet simply drawing one up for myself has been instructive to me because it's made me think – honestly and without elaboration – about what I can offer as a friend and what I cannot. This kind of formalised exchange is widely accepted in other areas of life. In WHSmith, you can pop in and buy a starter pack for your own legal documents. Tenancy agreements and wills are right there on the shelves for you to pick up and sign. Married couples or civil partners sign certificates and even pre-nups. Employers require you to sign a contract. I signed one for this book which stated a minimum word count and when I had to deliver the manuscript by. In all of the above instances, we're clear about what our responsibilities are and where they end.

But there aren't any friendship contracts. Or so I thought. It's at this stage that I have to admit to another addiction, not to friends but to reality television. I consider myself a fairly early adopter of the genre, having been riveted by the first ever season of *Big Brother*, which aired during my second year of university. For three weeks during the summer of 2000, I went travelling to Tunisia with Rich, who was then my boyfriend, and was kept breathlessly updated on the latest scandals in the *Big Brother* house via email from my mother. This being the early days of the world wide web, Rich and I had to track down internet cafes wherever we could find them to keep abreast of events. I vividly recall being in a hot, dusty North African town, wearing denim cut-offs, my thighs clammy on a plastic chair as I clicked on the mouse of a shared computer to log into my hotmail.co.uk account and read the most recent missive from my mother.

'Oh my God!'

'What's up?' Rich asked, on the computer next to me.

'Apparently Nasty Nick has been *writing letters* trying to influence the others' votes. And they weren't even allowed to bring pen and paper *into the house*!'

'Wow. That's huge.'

Rich wasn't even being ironic. We genuinely both viewed it as huge news. So did my mother, who didn't usually share my taste in TV.

What that series of *Big Brother* showed, I believe, is that reality television, when it's done right, can be one of the most compelling, anthropologically satisfying things to watch. It is a study of human behaviour, with all its inconsistencies, eccentricities and contradictions. And while reality TV undoubtedly shows some of the worst excesses of human behaviour, it also to my mind showcases some of the best. For every fuckboy on *Love Island*, there is also a lasting friendship being forged in the background. For every fame-hungry contestant on *X Factor*, there is also the undiscovered talent finally getting their due. For every terrible meal on *Come Dine With Me*, there is also the sweetness of an unexpected connection over the dinner table.

Within the pantheon of reality television, there is for me one main temple where I go to worship, and that temple is *The Real Housewives*. I could genuinely write a whole separate book on *The Real Housewives*, so I'll try and keep this relatively brief. For the uninitiated among you, *The Real Housewives* started out as a fly-on-the-wall documentary called *Behind the Gates*, following the lives of wealthy women in Orange County, California. The tapes were picked up by an enterprising young producer by the name of Andy Cohen and recut into something with broader appeal. It was called *The Real Housewives* to capitalise on the success of a comedy drama called *Desperate Housewives* that was popular at the time. As the franchise has grown to incorporate multiple other locations, most of the women featured are not, in fact, housewives (and the ones in Orange County are arguably more plastic than real) but the cast members range from businesswomen (Bethenny Frankel, who made her name on *The Real Housewives of New York* is worth an estimated \$80 million) to music moguls (Kandi Burruss on *The Real Housewives of Atlanta* is a Grammy winner who wrote 'No Scrubs' for TLC) to actresses (Garcelle Beauvais from *The Real Housewives of Beverly Hills* starred in *Coming to America*). The main thing they have in common is a penchant for the finer things, a healthy disposable income and a tendency towards fabulousness. The set-up might be camp and over the top, but the emotions on display are often relatable and the storylines, for my money, are more compelling than almost anything you're likely to watch in scripted drama. *The Real Housewives* was where I first saw the reality of IVF depicted on screen. It's also one of the only shows to pay proper attention to women in their fifties and sixties as they navigate divorces, widowhood, dating, singledom and the menopause. It's no coincidence that writers on *And Just Like That*, the comedy drama revival of *Sex and the City*, which featured the main cast members now in their fifties, were given *The Real Housewives of New York* as a reference point for inspiration.

The Real Housewives was also the first (and only) place I ever saw a physical friendship contract. It was drawn up by the former supermodel Cynthia Bailey for her close friend, NeNe Leakes, in season three of *The Real Housewives of Atlanta*. The two of them had been having issues, and Cynthia thought it would be a good idea to clear the air with the gift of a scented candle and a contract which contained a number of rules such as: 'If we get mad at each other, we cannot go to bed mad. We must talk it out' and 'Can't get un-befriended by one another unless it is a really good reason. Example: if one of us is unexpectedly killed and dies.'

The contract was, Cynthia insisted, meant in jest, but watching her talk on screen you can't help but be struck by the seriousness behind it.

'Cynthia,' NeNe said, laughing. 'We're not married.'

'But we're good friends though,' Cynthia replied, earnestly. 'I didn't like how I've been feeling the past few days.'

Both of them signed it. NeNe was somewhat reluctant, especially when Cynthia joked that 'the whole thing is a one-year contract. You can't break it unless you send a notarised letter saying you want to abort the contract and then it has to be signed by, like, the President.'

When I first watched that scene ten years ago, I thought it was wildly absurd. I watched it for laughs, as the producers intended. NeNe said she thought Cynthia was 'a single Black female' in a later confessional interview. It seemed overly intense and a bit unhinged and the viewer response was such that Cynthia was prompted to write a blog defending herself, claiming the whole thing had been blown out of proportion.

But now, returning to that scene after thinking about my own friendships, I wonder if Cynthia Bailey wasn't actually on to something. Was Cynthia Bailey a genius who, like so many geniuses, was able to solve a problem the rest of us couldn't even see yet? Was it simply that we all had to catch up to her more sophisticated way of thinking?

In search of answers to this question, I called Danielle Bayard Jackson, a friendship coach. Yes, that's right, Danielle is someone who specialises in helping women create sustaining and meaningful friendships. She started her own coaching programme specifically to help other Cynthias – the women who wanted a way to express conflict or disappointment or confusion in their friendships but who struggled to find the right words. When I spoke to Danielle, she was about to give birth to her second child, but it says something about her enthusiasm for discussing the intricacies of female friendship that not only did she find the time to talk, she also knew *exactly* what I was referring to when I mentioned the Bailey–Leakes friend contract.

'It's so funny because yes, it sounds ridiculous, and I remember that scene and being like, is this girl serious?' Danielle said. 'But I think the idea offers a lot of assurance – friendship is so elective and voluntary and fluid and undefined, that I understand the idea of a friendship contract offering some sense of security in a relationship that is not so easily defined.'

Danielle went on to add that we 'fall into friendship as quickly as we exhale, unlike a romantic conversation where it's expected that you'll have some kind of defining conversation beginning and end and have certain milestones – that does *not* exist with friendship. Before we know it, we're hanging out a lot, then we're not feeling it any more. We can leave without saying goodbye. We shouldn't be able to, but we *can*. And so you never really know: "Are we on the same page?", "Do we like each other the same?", "Is this a thing?", "How long are we going to do this?" Then there's "Are there expectations that it'll just be you and I?", "Are you gonna have other friends too?" and "Here's what I need – I need you to commit to offering this to me."

'So I wonder if a "friend contract" sounds so ridiculous because the application of that kind of structure on a friendship feels so restrictive. I think that a lot of us see friendship as recreational and fun and optional, and an escape and a refuge. And so if we see friendship as this fun thing and less of a commitment, which would be contractual, it just sounds really crazy. But I can see how a lot of women would find comfort in something that was spelled out and remove a lot of the mystery surrounding their friendships.'

Incidentally, the Bailey–Leakes friend contract was so instantly iconic that it has subsequently become something of a *Real Housewives* trope. In the 2022 season of *The Real Housewives of Miami*, we saw Julia Lemigova get down on one knee to propose a 'friends-engagement' to her co-star Adriana de Moura. Although there was no contract on this occasion, there was a ring offered as a symbol of their closeness. Julia's actual wife, the tennis legend Martina Navratilova, said afterwards she didn't feel at all jealous of the pair's closeness. The distinction was clear: Julia was married to Martina, but wanted to mark and secure a lifelong platonic bond with Adriana.

'I'm happily married, and love Martina,' Lemigova said. 'And, you know, Adriana is my best friend.'

The definitions were clear. But it isn't always the case. An inescapable part of the problem is that when you meet a likeable stranger, it's almost impossible to know what kind of friendship you might be embarking on because there is no consensus on what, exactly, friendship is. As a label, it encapsulates so much – an infinite, nuanced spectrum from passing acquaintance to bosom buddy – that it loses all specificity and so ends up meaning almost nothing.

When I asked Danielle to proffer her own definition of friendship, she immediately knew what to say – but that's because she's spent her adult life thinking about the concept and being trained to understand it. Most of us don't take time to do the same.

'As a reciprocal affection and feeling of goodwill toward another person,' Danielle said without even pausing for breath. 'And you know, I actually thought about that a little bit during your question about the friendship contracts and outlining expectations. Even the use of the word in general, we're all walking around here using the same language and talking about totally different things. And so, when people mention to me, "I need friends" often I ask people, "OK, are you looking for activity buddies? Or are you looking for a friend?" Because that's just going to be two different conversations. If you want somebody to do a bunch of cool things with, or if you want friends – to me, those are totally different, but we use them interchangeably. And so even the expectation of what a person should offer and what should be required of you, are maybe not the same and can be cause for conflict … So how I define it is a mutual, reciprocal affection for another person and feelings of goodwill that I want the best for you.'

While I was mulling all this over, I listened to a podcast episode hosted by the American writer Glennon Doyle, her wife Abby and her sister, Amanda, in which they defined 'friendship' as consisting of three criteria.[47] Firstly, that it is long term and stable. Secondly that it is positive. And lastly that it is reciprocal. What they meant by 'positive' was the neatly expressed idea that a good friendship should be like a mutual charging station, where you can each go to renew your emotional and energetic resources. A 'negative' friendship, by contrast, would be one where you felt drained or exploited: the person who routinely uses you as a dumping ground for all their dissatisfaction without ever asking how you are.

The same podcast discussion also introduced me to the helpful concept of 'social homeostasis'. Homeostasis is a term coined by a physiologist called Walter Cannon in 1926 to describe the body's need to reach and maintain a certain state of equilibrium (fun fact: he also coined the term 'fight or flight response'. He knew what he was talking about, did Walter)[48] – so, for example, the body's capacity to regulate its internal temperature or blood sugar levels. When applied in a social sense, what this means is that humans have an internal trigger point to determine the ideal balance of relational connections. Our brain, if it's doing what it's supposed to, is wired to adjust itself according to its optimal conditions. If we have too little social interaction, it triggers feelings of loneliness, anxiety or heightened stress, which set off an internal alarm system that encourages us to go and seek out our friends. The cruel irony of this, of course, is that many of us do not feel like making friends at the precise point we really need to. That's why mental health campaigns focus on it being 'good to talk'. Connection can be most important when you least feel like pursuing it.

But it's also important to acknowledge that we all have different levels of social homeostasis and the key to a lasting friendship is to determine what yours is and what your friend's might be. I, for instance, need much less face-to-face contact than other people might require. For whatever reason, I can feel deeply loved and connected to a friend even if I haven't seen them in person for months. My friend Bex, for example, is someone I count as one of my innermost circle. But we both have similar levels of social homeostasis and don't see each other all that much. We show our love through unconditional – and, yes, verbalised – acceptance of the fact that we do not expect contact with any kind of regularity. When we do get in touch, it's because we genuinely want to and we do so without any expectation that there will be a reply. Our texts are sporadic and infrequent, often separated by gaps of several weeks. When we do meet up, it's generally to have a night sitting next to each other on the sofa eating takeout, watching TV and feeling wholly understood and accepted for the introverted individuals we are.

Another friend, Minnie, has a different social homeostasis setting and is a generous and active companion. She will always be the one to pick up the phone to me, or leave me a message suggesting we meet up, but she does so with the full understanding that I have zero obligation to feel guilty if I can't make it. Minnie has never once, in over twenty joyous years of me knowing her, made me feel bad for not being a good enough friend. Her daughter was my first godchild, and I adore her too, and it's a point of pride that

I will never miss her birthday or forget to send a Christmas gift. In this way, I hope I show the depth of my love, even if I'm an inconsistent physical presence.

So if we are to draw up friendship contracts and CVs (albeit metaphorical ones) these are the things we need to think about before signing off on a wholesale commitment. Otherwise we run the risk of being stuck in friendships we never fully wanted or intended to pursue, with no clear means of ending them.

What I learned from my experience with Maggie was to apply a little more caution and discernment when launching into a new friendship. I shouldn't seek to give all of myself in one air-dropped knowledge dump. Nor should I expect other people to intuit this or have the same friendship belief systems as I do.

Plus, I learned that *The Real Housewives* is actually educational television. Those women have taught me a lot. Whether we'd be friends in real life, though … now that's a different story.

The Friendship Tapes
DANIELLE

Danielle Bayard Jackson,
35, friendship coach

'One specific case, I remember, was two best friends who had been together for years, and they essentially were having an issue. We discovered through the course of the call that one wanted to remain as friends and the other did not. And it was really hard and we didn't get to that until the very end of the session where the other friend just kind of broke and said "I don't know that I want to keep doing this." It was hard. It was hard to even watch the other friend get that news. What was happening, it looked like, was [that] one had outgrown the other. So while the one who booked the session for the two of them was hoping that this situation would help them overcome their misunderstandings and be closer, it turns out that the friend was just over it. From my observations, it looked like she had evolved a lot: had a new relationship, had a new career during this time, had new ideas of what was fun and what's not fun. And the other friend said multiple times during that session, "Remember, we used to do this, we don't do it any more," and "You used to call me every day, we don't even talk any more, you have new friends," and it was really painful to watch that happen and to watch one friend plead for the past with the other and the other finally say, "I'm so sorry, but I just can't do that any more. I'm not that person any more". And it was heartbreaking, but it was also kind of liberating for her to finally say that, because it was obvious she felt so guilty about admitting it but also so relieved to finally say it.

'If I had to rank the top five issues that women bring to me for their friendships, one of them would be feeling like they've outgrown the friendship or the other person is in a different life season, or that they've evolved in some way, and the friendship no longer fits. And that's why I like to emphasise that friendship research actually tells us that we replace half of our friends every seven years.[49] So to some extent you almost have to expect that you're going to outgrow some of your friendships. There's almost a natural pruning that takes place with your friendships and that can be a *good* thing.'

7.
SHARMAINE

The Joy of Clarity

A few months ago, I got a text from my friend Sharmaine.

'Hi. Can we talk?'

If you've read this far, you'll know that a message like that strikes fear directly into my cerebral cortex. Not only did I automatically assume I'd done something wrong. Worse, someone wanted to *talk to me on the phone about it.*

But if I knew one thing about Sharmaine, it was this: she is a friend who values absolute clarity of communication. I became friends with her at a time in my life when I needed this in ways I couldn't yet fully understand. I was in my mid-thirties. My first marriage had ended. I had left my job as a staff feature writer on a Sunday newspaper and taken a leap into the unknown world of freelancing. I was in the midst of writing my fourth novel. I didn't know it then, but a couple of years later I would also launch a podcast that would change my life. I would find that clear boundaries between private and public were increasingly necessary as my profile grew. But I would also discover that I was rubbish at boundaries, which was a problem. I needed friends who saw me, truly, deeply and authentically, as I was.

Sharmaine was one of those. We met at a dinner laid on by a fancy magazine and sat opposite each other, on either side of an overly wide table. The magazine had chosen us to be there as a select group of 'taste-makers' who could help them forecast future trends. I was flattered to have been included, given that most of my taste could be summarised by the words 'cheese' and 'reality TV', and as soon as I got there I felt out of my depth. By the time the main course had been served, the guests were discussing Beyoncé's seminal visual album, *Lemonade*, which had just been released. I was in love with every single track (and still am) but there was one person who disagreed. He happened to be a white man and his main issue was that Beyoncé was 'derivative' and 'didn't write her own songs' (and if you're reading this, white dude, both of these statements are untrue).

I saw Sharmaine gather herself up, internalise an eye roll that I could sense like a sonic boom across the table and then listened as she launched into a lethally calm deconstruction of every single point he made. It was so precisely done that I ended up feeling a twinge of pity for the man in question. I noticed that she never once raised her voice or altered the pace of her speech. It was a masterclass in cool. At one point, Sharmaine used the phrase 'with all due respect' and I wanted to hug her. Later, after the plates had been cleared, I did just that. We've been friends ever since.

I don't think it's any coincidence that I was drawn to her.

It wasn't just Beyoncé. It was that the older I got, the more I was attracted to clarity in others. On a subconscious level, I think I knew that if I couldn't put a reasonable friendship boundary in place, then I needed the other party to do it for me. Otherwise I would end up imagining I had to take emotional responsibility for how my friend was feeling even if they didn't express it. And often, in my imaginings, it wasn't actually how they were feeling anyway – it was a twisted projection of how I *believed* they might be feeling in my worst thoughts, which were designed with impressive attention to detail by my ever-versatile inner critic to make it seem like the friend in question might actually hate me or be furious for some relatively minor infraction I never even knew I'd committed.

Conventional wisdom has it that thinking in this way is a form of thoughtfulness (look at empathetic little old me! Constantly worrying about everyone else!) but writing it down makes me realise it was the opposite. It was a way of centring myself in a narrative that didn't, in truth, revolve around me. Was there an unexamined part of me that preferred the idea of a friend being angry with me to the idea of a friend not thinking of me at all? Was it better to be thought of with rage than forgotten about with neutrality? Maybe.

Although I couldn't have expressed it then, I think this is why I needed to be friends with Sharmaine. If I were more like Sharmaine, I never would have got myself into the pickles I did with Ella or Maggie and maybe I would never have been ghosted by Becca. I wouldn't need a friendship

CV or contract. I would simply have been more forthright and clear from the off.

As my friendship with Sharmaine developed, I came to realise that her clarity meant she also held a safe space for me to express how I felt. She encouraged me to say what I really thought, rather than what I believed someone might want to hear. She also had an uncanny knack of getting right to the heart of an issue I hadn't even vocalised to myself. When the podcast I'd launched started to get bigger and take up more of my time, she took me aside at a summer lunch party and stated baldly that I needed to ensure I wasn't having my attention diverted from writing books 'because that's who you really are and you should remind people of that'. Influencers who had podcasts were ten a penny, she continued, but I'd been writing books long before they'd ever come on the scene and that's what I should be known for. By this stage, Sharmaine was heading up her own publishing imprint and she believed in me as an author. In some respects, her belief in me was stronger than my own. I paid attention to what she said because I knew it came from a starting point of love. She cared about me and she cared about my career. I went away and restructured my diary so that I could spend more time writing. It turned out Sharmaine had been right: I was more fulfilled when I took my writing seriously, rather than fitting it in semi-apologetically around everything else I was doing to pay the rent.

So I knew, when I got the text from Sharmaine asking to talk, that she would not be sugar-coating anything she needed to say.

'Of course,' I replied, telling myself there was nothing to be worried about. She called me immediately on WhatsApp (it's a quirk of our friendship that she is the only person I know who uses WhatsApp for audio calls). Sharmaine had seen me post something on Instagram quoting a newspaper headline about a celebrity who had recently stated her family felt 'complete' now that she'd had a baby. I had made the point that women did not need babies to complete them, and there'd been a caterwaul of both support (people without children can be fully realised human beings too) and outrage (who was I to judge?). A follower had shared my post condemning the use of the word 'complete' as exclusive language. She had said another example of exclusive language was the oft-quoted idea that 'there was no love that could compare' to the love between a mother and her baby.

Sharmaine, who at that stage was a mother of one and pregnant with twin girls, wanted to know what I thought about that comment. Because Sharmaine's point was that there *was* no other love comparable, but that didn't mean the love itself was better or bigger in any way, simply that there were different kinds of love we felt in different situations for different people and for different reasons.

I reflected on this. I told Sharmaine I agreed with her, but the idea that motherly love was in any way 'the greatest' or 'the best' made women who did not have children feel as though their experience of love could not compete. It made us feel less than, as though our lives were never going to be quite as rich or full as those of our fertile counterparts.

'Yes, I totally get that,' Sharmaine said.

'And I completely understand what you're saying,' I replied.

That was that. We both ended the conversation feeling better and clearer about what we thought. Instead of letting the anxiety fester until it turned into distance or misunderstanding or resentment, Sharmaine had immediately addressed it. In doing so, our friendship grew even closer, not just because we knew a little more about each other but because we felt secure enough to raise challenging issues within our friendship. It had been the perfect example of clear, loving communication. It turned out I hadn't needed to be fearful of the phone call at all. And that's saying something.

I could learn from that. I wanted to find out how Sharmaine was able to bring candour to friendship without fear of causing offence. So I did what Sharmaine would have done: I asked her.

SHARMAINE: I basically can't deal with any fakeness or one-sidedness. It has to be entirely equal. The thing with making friends later in life for me is that there's been a true sense of equality in our friendships ... And that level of openness and acceptance and seeing you for who you are and not judging you because of age or race or whatever is hugely important to me.

She was in her home in Berlin when we talked; I was in mine in south London. It was a Saturday morning and Sharmaine, a few weeks from giving birth, looked in her element: statement earrings, hair wrapped up in a scarf, a familiar easy laugh.

I've already written about the fact that Sharmaine found herself homeless as a teenager after an estrangement from her mother. Now she went into more detail about how her friends were essentially her chosen blood. They were the ones who gave her the unconditional love that had been lacking from her home. And that was why she needed to trust them, above and beyond the trust required by others who might always be able to rely on their family. As Sharmaine entered her adolescence, that crucial time in finding one's own identity, she leaned more than ever on her friends to accept her both for who she was and who she was becoming.

SHARMAINE: When I was growing up, a lot of my friends were in the gay scene. It had to be a family because we had to protect ourselves from the homophobia and racism of the world … And that's been a really important aspect for me with my friendships: to understand and not judge.

I need a lot of emotional intelligence to be imparted within my friendships. And it's really important to me that there's trust and truth and that there's safety – on both sides. And that if there's something that I say, it's not going to go anywhere else. I need to be able to be really candid and I want my friends to be able to do that with me.

As a result of the powerful position friendship holds in Sharmaine's selfhood, loyalty carries a particular premium for her. If a friend displays duplicitous behaviour, she will end the relationship with no qualms. She gave me a couple of examples – one former friend who she'd invited to countless parties, introduced to many of her own circle, only to find that this same friend was deliberately excluding Sharmaine from her own events; another old friend who repeatedly closed off important chunks of her life from Sharmaine and, when confronted about it (because Sharmaine is clear even in her disappointment) didn't realise what she'd done wrong.

SHARMAINE: That's why we're not friends because you can't even understand that that kind of behaviour would really hurt me.

ELIZABETH: Do you feel guilty after a friendship break-up? Do you feel—

SHARMAINE: No!

We both laughed at the alacrity of her response. I mean, I hadn't even finished formulating the question.

ELIZABETH: Teach me your ways.

SHARMAINE: I don't feel guilty, I feel totally vindicated because I feel like my morals and values are really, really important to me and how people treat you in this life is so important. If someone doesn't fit in with your morals and views, if someone can't be respectful … And I don't think I ask for much, like – be loyal, be a good person, be open, and communicate. Those are the basics of relationships, right? And so if someone can't do that then they're just not right for my life. That's not my problem because I have other people that *can* do that. It's not that I'm setting my friends an agenda or code of conduct, like, 'Hi, could you please just sign here before we embark on this friendship?'

Oh Sharmaine, I wanted to say, if only you knew how much I'd been thinking of doing just that … But she was on a roll.

SHARMAINE: It's not like that. The chemistry of what brings people together is the shared values and morals and outlooks, you know? And that's a really amazing thing because that could be from anybody. It's an intersectional quality. You can have the same values as someone that has a completely different life and trajectory to you.

For Sharmaine, friendship is not about sharing exactly the same politics or the same opinions so much as being able to share a similar ethical underpinning to how we think about and approach the world. Sharmaine values discussion and disagreement, as long as it starts from a place of open-heartedness and equal respect. I'm in a WhatsApp group with Sharmaine and her friend Anna, a producer and screenwriter, and the three of us will quite often disagree about an issue but we do so with generosity because we try to understand where each one of us might be coming from. While I might say something wrong-headed, the other two will know it's not malicious.

One of Sharmaine's other friends had right-wing political beliefs. Although Sharmaine didn't agree with the way he voted, this didn't matter to her as long as he could argue his point with a full and loving understanding of who she was as a person, how her life had shaped her and how this made her perspective necessarily different from his. They had been friends for two decades in this way, but then he voted for Brexit and claimed Sharmaine was a living example of Thatcherite success and she felt wholly and utterly misunderstood.

SHARMAINE: If you don't understand that about me – if you don't understand my heightened level of empathy towards those that don't have or can't or are failed by the structures and institutions of our society – then I don't know what we've been doing for twenty years. We didn't speak for a really long time. But we're friends again now – he is who he is.

If all this sounds slightly disarming or scary, it's probably because you – like me – have so few boundaries in your friendships that the thought of introducing any, let alone strong ones that protect your core values, is anathema to you. Prior to meeting Sharmaine, I would have thought so too. But what she has made me realise is that being clear about your friendship values from the outset is a necessary precursor to the trust and safety she values so highly. You cannot feel secure in any relationship that has no boundaries, because that relationship will have no solidity. It has nothing to define itself *against*. It goes back to what Sathnam was saying: if your status as a friend is to have any worth, you need to stand up for the things you believe are integral to lasting friendship and only admit those who respect the entry requirements and the code of conduct. If friendship is a nightclub and you are the manager, it is up to you to decide what kind of music you want to play, the crowd you want to attract and who you're going to throw out for acting like a drunken prat and ruining it for everyone else. The more drunken prats you keep around, the less other customers will want to come and hang out. It's up to you to keep your house in order.

Sharmaine's nightclub is built on trust. She has to feel her friends accept her without judgement and with an understanding of where she comes from. Sharmaine is a Black woman, but to reduce her need for this acceptance to this single element of her identity would be wrong. Still, it is undoubtedly part of it.

She tells me the story of one of her friends who, out of the blue, called her in the middle of the night to help settle an argument about whether Prince Philip was racist. This wasn't a close friend – more an acquaintance she had got to know through someone else – but Sharmaine was, as ever, open to the conversation. The woman calling was in the midst of a heated disagreement with her boyfriend. She wanted Sharmaine to tell them who was right. And Sharmaine is never one to turn down the chance to enter a lively discussion.

SHARMAINE: I got in their debate and mediated between them. Then she said, 'Oh my God, I've just called one of my best Black friends and asked them their opinion on race! I'm going to let you go.' And I was like, 'Errrr, I hadn't thought that that's what you were doing, I actually thought it was because I really like debating and have an opinion on everything that you were asking me. Not because I was Black. And also I didn't have your number in my phone, so you're not one of my best friends!'

ELIZABETH: Bloody hell.

SHARMAINE: Now you've just called me one of your 'best Black friends'. I didn't even know what to think about that. She texted me in the morning saying: 'I love you so much …' I was just like, 'I can't even be bothered to answer this.'

ELIZABETH: 'New phone, who dis?'

SHARMAINE: Exactly!

Sharmaine found this kind of interaction happening with even more alarming frequency when George Floyd was murdered by a white police officer in May 2020. In the wake of his death, there was a resurgence of Black Lives Matter protests across the globe. Many of us were rightly shocked and outraged. Some of us took to the streets. But not all of us were re-traumatised in the way that any Black person who has experienced institutionalised violence or racism could have been. While well-meaning white liberals (myself included) were wringing their hands and posting black squares on Instagram, Sharmaine found herself fielding calls and messages from people she barely knew, asking her what they should do. They wanted to be 'a better ally' and while Sharmaine was sympathetic to the desire, there was part of her that wondered whether they truly understood what the word ally actually meant.

The experience was, she told me now, 'really hard'.

SHARMAINE: It's been really difficult to navigate with periphery friends and acquaintances who suddenly want to get into your orbit because you are their one Black friend. But I don't feel that with my actual friends because of that equality I was talking about. Essentially we wouldn't have a friendship if I didn't feel equal. The foundation is already there. So if my closest friends do come to me and talk to me about things like race then of course, of *course* we should talk about it because this is an equal conversation and you know that I have an opinion on it.

Her point was also that simply because a whole heap of white people were suddenly taking notice of racism, it didn't mean that the horror of it hadn't existed before; that it hadn't, in truth, existed for centuries before that.

SHARMAINE: Black people die every day, literally. Black people die because of inequality and injustice *every day*. So this idea that this is a moment … I'm like, 'Well, why is George Floyd more of a moment than Breonna Taylor?'[50] Everyone was talking about it [George Floyd]. A friend texted me when Ahmaud Arbery[51] died and the difference between that and the 400 messages I got when George Floyd was killed was amazing. But they were both killed by white people. They were both going about their business and were murdered by white people.

I told Sharmaine I had recently read *Big Friendship*, jointly written by US podcasters Aminatou Sow and Ann Friedman.[52] Sow, a Black woman, had recalled an incident where she had been invited to a birthday party at Friedman's house in Los Angeles. At the party, Sow noticed all the other guests were white. She described it as a stomach-lurching 'trapdoor' moment, referencing a term coined by the cultural critic Wesley Morris.

'For people of color,' Morris wrote, 'some aspect of friendship with white people involves an awareness that you could be dropped through a trapdoor of racism at any moment, by a slip of the tongue, or at a campus party, or in a legislative campaign. But it's not always anticipated. You don't *expect* the young white man who's been seated along-side you in a house of worship to take your life because you're Black.'[53]

Although they were extremely close friends, Sow and Friedman had never before explicitly talked about race within their friendship. The party, and Sow's experience of it, prompted a conversation they might not otherwise have had.

I realised when reading this passage that although Sharmaine and I talked about a range of issues, I had never explicitly asked her whether she had experienced any trap-door moments in our friendship. And I really wanted to know if I was failing her.

ELIZABETH: Can I ask you about that?

SHARMAINE: Yeah. It's a really difficult one because I'm just very aware of the society that we live in and the experiences that people have. I've always been the only Black person in the room. And what I fight for, in terms of my work, is that people from different backgrounds, races, ethnicities, etc., are included. I also maintain that I don't believe that when I'm in a room of Black people that I'm going to be *more* understood by them or agree with them because of our race.

I want there to be other Black people in the room, but not because I think they can understand me. I want them to be in the room because people should have opportunities and I don't understand why we're excluded – my thoughts around it are that basic!

I have no expectations that my friends will have other people from the same race as me there. And then there's also another thing: is it really about race? Or is it about class? As a middle-class Black woman, I'm aware of how few of us there are of my age group because of the logistics of that – I'm third generation and have parents who were born in the UK. Most people my age have parents that were born elsewhere.

My Britishness is equal to my Blackness. And then there's the question of what *is* 'Blackness'? In the end it's *like* a race but it's not one culture. I have all of those questions. So I don't think it's as easy as that. And I would have to be like, 'Where are my Asian friends?' for example … I have a lot of white friends and I have a lot of Black friends and there's lots of people that are missing from that from different ethnicities. Because of the structures and inequality and racism of our society it *is* harder to find people from different ethnicities who have a similar viewpoint or whatever. So no, I don't judge it. I only judge how I'm treated equally … I mean, do you think you've let me down on issues?

ELIZABETH: I don't. But I also am aware that I *can't* know at the same time. And, it's not your responsibility to educate me … Also, what I really value about you is clarity. If something is important to you, you'll say, 'This is important to me, please do this, or ask me this.' You'll just say that, which is so helpful as well. About anything.

SHARMAINE: Yeah, but it's the same with you, you know, being on a journey where you have been divorced, where you've had miscarriages, where you have been looking for fulfilment in a familial sense outside of your work. You're really open to me about those things as well. And there's an equality in that you've been through things that I haven't experienced and I've been through things that you haven't experienced. And so, you know, what I value is that you're never walking on eggshells with me and I don't equally have to walk on eggshells with you, which means that that's where the trust, honesty, authenticity, comes from.

I was reminded, as she spoke, that when Meghan, the Duchess of Sussex, had written an op-ed piece for the *New York Times* revealing she had suffered a miscarriage, Sharmaine had immediately texted to say she was thinking of me. It was an astonishingly sensitive and humane thing for her to do – she knew that, some months previously, I had gone through my third miscarriage and she understood, without my having to say anything, that any time a public figure opens up about their own experience of infertility or baby loss, it can be upsetting. At the same time as I welcome more and more women (and men) talking about their struggles to conceive, there are some days when it carries more personal weight for me than others. This happened to be one of those days. Instinctively, Sharmaine knew. And she knew, I think, because every time a Black person was killed and their death made the news, there was an element for her of resurfacing trauma. I am not for a minute comparing racism with infertility. One is the product of centuries of systemic discrimination from which all white people benefit, whether they acknowledge it or not. The other is painful bad luck: a deck of cards shuffled by the randomness of biology. But it was the first time I fully understood the depths of Sharmaine's empathy. She knew because she *knew*.

It's no coincidence that when Sharmaine found herself pregnant at the age of forty with a pair of miraculous twins, she took great care of how to tell me. When you are a woman who has tried and failed to have babies, it can be painful to hear of other people's seemingly effortless pregnancies. I became used to a near-constant stream of happy Facebook posts revealing growing bumps and bemoaning first-trimester morning sickness. I would watch Instagram Stories charting the progress of a pink- or blue-themed baby shower complete with helium balloons emblazoned with 'Mum-to-be' and a cutesy chalkboard where guests had been invited to make a guess as to the child's gender. Sometimes, expectant parents would just WhatsApp me a picture of a scan with the caption 'Some news!' while I tried not to cry. Every single one of those impersonal announcements felt like a kick in the gut. That wasn't my friends' responsibility, by the way. I'm not saying they should have done anything differently. I'm simply saying what my experience was.

To begin with, I tried to be nonchalant: it didn't matter; that was their baby, not the one that was waiting for me.

Then when that didn't help, I attempted cynicism: ugh, who would have a baby shower? It was so sentimental, so over the top, so *American* – who did they think they were, the Kardashians? As the years passed and my failed IVF attempts and miscarriages accumulated, cynicism turned inevitably to bitterness: imagine being so sure of your pregnancy that you post about it without fear of it going wrong. Imagine being so unaware of your privilege that you don't give anyone less lucky than you a second thought. And so on.

Eventually, I dropped all pretence and allowed myself to feel the uncomfortable emotions I was trying so hard to mask. Of course, there was part of me that was thrilled for my friends when they announced their pregnancies, but it wasn't straightforward. I realised that it was possible to feel joy for a loved one at the same time as feeling like an emotional bruise was being pressed. I could be happy for someone else who was having a baby, but I could also feel the resurgence of my own grief that it hadn't yet happened for me.

I understand it's hard for people to know what to do when they have a friend who has struggled to conceive, and I don't think there are any rules because everyone has an individual experience of infertility. But I do believe that the one thing that makes a difference is to personalise how you do it. Instead of simply sending out a mass text or social media post, it is far more meaningful for the recipient if you send a message that says something like, 'I wanted to let you know before you found out from someone else …'

or 'I know this journey hasn't been easy for you, and so I'm aware that this news might give you complicated feelings, but ...' or a simple 'I love you and am thinking of you and I wanted to tell you ...' A text gives the recipient time to manage their own feelings before they respond. But a phone call in which you leave space for how the other person is feeling can also be a very loving act.

Sharmaine did both. First, she sent a text, asking if I had time to chat as she had something to tell me. Already, that gave me a sense of what it would be. I knew that she and her husband had been thinking of expanding their family for a while. When she called, Sharmaine told me that she was in the early weeks of a pregnancy with twins, and that she wanted me to be one of the first to know as she understood it might also produce conflicting feelings in me. It was an object lesson in active compassion. She was so kind and thoughtful in how she said it that I genuinely felt nothing but love for her wonderful news. It had been delivered in a way that simultaneously acknowledged and respected my pain, and it meant I didn't need to hide or disguise my emotions. There was space here to face all the things we *both* might be feeling (because unexpectedly discovering you're pregnant with not one but two babies is pretty complicated too).

When, some nine months later, her gorgeous daughters were born, I was honoured that she asked me to be a guide (rather than a god) parent. This invitation came via email because Sharmaine felt I might want a chance to say no rather than being put on the spot. But I couldn't wait to be a part of these girls' lives. I knew already what a blessing they would be given what their mother was like. I said yes without hesitation.

Friendships like the one I have with Sharmaine are rare because you need to trust in each other's emotional honesty, and that's not always an easy place to get to. But for whatever reason, I knew almost as soon as I met Sharmaine that I could trust her with my heart. We were lucky that we randomly ended up at the same dinner and bonded over Beyoncé, but both Sharmaine and I have friendships in our lives that do not live up to this exacting standard. Sharmaine categorises them as 'White Wine Wednesday' friendships. A White Wine Wednesday friendship is between people who you met at university or at some point in your twenties. You spent drunken evenings together at a time when you had vanishingly little responsibility. You had a lot of self-conscious *fun*. But as life moves on and each of you starts taking work more seriously or begins having children or moving away from the city in which you once lived, you realise that you have less time for each other. And yet it seems somehow important to keep the group going – because you have so much shared history and so many good memories and you all used to be so much *fun*. So a group email goes out and you spend an interminable amount of time trying to find a date that you're all free. It takes a lot of admin because, as you tell each other repeatedly, you're 'so, so busy'.

SHARMAINE: You meet on a Wednesday because Tuesday is too early. Thursday there's normally a work thing and Friday you're doing other stuff. Wednesday is good, after work, you know. And then you meet somewhere for dinner, it takes ages to work out which restaurant ... When you meet, you're basically downloading what's happened to you by every quarter, so it's like a financial report. The agenda of the evening is who takes it in what turn to discuss the things that have happened in their lives. You drink a lot of white wine and you don't eat much and by the end of it you're completely in love with each other again. Or one of you might leave slightly pissed off that the other didn't give them quite enough time to discuss whatever thing was happening in their life in that quarter.

ELIZABETH: [laughing] It's so accurate! And you always have a terrible hangover and the hangover is never worth the experience.

SHARMAINE: Exactly. I mean, I don't get hangovers ...

Allow me to interject here and confirm that you did read that correctly. Sharmaine has never once had a hangover. And believe me: she has drunk enough to warrant one. I've been there. Truly, she's a medical miracle.

SHARMAINE: But there's definitely regrets. You do come away sometimes thinking: how is this person in my life? Other times you come away [wondering] do you want to see them again? Do you really care about them? But you make a promise like, 'We should do this more often. You only work around the corner! We should do this once a week!' And then you don't see them again for another four months. And it is always the same. Like, 'Why don't we see each other? We should go for dinner with our families! I would love to see you on a Saturday!' And then it's just like, don't overstep the mark, don't overstep the mark by trying to bring a *Saturday* into it.

By this stage in our conversation I was almost crying with laughter. Yet Sharmaine had made a serious point: the reason White Wine Wednesdays are never satisfying is because there's a lack of depth. The stories over the restaurant table in a group of people you don't really know any more can only ever scratch the surface. Without getting deep, neither Sharmaine nor I feel the conversation is truly honest. So it can't be equal either. Our Zoom call came to an end and I shut my laptop feeling as I always feel after a chat with Sharmaine: I felt seen.

A few months after that, Sharmaine and her family travelled from Berlin to London. She and her husband and the girls came for dinner at ours. It was the first time I'd met my new guide-children and although all adults are more or less legally obliged to say something sweet about babies that aren't theirs, I was relieved that the compliments came naturally. These were two ravishingly cute babies.

My thirteen-year-old stepdaughter was staying over and joined us for dinner and I was struck by how instantaneously Sharmaine could strike up a connection with her. Children are extremely good at sussing out inauthenticity or any whiff of falsity (and a savvy thirteen-year-old girl is probably the most adept at it: if MI6 knew what they were doing they'd start recruiting from single-sex London day schools). With Sharmaine, there was no need for my stepdaughter to be wary. Sharmaine simply asked the questions she wanted to know the answer to with no agenda or guile. Then she shared her own memories of going to school in the same city. At one point, the two of them had an impassioned exchange about the best bus routes.

The twins slept sweetly through dinner, as if to prove that they really were too good to be true. When they woke, they didn't cry but treated us all to matching gummy smiles. The night was long, fuelled by laughter and shared stories and great conversation. It was so good to be around Sharmaine again and it was the antithesis of White Wine Wednesdays.

Reader, it was a Friday. And we drank Pinot Noir.

The Friendship Tapes
ANONYMOUS

Anonymous, mid-40s, mum of two

'There are definitely friendship groups that as a mum you get thrown into, like the NCT group ... We're a group of eight – one mum was early, we all were meant to be roughly the same time but she had a baby, like, four weeks ahead of us. So she went through all that shit on her own, like breastfeeding and giving birth and panicking and not sleeping and so basically, the rest of us fed off her.

'We're still good friends – we meet up once a year and I come down [to London] for lunch [from Oxford] because I'm the one that gets everyone together. In my head they're all going out without me, but no! And we've all drifted but it was such an intense time and friendship – they've seen my boobs more than any other friend on the planet! If they asked to see my bits, I would show them anything because it's a very open, physical trip. And you are weep-ing because you haven't slept, you're all struggling and you *all* think you're failing.

'They're very different, but ... we meet up once a year. It's lovely and we again share really very personal stuff but then that's pretty much it for the rest of the year. We all do things and there's a few messages on WhatsApp, but there's not much as a group outside [that].

'My daughter, bless her, she's got a new friend at school, and so the mum and I are getting friendly. I knew we were going to get on when she turned up to the first playdate and said, "I haven't baked anything. I know probably I should have done that. But here's a box of Gail's pastries," and I was like, "Oh, we are going to get on just fine."

'I know that some of the mums from my son's school, when he moves on to secondary school, we won't keep in touch. We see each other at the gate. It's all very friendly. You will have a laugh and they're lovely people, they probably think I'm OK too. But that's it. You're there because your children are there at school and because you're seeing them frequently so you're up to date, but it's not a deep friendship. It's not a friendship that I've got with other people where you celebrate all the other stuff that goes on.'

8.
FRENEMIES

When Friends Don't Want
the Best for You

The opposite of Sharmaine's clarity is a friendship that is so confusing you never quite know what you're going to get. They're the ones guaranteed to tell you a new haircut is 'interesting' rather than giving a straightforward compliment. They're the ones who are secretly threatened by your success rather than rejoicing in it. They're the people who don't want to integrate you into their lives but will enjoy striking up intimate acquaintances with your other friends that exclude you. They'll probably find a way of ensuring they're the centre of attention at any party you have. They will trigger feelings of uncertainty, because they're capable of both love and withdrawal, sometimes within a single hour. They offer backhanded compliments and passive-aggressive jabs and never seem entirely capable of being happy for you.

In academic circles, these are called 'ambivalent' friendships, after the work of the Swiss psychologist Paul Eugen

Bleuler, who coined the term ambivalence in the early 1900s to describe the state of having simultaneous conflicting reactions, beliefs or feelings.[54] An ambivalent friendship can therefore be one that contains multiple different impulses – they can be affectionate one day and combative the next. In popular culture, however, the verbiage is more straightforward. We call these people frenemies.

I previously thought that Gwyneth Paltrow had invented the concept after writing a 2009 piece for her Goop newsletter in which she revealed that she had once 'had a "frenemy" … This person really did what they could to hurt me.'[55] There was much speculation that she was referring to fellow actress Winona Ryder, who had been reading the script for *Shakespeare in Love* when Paltrow stumbled across the screenplay in Ryder's home and asked for an audition. Paltrow got the part and later rubbed salt in the wound by winning an Oscar.

But it turns out that 'frenemy' actually came into common usage as early as 1953, when the anti-communist journalist Walter Winchell used it in the *Nevada State Journal* to describe the tense relationship between America and Russia.[56] In the 1970s, the author Jessica Mitford, sibling of the more famous Nancy, claimed that the portmanteau was in fact invented several decades earlier by one of her six sisters 'when she was a small child to describe a rather dull little girl who lived near us. My sister and the Frenemy played together constantly, invited each other to tea at least once a week, were inseparable companions, all the time disliking each other heartily.'[57]

FRENEMIES

I have, in my time, attracted a fair few frenemies, both men and women. They have varied widely in terms of background and character, but the one common feature is that they made me feel being their friend was a precious and unparalleled gift – the equivalent of the toxic partner who tells you that you'll 'never find anyone who loves you like I do'. It takes years of recovery to realise you won't, and that this is a good thing because the way they loved you was unhealthy and controlling and not a little narcissistic.

With frenemies, I found it was often very difficult to become their friend because they had absurdly high standards for anyone who came into their orbit. They would criticise a stranger's clothing, or a colleague's halitosis, or the fact that the person they'd just gone on a date with had terrible taste in music. All of those should have been red flags, but then I discovered that to be allowed into their hallowed circle after passing these invisible tests – to be deemed 'worthy' of their attention – felt as though I'd won a competition I'd never even realised I was entering.

I have a friend called Ali, who is one of the most riotously funny people you could ever hope to meet. I've had some of the best nights out with Ali and some of the worst next-day hangovers. He is the kind of person you agree to meet for a coffee at 3 p.m. and end up on a dance floor with at 3 a.m. the next morning. He makes me laugh until I cry.

But he can also be unpredictable. Over the years, I noticed that any time something went well for me, he seemed to feel it meant his own life was lacking. As a result, he was constitutionally incapable of acknowledging anything I achieved. I would have understood the impulse a bit more if he had been unhappy, but that wasn't the case: he was professionally successful and in a long-term relationship. And yet when I published my first novel, he never mentioned it. Not once. Not even at the launch party, where he was one of the only guests not to buy a copy. Later, when the topic of my book came up, he breezily confessed he still hadn't picked it up because 'it's not really my kind of book'. I laughed uneasily because I didn't know what else to do. 'Just joking,' he added. But he wasn't. It's not that I expect all my friends to read whatever I write, but it was the way Ali was so conspicuously *not* doing it that bothered me. I published more books. With my third novel, Ali texted me to say he'd raced through it 'in the bath one night. It was such an easy read!'

I didn't believe anyone was capable of reading an entire novel over the course of one bath so I knew that Ali had either skimmed through it, not thinking the book worth his time, or that he had lied. Either way, it made me feel as though he had no respect for what I did. But instead of confronting him, I let it slide and never mentioned my books to him again.

Quite often, a frenemy will say something mean under the guise of humour. When I got engaged to my first husband, Ali made an acerbic comment about how he was surprised I'd found someone to 'take me on' and again, when I looked hurt, he squeezed my shoulder and said he was only joking. In my twenties and early thirties, I had a horror of seeming humourless or like I took myself too seriously, so I forced out a giggle and told myself not to be so sensitive.

I understood that, at some level, Ali's passive aggression came from a deep-rooted insecurity and because I could empathise with that, it kept me in the friendship. It was also true that Ali was capable of great acts of generosity. He once sent me a beautiful orchid for no reason other than it had 'reminded me of you'. Although he might not always have been nice to my face, I knew from mutual acquaintances that he was loyal and protective behind my back, and this meant a lot to me.

I would be grateful for these unanticipated gestures: all the more so because I was relieved Ali was in a phase of being nice to me. The push and pull of his affection kept me oddly entranced. When I had his loving attention, it was gorgeous to be in the warmth of that gaze. When it was taken away, I wondered what I had done wrong and endeavoured to set it right. I kept performing and performing and performing until one day, another friend asked me why I put up with it.

'He's so mean,' she said.

'Oh no, he isn't. That's just Ali.'

'But why would you want to be his friend if he treats you like that?'

I couldn't explain it back then, but now I realise that for me, it was a bit like the person you're dating not being that into you. When Ali undermined me, I wanted to prove him wrong. On the occasions that he cared for me, I wanted to live up to his belief in me. I did not have a clear sense of who I was, so I relied too much on his opinion of me to give me validity. He was leaving me emotional bread-crumbs, and I was picking them up and storing them in the hopes that one day I'd have enough for a full sandwich.

My need for this kind of friendship clearly had its roots deep in my own psychology and when Ali moved out of London and bought a house in the countryside a three-hour drive away, it gave me a chance to reflect more deeply on what that might be. The distance was good for us. Removed from the same social circles, Ali became less competitive and his newfound isolation in a small rural village meant he was more appreciative of my friendship. He would book dinners in with me weeks in advance and when we met he genuinely seemed to want to hear all my news. Occasionally there would be a flash of the old Ali – once, he took me to task for not having called him on the day he returned from holiday, as if the date should have been engraved on a plaque hung above my front door – but generally speaking, the interactions between us were smoother and nicer. It meant that when he did say some-thing mean, I was more aware of it.

So why did I put up with it?

Let's say you are someone who has grown up around unpredictable moods and atmospheres. Let's say you get so accustomed to the febrile nature of these shifting tensions that you begin to equate love with uncertainty, with the idea that you're never quite sure of what you might get. And let's say, hypothetically speaking, that this conflation had such an impact on your romantic life that you found yourself in an emotionally coercive relationship without realising that's what it was because not even the language existed back then.

Let's say your partner was prone to jealous fury. Let's say he did things like check your laptop to see if you'd been googling your ex's names. Let's say he probably cheated on you because he evaded the question once you asked him about a particular woman he'd been flirting with. Let's say he believed you should be grateful that you were with him. Let's say that once, when you told him you couldn't babysit his children as you usually did at the weekends, he was so angry he pushed you up against a bedroom wall and raised his hand as if to strike you. Let's imagine that in this moment you are so shocked you can think of nothing else to say other than 'Go on, then,' and his eyes flicker and he realises what he's doing and drops his arm. Let's say, the next day, you are so ashamed of what happened that *you* are the one who apologises. Let's say you only tell one other person of this incident, carefully selected from your outer circle of friendship to be someone who doesn't tell you to leave.

Let's say, in this hypothetical exercise, your partner then claims what happened was an example of passion inflamed to an irrational degree. This reminds you of domestic abusers on television soaps who say they only beat their wives up because they love them so much. Let's say you're aware of this comparison but you don't explicitly *make* it because you're busy telling yourself it wasn't that bad, was it? It was only words, in the end. He didn't actually hit you, did he? And besides, it would be hard to leave, wouldn't it? Because he gets so angry, and you spend most of your time together trying not to trigger his rage and – here's the thing – you're normally so good at avoiding it. You're excellent at treading lightly on eggshells so that the thin membranes don't crack or splinter. You know how to do it, somewhere deep in your muscle memory. Truly, it is one of your greatest life skills. You can tiptoe around the contours of his damage. You can weave together the threads of his excuses into vast, colourful tapestries of forgiveness. Where there is fear, you can choose to see it as love.

Let's say all this happened – *hypothetically*, of course. Not just once, but again and again and again until you gathered up the courage to pack a bag and go.

Now let's imagine you in a wider context. You will be in recovery for a long time. It will take years for you to unplait the strands; to understand that love is about acceptance rather than challenge; that passion stems from safety not anger. In the time it takes you to do this, you are vulnerable to all sorts of relationships that echo their previous experience. Let's imagine a friend who is sometimes adoring and sometimes disengaged and sometimes resentful of a thing you never knew you'd done. Might you, once more, confuse those actions with a kind of love?

I embarked on this book because there is so little language around friendship. We don't have the terminology and until we speak it into existence, it is difficult to express what we mean with any precision. Yet here I am again reaching for the vocabulary of romantic love.

I suppose it's because an ambivalent friendship, which is so rooted in uncertainty, bears the closest resemblance to what we've (wrongly) been told is a characteristic of old-fashioned courtship. In classic novels or films or songs, romance is heightened by the will they/won't they ebb and flow; the sense that no one quite knows whether someone loves or hates them until the final, satisfying denouement. Mr Darcy and Elizabeth Bennet are the archetypal example of this, and Austen writes it so beautifully in *Pride and Prejudice* that their interactions on the page become as heart-pounding as anything you might read in a thriller.

Classic literature, of the sort we might have studied on the national curriculum, was mostly shaped by dead white men. It meant that friendship got vanishingly little attention – if it did appear, it was frequently a stolid alliance between male equals who had important things to discuss before going off to fight in the Napoleonic wars. Children's books of the same era are the exception – primarily because children didn't consummate love affairs in polite society, so one of the only things left to write about was amicable or familial relationships rather than romantic.

There are far fewer adult novels that take lifelong friendship as their subject matter. This is why, when I first read Elena Ferrante's Neapolitan Quartet, it felt so revolutionary. The four books, set over a fifty-year span, tell the story of Lenu and Lila – childhood friends from Naples whose lives intertwine and diverge as their selfhood is shaped over the decades by education, politics, love, feminism, family and ambition. Lenu and Lila love each other deeply. But they can't escape loathing each other at points, or feeling jealousy or anger and disappointment too. As such, it is the most brilliant and convincing portrayal of friendship ambivalence I've ever read.

Take this, from the first novel in the quartet, *My Brilliant Friend*, as narrated by Lenu recalling the two of them as schoolchildren: 'Lila knew how to read and write, and what I remember of that gray morning when the teacher revealed it to us was, above all, the sense of weakness the news left me with.'[58]

Lenu knows she should be happy for her beloved friend, and yet she's left with resentment. For Lenu and Lila, competitiveness proves to be an integral part of their friendship because they both have a desire to escape the limitations of their impoverished upbringings. Their life chances depend on being the best, which means they are rivals as well as friends. This is why Lenu feels undermined by Lila's reading prowess, and why – much later – she will ponder the duality of their friendship after returning from a holiday to the island of Ischia.

'I established convergences and divergences,' Lenu says. 'In that period it became a daily exercise: the better off I had been in Ischia, the worse off Lila had been in the desolation of the neighbourhood; the more I had suffered upon leaving the island, the happier she had become. It was as if, because of an evil spell, the joy or sorrow of one required the sorrow or joy of the other; even our physical aspect, it seemed to me, shared in that swing.'[59]

Convergence and divergence. The forces that push us together, and the jealousies, resentments and disagreements that pull us apart. It's all there. Ferrante conveys the intensity underpinning such friendships – the way that sometimes we forget where we stop and the other person starts. Working that out necessarily involves seeing ourselves in counterpoint: Lenu can only become self-actualised by defining herself separately from Lila, and this is the fatal flaw of their friendship. By the final novel in the quartet, Lenu reflects that 'every intense relationship between human beings is full of traps' and calls her friendship with Lila 'splendid and shadowy'.[60]

What Ferrante so accurately identified is that ambivalent friendships contain within them the capacity to be both splendid *and* shadowy. And yet it turns out they are just as bad for our emotional wellbeing as a full-blown toxic relationship.

In 2003, several thousand miles away from Ferrante's Naples, two psychologists from Utah called Julianne Holt-Lunstad and Bert Uchino conducted an intriguing experiment. They asked 102 participants to wear blood-pressure monitors for three days and to record every social interaction lasting more than five minutes, noting their feelings and responses. Holt-Lunstad and Uchino found that blood pressure was raised when the participants interacted with people they disliked but could not avoid. But the really interesting discovery was that when these people met up with ambivalent friends, their blood pressure was even more elevated than when they spoke to the straightforwardly awful ones.

The study's authors concluded that this was because we expect very little from people we loathe. Unpredictable friends, by contrast, can encourage your resilient optimism: you give them the benefit of the doubt because sometimes they are kind and loving and generous and sometimes they're not. They raise your hopes and dash them with no warning.[61]

Holt-Lunstad and Uchino went on to do several more studies in this area. In 2014, Holt-Lunstad wrote that 'concurrent positivity and negativity' in ambivalent friendships was associated with higher rates of depression[62] and greater cardiovascular reactivity to stress.[63] Uchino found in 2012 that that the more ambivalent ties a person has in their social network, the more likely they are to have shortened telomere lengths.[64] Telomeres are the caps at the end of each strand of DNA that protect our chromosomes, like the plastic tips at the end of a shoelace. They are an essential component in determining how our cells age (and yes, I did have to look that up because I did Single Science GCSE and essentially only understand that chlorophyll is green and the earth is round). Shorter telomeres are strong predictors of mortality across different diseases including cardiovascular disease, cancer, and infectious diseases.

In brief: frenemies are bad for your health. Not just that, but they are actively worse for you than hanging out repeatedly with someone you hate. At the same time, these relationships are difficult to disentangle yourself from, because the good memories affix themselves to you like burrs on a hemline and the bad ones are frequently too subtle to identify as obviously negative. For me, the clearest way of identifying an ambivalent friendship is to take note of how I feel after I've seen them. If, on paper, we've had a perfectly nice evening but I'm left feeling inexplicably drained and a bit low, the chances are they fall into that category. Holt-Lunstad and Uchino would doubtless advise me to cut Ali and others like him out of my life. But, as previously established, I'm conflict avoidant and, I don't know if you've heard, but I'm also a friendaholic. When a friend offers me even the slightest glimmer of niceness, it's hard for me to turn my back on them unless it's a consistent pattern of repeated bad behaviour over decades of knowing them. It takes a lot to push me to a point of no return. It does occasionally happen (as it did with Ella and Becca) but the fact that I can count these break-ups on the fingers of one hand tells you everything you need to know.

One evening, when I'd just come back from another desultory dinner with Ali, I was sitting in the kitchen with a cup of tea, decompressing from the night.

'How was it?' Justin asked.

I gave a sigh as heavy as my spirits, and then proceeded to list all the perceived slights and passive-aggressive jabs; all the things Ali had said that made me feel less than and stupid; all the ways in which he'd sought to undermine me.

'Don't ask me why I'm friends with him,' I said, because I knew that's what Justin was already thinking. 'He's had a really hard time and he can be really lovely sometimes.'

Justin sat down opposite me and nodded, not saying anything for a few seconds.

'He's great when you're sad,' he said. 'But he's not happy for you when you're happy.'

He was right, of course. And I was coming to understand that one of the foundational tenets for real friendship is generosity of spirit and meaningful reciprocity. I protested.

'But he doesn't have that many friends or family and I feel sorry for him …'

I let the sentence trail, aware how pathetic it sounded. Besides, Ali wouldn't want me to feel sorry for him. He'd be horrified at the thought.

'OK,' Justin countered. 'So then maybe you can think of it as charitable service. Every year, I give a certain amount of my time and money to charity. Why don't you start seeing the time you spend with Ali as that? You're doing something nice for him because he needs it and presumably gets something from it. It doesn't matter if you don't get anything back because it's a charitable act.'

It made a curious kind of sense. There was part of me that felt uneasy with the notion that I was some Lady Bountiful, dispensing my friendship gold coins from atop my moral high horse, but the more I pondered it, the more I could see the appeal. It wasn't that I genuinely thought of Ali or myself in this way; it was more like a mental switch I could flick in order to re-categorise the friendship in a manner that made it more palatable.

By seeing it as service, I no longer expected anything back. More than that, I would no longer be as hurt by it. It would be a bit like parenting a tired child throwing a tantrum in the sweets aisle of the supermarket. A good parent in that situation would understand that their child was not acting on a set of conscious, rational decisions, but rather that they were responding to a desire they were not able to meet. An exhausted child with a yearning for sugar is unable to view their unhappiness as a consequence of their own behaviour in the moment itself. I don't think Ali knew what he was doing. Just as I had learned how to navigate affection – both its evolution and erosion – from damaged past relationships, he too had his own emotional pathology. In being aware of that, in deciding to exercise patience and to give him the benefit of the doubt, perhaps I would end up being a better friend than I thought. Not expecting anything in return meant that when I did feel seen and supported by him, it was a pleasant surprise rather than a measly sticking plaster applied too late over a wound that had festered for years.

So Ali and I are still friends. I have chosen to value him for what he is, rather than bemoan what he isn't. I am aware of the convergence and divergence and, broadly speaking, I've decided the splendour is worth the shadow. As much as I respect the work of all those clever psychologists, I have a sneaking suspicion that ending my friendship with Ali – ambivalent, though it is – would affect my health more negatively than managing it as part of my life. Ferrante was right: maybe some friendships are destined to be long, even if your telomeres are short.

The Friendship Tapes
MARK

*Mark Ford, 58, former TV executive
and co-owner of Sweat Box Soho,
a gay sauna which he runs with
his husband Jason*

'I don't have that many friends. It's almost a joke.

'I've never really reached out and made friends; if I make friends it is usually because I fancy them first of all, and then it becomes a friendship. If I allow somebody to make friends with me, they are the ones that have to do the work of courting. I think friendship needs a time to grow organically and it's quite hard to find the mechanisms for that to happen ... It's quite hard for somebody to just go "I'm going to be your friend"; you don't know quite what to do with that, so you have to find things to do together, which can feel a little bit false.

'My husband and I own a gay gym and sauna, so it's a very permissive and open environment, but I still have to be guarded about those around me: most of them are working for me. So we have our friendships outside of that, to protect that.

'I think the reason a lot of gay men find the most comfortable people to develop friendships with to be straight women, or gay women, is because there's no sexual energy, except for the mutual interest in men. So there's something to talk about! But there's a comfortableness.

'Straight men are awkward enough at making friends with each other, but it's even harder, I think, for gay men to be friends with each other, because you don't know whether you're dating or whether this is sexually based or whether it's platonic. It's not terribly natural.'

9.
FERTILITY

Not Having Children When All Your Friends Do

I have, at several points during the writing of this, alluded to my own struggles with fertility. I shy away from calling it infertility because it feels so judgemental and also inaccurate – my problem has not been getting pregnant as much as it has been carrying a baby to full term. Nor do I love calling it a 'fertility journey', but that's just because it sounds cliched and makes me think of a cheesy rock band beloved by high school a cappella groups. However, I'm aware that both these terms are among the only ones we have available – because fertility, like friendship, has a limited lexicon given that, for centuries, it has barely been spoken about – so I'll probably end up using them. Look, no one ever said I had to be consistent.

I have referred to my own fertility in previous chapters to provide the necessary context for a particular friendship or a particular realisation. The reason it keeps making an appearance is because, for the last decade or so of my life, it has been the canvas on which all else has been painted. Every friendship, every emotion, every moment of professional success or failure, every love affair, every social media post, every cat stroked, every book read and *Line of Duty* series watched has taken place against this backdrop. It has been a constant shadowing of my everyday reality. My yearning to have a child has not just shaped me as a woman: it *is* me as a woman. There is not a single day that I don't think about it. There is not a single day that I don't have to grapple with the sadness and the fear and the anxiety while at the same time mustering up the energy to maintain hope when it feels like all optimism is flagging.

A woman fighting a fertility battle has to wear an armour made up of all these linked, yet conflicting, pieces of chain-mail: we are told by spiritual guides to keep thinking positive, to manifest our children into existence by believing they will come to us when the universe decrees it so. At the same time, we are told by doctors we're not responding to the drugs, our follicles aren't behaving, our hormones are too low; we're told that we're too geriatric or it's too late or our womb is the wrong shape and in the face of all this failure, the only advice is to keep trying even though the probability is we'll fail again. I will never forget the revered fertility consultant who, on hearing I had miscarried three times, simply advised me to carry on attempting to get pregnant.

'My wife had ten,' he said breezily. 'But we got there in the end. Just keep at it.'

As if, really, it was my own fault for not trying hard enough. As if ten miscarriages were just something to be endured rather than investigated and, hopefully, avoided. As if women were mere vessels for pain and possibility.

We are told to have hope while simultaneously limiting expectation so that we're not disappointed. We're told it will happen in the same breath as we're told it won't. Living in this state of ambiguity is exhausting. There is faith and there is doubt and between is the weight which holds taut the tension between the two. We carry that weight, each and every one of us. Even if there is eventual resolution, we can never forget the slow-motion trauma which has embedded itself into our souls, which was part of our daily survival to get there.

I've written extensively about my early encounters – namely, IVF and my first miscarriage – in a previous book.[65] But my journey (dammit) has continued beyond the publication date of that sort-of memoir, and there is so much more to say, especially because the longer a woman tries for a baby, the more her biology denies her an easy conclusion. I'm talking specifically of the attempt to conceive a child here, not about those admirable men and women who are adoptive parents or who live a contented and accepting childfree life. I have nothing but respect for them, but I can't talk from a position of first-hand knowledge about their situations, and if I did, the words would land hollow on the page.

Sharing what I went through, in all its specificity, means revisiting some of the darkest times in my life but it is also the purest way I have of understanding and bringing meaning to the process. The truth is, in any discussion of friendship in my life, I absolutely have to include this part. How others responded to it, or how I navigated their reactions, has been vital to my understanding of what a friend is. So. Take my hand. Walk with me. Here goes.

On 23 March 2020, the UK entered its first national lockdown to help prevent the spread of Covid-19. Somewhat less momentously, my period was late. Only by a day or so but I was usually pretty regular and immediately a fissure of uncertain possibility cracked open in my mind. Could I be …? Was it possible that …?

The following day, I took a pregnancy test in the afternoon. It was one of the expensive ones that claims to be able to tell you with 99 per cent accuracy how many weeks you are. The digital display returned its brutal verdict: 'Not pregnant', typed in letters so tiny it was as if I'd been stupid to think otherwise.

The previous December, I had taken a different pregnancy test. The result had been positive. I remember sitting on the loo in our bathroom, crying and laughing as Huxley, our ginger cat, looked on with bafflement. I couldn't believe it. After my previously challenging fertility journey, I had frozen my eggs at thirty-seven. I got a grand total of three. Most women my age got an average of twelve. Those under thirty-five freeze around fifteen.[66] When I met Justin, I was thirty-nine. All of the indications were that my fertility was compromised and that it would be extremely difficult to conceive naturally. If it happened, we would be happy, but we didn't expect it. At that stage in my life, my lack of children caused me sadness, but it was a muted sadness and I thought that maybe I would be able to live with it.

Sitting on the toilet with that positive test in my hands, it seemed utterly miraculous to have a surprise pregnancy at forty-one. I realised that I had been suppressing how much I wanted it for fear of another disappointment. We were both overjoyed but Justin had more faith in my pregnancy than I did. I knew things could go wrong and as a result was highly anxious. He, already the father of three healthy children, did not have the same worries and would be so cheerfully positive about it all that I almost believed him. When I miscarried at seven weeks, I felt double the guilt: firstly, for not being able to hold on to our pregnancy and secondly because I had initiated Justin into a group no one wanted to be part of.

They say that children often teach you what you need to know. That pregnancy taught us both we wanted a baby more than we'd been admitting until now. I realised I would need some help. My best friend Emma did research into fertility clinics at the cutting edge of medical research and sent me the details of one in Greece.

The clinic appealed to me on three counts. It was considerably cheaper than the British alternatives. Plus, it was a one-stop shop: you could have a consultation in the morning and any necessary procedures in the afternoon, whereas most fertility clinics had to refer you to specialists in different hospitals. The final and most important point was that it was run by a woman. This was rare. It is a perpetual irony that in a medical field that mostly affects women, the consultants are overwhelmingly male. That's not to say they aren't good at their jobs – many of them are – but natural empathy has its limits. Not many men can understand what it is like to experience a menstrual cramp, let alone a miscarriage, in much the same way as I will never fully be able to comprehend the pain of being kneed in the testicles. A lot of the care I had been given at the hands of men had not been *careful*. At best, it had been sympathetic – a tilted head and an understanding expression as I recounted my litany of failed attempts at motherhood. At worst, it had been dismissive and callous. The male consultant who refused to turn away as I wiped myself after a briskly administered ultrasound, pulling on my knickers as quickly as I could to avoid his gaze. The male doctor who told me having children wasn't all it was cracked up to be within minutes of informing me that my chances of natural conception were minimal. I could pluck out a dozen more examples.

But when I called Alexandra, the woman in charge of the Greek clinic, I was struck immediately by her warmth. She had endured many years of infertility herself and she was able to apply neutral language to my situation. I told her that my uterus was bicornuate – a congenital abnormality affecting around 3 per cent of women and commonly referred to as a 'heart-shaped womb', because it has a deep V-shaped indentation (or septum) at the top. Alexandra refused to call it an abnormality. Instead, she asked me to visualise my womb as a room that we needed to get ready for my baby. There were beautiful columns on one side of this room, she continued, and removing them would give more space for any embryo to develop. The kindness of this language made me cry. It was so simple, but describing it in this way immediately absolved me of any sense that my body was failing me. My womb was a beautiful room! With columns!

Some of my previous doctors had said my heart-shaped uterus might have contributed to my fertility problems, but then again it might not have done, so I just had to live with it. But Alexandra thought it might be the cause of my recurrent failure to hold on to a baby. This was why Justin and I had found ourselves on a flight to Greece on a dark, windy night in February 2020 just as Storm Ciara threatened to ground all aircraft. The plane soared shakily into the sky.

We arrived at the clinic the following morning. The waiting room was filled with pale-faced couples and one woman in her fifties who we later found out was having a baby via egg and sperm donation. We were weary warriors sitting in cheap fake-leather armchairs that squeaked against our clothes. We made no eye contact because, at a certain point, you just can't take on anyone else's sadness on top of your own. Everything was running late. In fertility clinics the world over, lateness is the one thing they have in common.

Justin and I were eventually taken in to see Alexandra. She was just as warm as she had been over the phone and increasingly firm that the most obvious course of action was a surgical procedure that would remove my septum. Within hours, this had been arranged at a local hospital for the next day. I was told I wouldn't be able to eat or drink anything beforehand, and to ensure that I had no nail polish on. I looked down at my shellac manicure. The remainder of the afternoon was spent trying to find a salon that would take it off for me, and then a rushed visit to the Acropolis because, well, it seemed rude not to.

I wandered around the temple of Athena and thought of the ancient virgin goddess, who was lusted after by Hephaistos. According to legend, he ejaculated over Athena, but she wiped the sperm away and it fell onto Gaia, the goddess Earth. Hephaistos himself had supposedly been conceived when his mother ate lettuce leaves, a plant associated with semen because of the milky white fluid in its leaves. Athena was also the product of an unusual conception: her father Zeus had eaten his lover Metis while she was pregnant and was said to have given birth to Athena from his own head.[67] I found the Ancient Greek mythology strangely comforting. Compared to all this, my quest for a child seemed relatively straightforward.

The next morning, we woke at 5 a.m. We got a taxi to the hospital and I was given a gown and forms to fill in and then wheeled off on a gurney by people who were talking to me in a language I didn't understand. Justin was left anxiously sitting on a plastic seat in the waiting area. It all seemed to be happening so quickly that I momentarily panicked. Was it unwise to have handed myself over to a surgeon I'd not even met yet and put all my faith in the judgement of a woman who'd described my womb as a room? Well, it was too late to do anything about it. The anaesthetist was knocking me out and all I remember thinking was that the surgeon looked like an actor playing the part in an American hospital TV drama.

I came round shortly afterwards to find two plastic tubes hanging out of my nether regions. These, I'd been told, were attached to an inflated balloon inside my womb which would ensure that it kept shape while the scars healed. I had to wear that thing for five days and I cannot tell you how disconcerting I found it. The tubes looked like something a coked-up *Blue Peter* presenter might have assembled with sticky-backed plastic and a roll of double-sided tape. Sometimes, for no reason, they filled up with blood and I had to drain them in the shower. If that sounds gross, it's because it was.

Alexandra sent us back to London that same evening. I was still dazed from the general anaesthetic and both of us were grim-faced with the emotional weirdness of the previous forty-eight hours. It was a relief to be home.

A later scan revealed the operation had been successful: my septum had shrunk from 7 mm to a little under 2 mm. A week or so later, I flew to New York to visit my friend Clemmie, who had suffered a brain haemorrhage that left her re-learning how to walk and talk. I sat beside her in hospital, sometimes lying next to her in bed, as we clutched each other's hands. The days passed. The nurses were talking about Coronavirus but I still felt it wasn't really anything to worry about. It would fizzle out, I thought, like bird flu. But before I left to get my flight home, a nurse handed me a travel-sized bottle of hand sanitiser. I didn't know then what a generous gift that would turn out to be – within weeks, supermarkets back in London would have sold out of hand sanitiser and toilet roll. I still have that travel-sized bottle, refilled countless times over the last two years.

I give you all this background to underline the surreality of the times we found ourselves in by March 2020. Still, the pregnancy test said negative. Although my period was late, there was clearly some other explanation. I texted Emma.

'Maybe do another one tomorrow morning just to be sure?' she replied.

So on Wednesday, 24 March, I did another test – in the morning, because that's when anti-Müllerian hormone levels (AMH) are at their highest. And this time, the digital display said I was pregnant. Two to three weeks pregnant, to be exact. I went upstairs to tell Justin who was, by now, working from home. We were both shell-shocked. When the world is facing an unprecedented crisis and a frighteningly uncertain outcome, it's an odd time to find out you're expecting a baby. It's even stranger if you have a history of infertility because the uncertainty becomes internal as well as external.

The following weeks saw me dazed and confused. I was in a state of semi-denial, while at the same time daring to believe that this pregnancy would work because of the operation I'd had the previous month. My pandemic-induced empty diary made it easy to relax and ensure I wasn't doing too much. It felt almost serendipitous.

I emailed Alexandra to tell her. She replied asking me to

get my bloods tested for her to monitor my progesterone levels and sent a prescription for Heparin, an injectable form of aspirin that would prevent clotting. I drove through the empty London streets to get my blood test. It felt like the apocalypse, except it was sunny and the sky was tauntingly blue. When she got the results, Alexandra was satisfied. The progesterone was rising nicely. Everything seemed to be going as well as it could.

At seven weeks, we had an early scan. I remember it was the first time I wore a face mask in public – they hadn't yet become routine and I'd had to order mine from a woman on Instagram who had turned her hand to making cloth masks for purchase. I lay back on the reclining seat as the sonographer prepared the ultrasound wand. I gripped Justin's hand and braced myself for the worst. I had been here before. Scans were not happy moments for me. But this time – a miracle! – the sonographer smiled as she told us all the good news. The baby was developing as she would expect. We listened to the baby's strong, healthy heartbeat. We were given a video with the swooshing, metronomic sound. We listened to it again at home, hugging and crying and laughing.

Relief swept through the house. I allowed myself to feel pregnant for the first time. I noticed symptoms I had deliberately ignored before in case it was dangerous to believe they meant anything – sore breasts; a gurgling stomach; an urgent need to pee during the night.

The following week, we returned for another scan. I was anxious, but more out of habit than anything deeper. The sonographer had said it was just a precaution. I went through the same routine: jeans off, lying back, legs spread, wand inserted.

And then … No sound.

No heartbeat.

A long pause from the sonographer as she angled the wand to the left and then to the right and then back again.

'I'm so sorry,' she said.

Justin gasped. Deep down, in the darkest part of me, I told myself I had already known this would happen. But I hadn't. I had thought this was the one. I had allowed myself to hope.

'I still feel pregnant,' I said.

'That can often happen because you've still got all the hormones,' the sonographer said kindly. 'I'll give you a moment.' She left the room.

I didn't think I was crying but I was. I released myself into the certain understanding that I knew how to do this bit. This was the bit I was familiar with. It was the other part – the part with a happy ending – that I had felt lost in.

I was offered two options: either wait and miscarry naturally or take pills to hasten the process. I couldn't have a surgical procedure to remove early pregnancy remains because the pandemic meant that all non-essential operations were rightly being postponed or cancelled. I took the drugs because they afforded me clarity. I was done with the headfuck of being simultaneously pregnant and not.

Back at home, I googled what to expect. The forums were not reassuring. A close friend, who had been through the same, texted me to say that it could be painful and not to panic if it was. The following twenty-four hours were among the most brutal I've ever experienced. It was, hands down, the worst of all three of my miscarriages. The pills prompted cresting surges of pain so vicious they made me throw up. The pain would climax then recede as I gathered up my energies for the next wave. I was grateful that Justin was working from home. He would appear at the bedside to hold my hand and ask if there was anything he could do. His presence was an unbelievable comfort. But it was a lonely journey.

This, then, was the place I found myself when my truest friends revealed themselves. Emma was constantly in touch via text and FaceTime. She also called Justin to see how I really was and, in the weeks that followed, the two of them kept a lovingly close eye on me. Others followed suit. Our friends Bette and Sinead immediately offered to do a grocery shop and leave it on the doorstep. They came round in their car and I waved at them through the bedroom window, feeling so blessed by their kindness. Roya left a tote bag filled with tulips and aubergines (listen, I *love* an aubergine). Sally, who I hadn't seen for years but who – bizarrely – had been in the same online pregnancy yoga class as I was a few days before, drove round and left a bunch of beautiful flowers. There were countless other texts and acts of kindness from the people I love. They seemed truly to share in our devastation. They told us how sorry they were. This was all I needed to hear. It was the most loving thing to say.

What I had learned over the preceding years was that friendship, in these circumstances, was not about the doing as much as the being. It was so lovely to get those aubergines and flowers, but the real meaning lay behind the action. It was the intent to mark and acknowledge what we were going through that was important. So often a miscarriage can feel like a silence that others gloss over in their rush to move the conversation on. It was important – for both of us – that the existence of our too-short pregnancy was respected.

Knowing that people were thinking of us was crucial to my recovery. Infertility is the grief that dare not speak its name. When you're mourning a pregnancy that ended before birth, you're mourning an absence. But the moment you get a positive result on a test, you start imagining your future with a child. You can't help it. Believe me, I've tried. I've tried not to hope, aware that this might make it more painful in the long run, but it's inescapable. That leap of faith, that vision of parenthood complete with potential names for your child, kicks in along with the hormones. Perhaps, in fact, it's *part* of the hormones. Perhaps nature in its infinitesimal wisdom, is equipping us to care.

When you're facing this absence alone, it can feel unmooring: a dream-like state where you wonder if you made it all up. This was what it was like the first time I miscarried in October 2014. I'd had an eerily similar experience – a heartbeat seen at seven weeks that disappeared just before my twelve-week scan. Back then, I didn't understand what I was going through, and I tried to ignore it. Besides, my marriage was breaking down, and I needed to resolve that issue first. I delayed my grief. Worse, I denied it. I did not believe I deserved the time to mourn what had never been.

I can't remember the first time I decided to speak publicly about my fertility. But when I did, it gave my loss substance and shape. It was my own acknowledgement of what had been and what was no longer. To my astonishment, hundreds and then thousands of women (and some men) got in touch with me to say how much they valued my words. They saw their own experiences reflected in mine. They felt they had a voice.

It was as if, by naming our collective sadness, I wrote those babies into existence. I realised that a deeply personal feeling that I had, for some time, wrongly labelled as shameful was turning out to have far more universal resonance than I had ever anticipated. And this made me feel less alone. It made me understand, for the first time, the power of solidarity forged in the fire of vulnerability.

Brené Brown says that 'shame cannot survive being spoken'.[68] She was right. Once I had started speaking, I couldn't stop. My sense of personal failure dissipated. Sharing became a necessity. I talked about fertility on my podcast. I penned columns on miscarriage. I was asked to comment on the radio about women's health issues, and fertility charities wanted me to chair events. The more I opened up, the more other people opened up to me. I felt seen. And the more I talked, the more my close friends who had never gone through fertility problems could understand. The more they knew what to do.

Grief is uncomfortable and spiky to look at. People often don't know what to say and would therefore rather remain silent in order to avoid further hurt, as if grief can be heightened by an ill-judged comment. It can't. Grief is absolute. It can't be made any worse than it already is, any more than an animal can become less extinct. By being open about my miscarriages, I think it assuaged the fear my loved ones had that they would say the wrong thing. They now knew it was more important to say something than nothing. And in order to set things out even more clearly, I wrote a piece in a national Sunday newspaper entitled 'What Not to Say About My Miscarriage', ending with the one thing you *could* always say, which was 'I'm so sorry.'[69] That's literally all it takes.

My closest friends got this without question. I am constantly surprised by the depths of their love for me and the way they find space to give my experience a place in their own hearts, a candle that never goes out. They will remember what would have been my due date. They will voice note me when a mutual acquaintance starts posting an endless stream of baby photos. They will text on Mother's Day to say they're thinking of me. They hug me when I well up unexpectedly. They are deeply sensitive to how I might feel around their children – sometimes so sensitive, in fact, that I have to plead with them to be allowed to see their kids. They meet me wherever I happen to be on any given day (psychologically speaking, that is. I wouldn't ask them all to travel to Vauxhall).

But for every person who got it, there were inevitably those who didn't. One of the deep injustices of infertility is also an obvious statement of fact: at the same time as you are struggling to conceive, others in your peer group will be doing so with seeming ease. And some of them will do it repeatedly, popping out babies like Pez dispensers. You will marvel at their confidence. I remember talking to one friend, in the early stages of her pregnancy, about any anxiety she might be experiencing. I wanted to tell her that I understood, that it was a time laden with worry, and that it was OK.

'Yes, I am feeling really worried,' she said over dinner.

I reached across and took her hand.

'Because if I'm having a girl, I just worry so much about how to raise her to be an empowered woman in these times we're living through.'

I was stunned.

'And I have three younger brothers,' she continued. 'So most of my experience with babies is of the male kind. It's very different.'

My friend is a lovely person who will constantly think of the bigger-picture issues of any given situation – and this was no exception. My reaction was entirely informed by my own personal history and my surprise was simply that people could think like this. That they were allowed to. That they were so blissfully convinced of their pregnancy's happy outcome that they were able to project several years into the future, long after their child would be safely delivered. That their worries were not about miscarriage or unexpected bleeding or pregnancy complications, but about how to raise the child they already believed they were guaranteed.

Wow, I thought, *imagine*. Imagine the peaceful certitude of that.

I had a similar feeling when I read Sheila Heti's book, *Motherhood*.[70] People had been recommending it to me for years and when I finally picked it up I thought I would find myself among Heti's pages. Instead, I endured hundreds of pages of an unnamed narrator throwing dice to decide whether or not she wanted to have a baby and whether getting pregnant would take her away from her art. The navel-gazing philosophical angst did not for one minute take into consideration that she might not be able to get pregnant, and that for millions of women around the world, the meandering should I/shouldn't I was a privilege they had been denied at the outset. We rightly talk a lot about privilege in this era of social change – an era marked by necessary protest movements such as Black Lives Matter and Me Too – but hardly anyone acknowledges fertility privilege. Those of us who have had complicated journeys to parenthood are only too aware of its existence. I don't think I'll ever forget how it feels to be the infertile one in a world of apparent abundance. I wouldn't post about my glorious babies on social media in much the same way as I wouldn't post about my expansive mansion or my fleet of Bentleys (not that I have any of those) because it's thoughtless to those who don't have these things. Forget the language of privilege for a second: isn't it just lacking in basic empathy or contextual awareness? Isn't it just being a good human?

Unfortunately, my difficulties with fertility coincided with the online fetishisation of motherhood in the 2010s. The internet afforded mothers the space to confer with each other across countries, oceans and time zones in a way they had never previously been able to. Suddenly, it felt as though our Western culture was awash with mummy bloggers exchanging everything from tips on teething to the perfect fashion-statement buggy. Mumfluencers encouraged us to buy organic cotton babygros and 'Wine O'Clock' slogan T-shirts through sunnily filtered Instagram tiles. The media pored over every detail of a celebrity's path to parenthood – from the artfully styled pregnancy photoshoot in the feature pages of a Sunday newspaper right through to the exclusive new-baby glossy magazine spread and then the inevitable scrutiny of the post-baby body in the MailOnline's sidebar of shame, posing the seemingly crucial question of whether a famous woman was 'snapping back into shape' in the number of weeks a male editor had deemed to be acceptable. It was a barrage of ovaries.

Mumsnet, the online community founded by the journalist Justine Roberts in 2000, became so influential that high-profile politicians fought to be interviewed on the site in a bid to connect with its largely middle-class female user base, seen as a valuable asset because of their tendency to be floating voters. In 2009, the then Prime Minister Gordon Brown took part in a Mumsnet web chat and was widely derided for failing to answer the pressing question of what his favourite biscuit might be. Roberts was given a CBE in the 2017 New Year Honours for services to the economy. Mumsnet is still one of the biggest parenting websites in the world and regularly attracts more than 10 million visitors a month.[71]

All of this simply emphasised the widening gap between my stage of life and the one where the majority of my friends found themselves. Many of them were actively engaged in the business of becoming parents, and then raising children. A small but powerful minority ran out of time for many other pursuits, including friendship, and so the expectation arose that I would be the one who would come to them. At this time in my life, I did not talk openly about my own issues and in fairness to this tiny handful of friends, I suppose that because I wasn't telling them what was going on for me, they were left to fill in the gaps. When they did, their logic was skewed.

I had fewer claims on my time, their reasoning went, so the obligation to make an effort would inevitably be mine. Because, as they repeatedly told me, parenthood was *hard*. It was the most challenging role they'd ever undertaken and therefore every other part of life must revolve around this central axis. I couldn't hope to understand until I'd experienced it myself, they said. I was lucky, they said, that I still had such a footloose and fancy-free existence. Make the most of it while you can, they said, while breastfeeding a newborn and complaining of disturbed nights and chafed nipples.

Of course, some of what they expressed (along with the milk) was implicit. But when they didn't speak overtly, the rest of society was ready to fill the gaps and speak for them. I was overwhelmed with information about how tough it was to be a parent, at the same time as I was being told it was the most extraordinary, blissful, transformative, rite of passage and that there was no other love like it. That I was, in essence, living half a life by not having children of my own, while simultaneously being so incredibly lucky to pursue a responsibility-free, martini-swilling, stiletto-wearing, girl-about-town, career-woman existence. And meanwhile, the social media algorithms ensured I was assailed on a daily basis by targeted parenthood adverts. Did I want to measure my natural ovulation rhythms? Did I need a stick to test my remaining fertility levels? Did I need personalised new mum vitamins delivered directly to my doorstep? And if I didn't – what was *wrong* with me?

I was confused by this mixed messaging, but I also felt the confusion was my fault. I added my lack of clarity into the box labelled 'not yet a parent', to be understood at some later date when everything would magically make sense because I'd been welcomed into the hallowed realms of motherhood. And while I left that question hanging, I tried my absolute hardest to be A Good Friend to those in my circle with children. I traipsed across town with personal-ised cuddly toys and bootees knitted in non-gender-specific white to welcome the arrival of a newborn. I went to birth-day parties for one-year-olds, where oestrogen bloomed like a noxious cloud and conversations were interrupted by caterwauls and nappy changes. I went to picnics in crowded parks on summer Sundays where my distracted friends would spend most of the afternoon chasing after recalcitrant toddlers and swiping half-eaten chocolate bars from their muddy paws. I was given baby after baby to hold, as though I were practising to play the part of a glad-handing minor royal in a straight-to-TV movie. Every time I held a baby, I worried I was doing something wrong, that this tiny, perfect person would intuit I wasn't a mother and start screaming and that I would be looked at as someone who didn't quite get it, but … *bless, it wasn't her fault was it, she just didn't have her own yet.* I found the smell of their milky newness so intimate, so embedded in the untouchable bond between parent and child, that I could barely breathe with the necessary exclusion of it. And all the time I felt it was my fault for not enjoying it. I felt I was un-maternal for not revelling in the company of other people's children. I felt ungrateful, wretched and selfish. I felt useless.

It took me years to understand that just as parents were allowed to state how they felt about having children, I was equally allowed to say how I felt not having them. When I started speaking up about what was going on for me – the IVF, the miscarriages, the egg freezing, the heart-shaped womb, the failure I'd been made to feel – it became startlingly apparent which friends were there for me and which ones simply couldn't get it (or worse: chose not to). It is often said that becoming a parent shifts your friendships irrevocably. In the intensity of those early post-natal months, many people understandably gravitate to others who are going through the same thing. And, when the children grow older, there is comfort to be had in peer groups who can discuss school catchment areas and screen-time allowances. Raising a family can be all-consuming and there is precious little time left over to nurture friendships with people who aren't on the same journey. By the same token, I came to discover that *not* being a parent also shifts your friendships irrevocably. It becomes obvious who cares and who doesn't.

Emma, for instance, would always make time for me separate from her children. I never once asked this of her. It was simply something she wanted to offer me. So if I went to stay with her for the weekend, she would ensure that her husband took the children for half an hour on the Sunday morning so that we could have an uninterrupted coffee. It really was as simple as that. But hardly anyone else did it. When I thanked Emma, she assured me it was what she most wanted to do: an act of self-care on her part to be able to connect with me properly.

Emma has never once asked me to babysit her children, which is something childless women get asked *all the time*, as if we must relish the opportunity to be around the thing we so desperately long for. Some childfree individuals might want just that. But for the rest of us, it is never other people's babies we desire, it's our own and expecting us to delight in looking after your progeny is rubbing our faces in what we don't have. When Emma asked me to be godmother to both her son, Thomas, and her daughter, Elsa, she made it clear she didn't expect presents or presenteeism and as a consequence, I immediately wanted to lavish them with both. Emma also comes to me for advice on parenting, in a way that respects my opinion as a thoughtful human being even if I don't have my own children yet. This makes me feel that I continue to have a purpose in her life and that I am valued for who I am, rather than for the babies I've failed to produce.

I am so lucky that several other close friends do this for me too. They accept what I have to offer and never make me feel guilty for what I don't. In fact, they are sometimes so sensitive to my state of mind that they pick up on things that completely pass me by. At a recent dinner with Emma and our mutual friend, Bex, I was updating them on my current fertility treatments. The conversation continued and Emma mentioned that Thomas had been made a school prefect. I was delighted to hear it. A few minutes later, I noticed Emma was being quieter than usual.

'Are you OK?' I asked.

'I was just aware that I mentioned Thomas being a prefect and you might not want to hear that given everything you're going through.'

I immediately reassured her.

'Oh my God! No, I love hearing about Thomas! I hadn't even clocked it,' I insisted, but I appreciated the thoughtfulness so much.

I don't expect my friends to hide the joy of parenting from me and nor do I find it insensitive if they need to offload about the tough times. What I do object to is binary extremity: the idea that something is either a flower-filled field of bounteous joy or a relentless trudge through a joyless gamut of colic and sleep deprivation. Both of these mindsets are exclusionary: I either can't hope to understand the happiness or I can't hope to understand the misery. The truth, surely, lies somewhere in between? I suppose if I had to summarise Emma's attitude in one word, it would be 'care'. Emma, and those like her, take care of my feelings. They treat them as valid. Maybe a better word is equal.

Others do not. They were the ones who, when I opened up about my fertility issues, either continued inviting me to toddler picnics and chaotic weekend mornings at their houses as if nothing had changed, or who began to view me sorrowfully as a wounded animal. Their pity was so strong I was winded by it. They would look at me, these parents, with self-conscious concern on their brows and a baby clamped to their breast, and I could see the smugness in their eyes. They didn't mean to be smug, but they were. They were relieved that they had their lives sorted while mine was falling apart. I discovered there was a difference between empathy and pity, between kind consideration and patronising sentiment. While Emma exemplified the former, these other friends would assume things about me I had never told them. They would assume, for instance, that I would never become a mother. They would say things like: 'I'm sure you can learn to live with that pain' or 'There are so many benefits to not having children – you can go on holiday at a moment's notice!' or 'Well, at least you've been able to pursue your career. It's so hard for mums to get back into work.'

Once I sat next to a woman at a wedding – not a friend exactly, but a friend of an ex-boyfriend who I had met on a handful of occasions. And because it was a wedding and we'd both drunk a fair bit of champagne, I found myself talking a little about what I'd been through and before I knew it, she was telling me about how she'd recently had her first baby and had found the experience of childbirth to be one of orgasmic ecstasy, a spiritual portal of bliss into an entirely different dimension of love.

'You've never known love like it,' she said, with breathy giddiness. (People say this all the time.)

No, I wanted to reply, I haven't. But that's not to say I haven't experienced lots of emotions that you won't ever understand either. You will never know this particular grief of mine. You will never know the specific loss of recurrent miscarriage. You will never comprehend the love you can have for children who never existed, the seeds you planted that never took root. You will never understand the resilience of hope, the way it surges greenly up again through the soil, the way it makes you realise that the power of creation and recreation goes far beyond the biological improbability of sperm meeting egg. You will never have access to the solidarity I feel with the hundreds of thousands of women who have walked through this same field and nor will you understand the courage I get from that, from knowing that whatever happens, we stand facing the sunlight in the cast of each other's shadows. I could feel sorry for you, just as you so clearly feel sorry for me. I could point out the chasm in your emotional landscape, just as you have pointed out mine. But I choose instead to feel empathy for your ignorance. I choose instead to leave that arrowhead there, where you have pierced my ribcage, and I will grow around it and this growth will be a deeper human experience than you could ever imagine.

I didn't say any of that. I mean, it was a wedding, after all. I didn't want to bring the mood down with talk of ploughed fields and arrowheads and pierced ribcages. I went to dance to Beyoncé's 'Crazy in Love' and tried to shake it off. But I couldn't, not entirely. Unthinking words leave an imprint like a trail of heavy footsteps trampling over your hopes, breaking their stems. The hopes can grow again, but each time it takes a little more energy, a little more patience.

I knew I had to let these friendships go. It was inescapable. Just as they could not understand me, so I'm sure they felt I was deliberately pulling away and refusing to understand their own difficulties. It was a bridge neither of us could cross and by the time I knew that, it was too late to make amends. It was easier just to chalk it up to 'one of those things' – a life phase that we all went through at one time or another.

I'm sure, if you were to ask these former friends of mine, they wouldn't understand why our friendship had grown fainter and fainter, like pencil markings fading from paper over time. I imagine they would say I'd been selfish or unclear or hurtful: anything that could project an explanation outwards rather than looking within because the other thing parenthood absolves you from is self-examination.

The fact you have a child is enough of a reason for you to occupy more space on this earth, for your opinions to carry more validity, for your votes to be courted by desperate politicians who can't even tell you what their favourite biscuit is. Being a parent is the access-all-areas card to human experience. And sometimes, in truth, I couldn't have found the words if they'd been willing to listen. It was too painful to explain unless the person I was talking to had been there from the start. There was too much to catch up on. Too many infinite, difficult nuances to convey.

But because life is full of paradox, I also found myself wanting friends more than ever to stave off an innate fear of ending my life in a state of existential loneliness. If I didn't have children, I would think, who would be there for me in my twilight years? I lusted after more friends, not fewer. So I put up with a lot. I would contort myself to meet a friend's needs even if my own were ignored as trivial. And because I had no children, I didn't feel my own needs carried as much weight as the time-pressed parents in my life. My needs could be ignored, I reasoned, all the while resenting the fact that they were being. I had made myself into a perpetual giver but there was precious little being given in return. They're busy, I reasoned. It's so tough having children. And on and on it went until I acknowledged my tank was empty. I was spent. There was nothing more left to squeeze out.

So I lost friendships during this time and I comforted myself with the thought that their lives were too busy for them to miss me. If they did miss me, they didn't tell me so.

I never really heard from them unless they wanted me to celebrate another one of their life milestones, which was how I knew I'd done the right thing. We both had, in our own way. A friendship ending doesn't have to be dramatic. It can, in fact, be a kindness on both sides to let it slip quietly away without much fanfare. If there are internal phases in the evolution of each individual friendship, there are also outward life phases that friendships will survive or be broken by. These external phases, like oceans, can encompass smooth seas or tsunamis, and arrival on dry land depends on putting in the work to build the right kind of vessel. Certain human experiences will lie beyond our own understanding. If you simply can't understand what your friend is going through, then possibly the most understanding act of all is to give them space to work it out for themselves. You are heading for different shores. Let their boat sail and wish them well as they go.

The Friendship Tapes
GRACE

Grace Latter, 28, writer, speaker
and body lover

'Friendship is finding the people who were missing and the people that you needed, or maybe sometimes you didn't know that you needed them. And then they come along and they fill that inexplicable void.

'I think during the pandemic, people thought that the people who had to shield were older or perhaps had a visible ailment or were more obviously at risk, but I was part of a huge community of people who had to shield that, from the outside, looked completely fine [Grace has a type of brain tumour – a low grade pilocytic astrocytoma, lodged unusually deep in her left temporal lobe. She also has mild IBS, sensitivity, pain and PTSD following bowel problems, which led to her having major surgeries on her intestines.]

'When I was told to shield, there was an outpouring of love and friends. It was lovely. Actually at the time my boyfriend was pretty useless! He didn't know what to do. But all my friends came swarming in.

'Friends are a key component of life. They are just your favourite people who you want to go to with good news and that you trust with the bad stuff, and they are people that you don't have to perform with, you can just be yourself.

'I do feel as humans we fear rejection. I struggle with what other people will think of me. One friend in particular who's so brilliant with all things mental health, when I see her we'll catch up, and then she texts me maybe like half an hour after we hang up and says, "I just want to let you know that you didn't talk about yourself too much. I really enjoyed our chat. It's so nice to hear what you've got going on. You didn't say anything stupid. You have no reason to panic."'

10.

CLEMMIE

Can Friendships Withstand
Big Life Shifts?

Everyone's life is filled with phases, but some of us experience more transitions than most. Ludolf Bakhuizen was one of these. He was a man with a mercurial sense of self. Although he was born in Germany, not even his date of birth is certain – some records say 18 December 1630 and others claim it was actually 28 December 1631. He was the son of a scribe and at first, Bakhuizen also made a living as a calligrapher. But he seemed to delight in reinvention, changing the spelling of his own surname several times over the course of his career.

By 1649, he had moved to Amsterdam and in the years that followed, he turned his attention away from the written word to painting. He began with elaborate pen drawings of ships, known as *penschilderij*. Eventually, he graduated to oils on canvas.[72]

He was married four times. His first wife was a widow fifteen years older than him: on their wedding day, she was forty-two (a crone by seventeenth-century standards) and he was either twenty-six or twenty-seven, according to which birth date you believe. The marriage lasted three years. Bakhuizen's second wife died within a year of their wedding. He was married to his third wife for fourteen years before she, too, died. It wasn't until tying the knot with his fourth spouse, Anna, in 1680 that he had a child. His son, Johannes, was born in 1683 when Ludolf was fifty-two or fifty-three.[73]

When his son was on the threshold of adolescence, Ludolf produced what is arguably his greatest work. *Warships in a Heavy Storm* was painted in 1695 and depicts several sailing ships buffeted by terrifying waves underneath a glowering sky of grey clouds. The tallest ship is keeling over, perched precariously at an angle on a crashing wave. And yet, amidst the chaos, the ship is keeping steady. If you look carefully enough, you can still discern candlelight glowing from inside the hull. The Dutch flag flies proudly from the mast. On the horizon, the steel-grey clouds are parting to make way for clearer sky and the promise of sunshine.

The painting is mesmerising partly because of its accuracy. Ludolf used to immerse himself in nature – often literally, as he took himself out to sea in an open boat to observe the effects of storms first-hand. There is an intense realism to his paintings, which serves to heighten their impact as allegories.

Ludolf's works were not merely decorative. According to the philosopher Alain de Botton, the author of *Art as*

Therapy, 'they had an explicitly therapeutic purpose to them: they were delivering a moral to their viewers, who lived in a nation critically dependent on maritime trade, about confidence in seafaring and life more broadly …

'Bakhuizen wanted us to feel proud of humanity's resilience in the face of apparently dreadful challenges. His painting enthuses us with the message that we can all cope far better than we think; what appears immensely threatening may be highly survivable. What is true of storms in the North Sea may be no less true of the turmoils in our lives. The storms will die down, we will be battered, a few things will be ripped, but we will eventually – as the sun rises over the spires of Alkmaar – return to safer shores.'[74]

Ludolf was making the point, as I did in the previous chapter, that life is full of changing weather. Some phases will be sunny and easeful. Others will be drizzly and uncertain. There will be storms that remind us of our ability to withstand turmoil, and cataclysmic thunder that will dampen or break our spirit, but most weather is survivable if we learn how to prepare for it. What I like about Ludolf is that he lived his life as he painted his pictures. In private and in public, the message was the same: that human experience is one of evolution and adaptive change. The key was to take opportunities where they arose and to respond to each shifting circumstance as best you could. Sometimes, that meant moving countries, making a substantial career change, marrying four different women and spelling your name in myriad different ways over the course of your life. Ludolf's adaptability served him well: he was courted by significant patrons including Cosimo de' Medici and Peter the Great, and he lived well into his seventies.

Friendship, too, is buffeted by life's changing weather. My own experience of this was not having children while all around me appeared to be having theirs. But there are other formative life phases which divide us. Divorce is one of them. When my ex-husband and I split up, I lost a handful of his friends who had also become mine over the course of our marriage. It wasn't all that painful to me because I understood it was their role to take his side and to offer him their support. They couldn't do that wholeheartedly while still maintaining my friendship and seeing things from my point of view. My friends did the same for me. It was simply one of those things.

But there are other cracks that are difficult to ignore: the physical distance that appears when friends move to different cities and countries or the metaphorical distance that creeps in when we don't warm to someone's romantic partner. Then there's disagreement over politics. We live in an age of extremes, where the personal is intermingled with the political to an overt degree. When one friend votes for Brexit or Donald Trump or reveals themselves to be unconsciously racist or transphobic, it is difficult for some people to consider their opinion separately from who they are. The combination of a twenty-four-hour news cycle, social media and a clickbait online culture means that we all know a lot of supposed facts about specific topics that speak to our own echo chambers. That makes it trickier to see a different point of view without attaching a bigger meaning to it. Opinions have become identity currency. There is a sense that when anyone airs a forthright opinion, they are identifying themselves with a tribe which you might or might not wish to belong to. In this binary, febrile environment, even *not* having an opinion can be seen as an expression of moral lack.

I've never lost friendships over political disagreement, either because any disagreement is within the bounds of reason or because I'm so conflict avoidant I seek to end any potentially combative conversation before it starts. Or it could also be that those friends have quietly phased themselves out of my life, knowing that we no longer have much in common. I do think that the most worthwhile friendships allow enough safety for challenge. If we never feel safe enough to say, 'I don't agree with you', the chances are that friendship is flawed.

But even if I haven't experienced losing a friend over politics, there are many who have. During the Covid-19 pandemic, public acts such as wearing a mask or getting a vaccination became a proxy for the kind of person you were in private. Suddenly, we were confronted with the disarming prospect that people we loved were capable of not caring in the same way that we did about big issues. Worse, we imagined their way was more dangerous and selfish than ours. It was a combustible time for friendships, especially because we were being told to act in certain ways by political leaders who were – in and of themselves – deeply divisive.

In Los Angeles, my friend Joan found herself considering her own relationships. Her husband, Michael, is older than she is and was therefore particularly vulnerable to Covid. She decided she was unable to continue nurturing friendships with people who refused the vaccine or who had voted for – and continued to support – the then President (and face-mask refusenik) Trump.

'I like to have diversity in the people I know – and I'm proud that I do,' Joan told me, 'but it's been … it's a bit of a bridge too far to travel to people who, say, support a fascist candidate. No can do. Or who are anti-vaxxers. It's just too hard.'

She gave me one example of a friend who had started sharing fake news stories about the dangers of the vaccine on Facebook. To begin with, Joan tried to reason with this person, commenting online in reasonable tones, attempting to point out inconsistencies in the arguments. But her friend didn't take kindly to this, and met Joan's questioning with anger and an overuse of the Caps Lock key. After a while, it became clear to Joan that her friend was not going to change her outlook. And neither was she. They unfriended each other on Facebook.

'We all have blind spots,' Joan continued, 'and people have told me – my husband included – that I'm too judgey. And I struggle with that, particularly with friends because … I guess I should be more accepting of people as they are, but I struggle with that with my closest friends when I feel like they have years – if not a lifetime – of self-defeating behaviours that they're unwilling to confront and certainly not willing to change. And that's where my judgey part comes in.

'Really, all I'm asking for is accountability on your decisions and your behaviour. And I want that in my friends, I want that in me, I want that in my partner and I certainly want that – and expect it – in my other intimate relationships.'

With every friendship, we have to decide, like Joan, what we can put up with and where our limits lie – it's that idea of 'stretch' I referred to earlier. With some people, we are willing to stretch further because the friendship at stake is more precious than any superficial disagreement. With others, the effort of the stretch is not warranted by the circumstances. And in certain contexts, no stretch can bridge the chasm. External phases – divorce, politics, distance – are one thing. But friendships have internal phases too – they have their own circadian rhythms, a warping and wefting of closeness, shared perceptions and mutual affections over the years.

We rightly talk a lot about mental and physical health, but I believe there is a third category that needs discussion. That is relational health. What is the status of our relationships? Do they need care and attention? Or are they draining our energy and making us anxious? How do they make us feel? How do we want to feel when we're in the company of friends? What measures can we put in place to make that so? If a friendship ends, how can we reassure ourselves that this does not automatically equate to failure or shame? And how much are we willing to stretch in order to prevent this from happening?

These are huge questions. To explore the answers, I turned to someone who had survived a life change so catastrophic that all of her relationships had shifted like tectonic plates in the aftermath of an earthquake. I turned to my friend Clemmie.

Clemmie was (and is) a legendary beauty who I knew *about* long before I actually knew her. For years after we graduated, I watched with awe as her star shot ever higher into the ascendant. This was a woman with so many talents, it was almost as though she had been constructed by an advanced alien race to show the rest of us mere earthlings how it was done. After graduating (with a double first in English from Cambridge), she pursued a number of brilliant careers. She was a concert violinist, an actor, a published author, the youngest ever columnist on a national broadsheet and a gifted television and radio presenter. For many of us, Clemmie seemed almost unreal. It was absurd how talented she was, and how striking, and how *clever*.

The years passed and I ran into Clemmie occasionally at parties and book launches. She was always lovely but I felt one step removed from her. What on earth could she hope to gain from talking to me, I would wonder? She was clearly just being kind to pass the time. There were a million other more impressive people she could be chatting to. Then, in 2015, I found myself at a wedding in Brooklyn where I didn't know anyone other than the bride. I was alone and single. It was hot. I was sweating. I had worn uncomfortable shoes. I found myself in the queue for the bar, willing myself not to panic at the hours of social effort and small talk that lay ahead. The woman in front of me turned around. I caught sight of her face and realised it was

Clemmie. She was also there by herself, and thrown together by this unanticipated coincidence, we connected immediately. When we got served at the bar, I remember her asking for a cocktail and a 'seltzer' which struck me as the acme of sophistication.

'What *is* a seltzer exactly?' I wondered out loud after years of seeing it spoken of in movies or written in the pages of American novels.

'It's just sparkling water,' Clemmie explained. 'I'm so bloody hot! I could have just said sparkling water. But Americans never understand me when I say water.'

'No, me neither!'

That was the start of our friendship. Meeting Clemmie again in this context after so many years of having known her from afar was like being presented with a precious gift. We discovered we had so many things to talk about that we ended up meeting the following day for dinner. All of those achievements she had to her name masked a sweet vulnerability that came from a lack of self-worth. I could *definitely* relate to that. The conversation hasn't really let up since.

Clemmie became a very close friend. Whenever we met, she seemed to be operating at twice the speed of anyone else. She had so much to say, so many ideas to share. She was fizzing over with the joy of living life, of experiencing every single moment and squeezing it for all it had to offer. She wrote books in weeks when it took anyone else years. She juggled presenting her morning radio show with raising a young family and enjoyed the challenge of fitting it all in. When we met up, she'd invariably just have come from an art exhibition or an Arsenal match (she's a devoted Gooner) and be on her way to host a concert at the Royal Albert Hall, or go to an after-hours gig for a band I'd never heard of. I once went with her as she got an ear piercing in London and she struck up a conversation with the piercer, getting him to agree to being interviewed on her podcast within about ten minutes.

Time, for Clemmie, seemed to possess an elastic quality. She could do five things in the hour it would take me to get dressed. Our friendship had this same intensity: if we had dinner we would *really* have dinner. I remember once we ordered almost everything on the menu in a restaurant just because we wanted to try it all. A plate would come and it would be so delicious we wanted to try the next one and the next and the one after that and, while we were at it, all the sides too. If we met for a drink, it would never just be one.

'I could have another, couldn't you?' Clemmie would say, eyes glinting. And I would always say yes because you could never say no to her irresistible spirit.

That is not to say her energy never flagged. Of course it did. You can't have an exceptional mind like Clemmie's and not also spend time in the shadows. There would be periods of anxiety – even of depression. During these times, she would call me and tell me she felt like a failure when the truth was she was anything but. It was simply that her own expectations for herself were so uncompromising. She never believed in her own value as much as she believed in other people's.

In 2018, Clemmie, her husband and her two young sons moved to Manhattan where she'd landed a prestigious job with New York Public Radio. She adored her new home. If Clemmie were a city, she would be New York: full of hectic opportunity and visceral speed, all human experience being lived simultaneously on subways and on street corners belching plumes of city steam.

The move marked the start of a new phase in many of her friendships. She was living thousands of miles away as she established herself in her work, which she loved, and she struck up easy connections but she missed the deep friendships she had left back in London. We kept in touch via FaceTime and voice note and Clemmie flew back to London regularly, keeping her hand in with her work on this side of the Atlantic. I would often meet her for lunch when she'd got off a flight that morning. She would turn up to a bustling cafe looking wide awake and perfect, wearing one of her beloved slogan sweaters and several tiny earrings, glittering all the way from lobe to cartilage. Her eyeliner was always so deftly applied I used to wonder how she did it.

'Years of practice,' she said drily.

'Aren't you tired?' I asked. 'You've just got off a long-haul flight.'

'Not at all,' she said. She told me she'd solved the problem of jet lag by listening to Bach variations or Roni Size throughout the flight. There was something about the melodic repetition and rhythm, she explained, that kept her brain energised. It's not a tactic I've ever tried myself, admittedly, but I believed her because it was impossible not to be caught up in her zeal.

In January 2020, I got a message from her telling me she was feeling very low and asking if I could talk. We did. It was a resurgence of her unfounded imposter syndrome: the sense that she was not quite good enough in any area of her life, compounded by the fact that she was working extremely hard, often hosting night-time events while also being there for her children and husband. I was worried about her mental health and we chatted it through as best we could. I told Clemmie that even if she never achieved anything ever again in her life, I would love her just the same. My point was that her value as a person was not determined by her performance, and that her worth was innate. It existed beyond all of her achievements. She did not have to do. She could simply be. That was why people loved her: for Clemmie, not for how well Clemmie did things.

I woke up on the morning of 21 January 2020 to a text from Clemmie. She was coming back to London the following week and we were meeting for dinner so I thought she'd want to discuss arrangements. When I clicked on the message, I realised it wasn't from Clemmie. It was from a WhatsApp chat that had been set up in her name. Her husband, James, was the one texting. It had been sent at 2 a.m. UK time.

'Clemmie isn't very well,' he had written. 'Her wonderful beautiful brain decided to bleed earlier today – on the left-hand side. The doctors have stopped that bleeding, but think it did quite a lot of damage to her motor and language functions. So we don't know how much of our Clemmie will wake up.'

I sat up in bed, the blinds still closed. I couldn't make sense of it. People sometimes say they are numb with shock. I wasn't numb. Every single nerve ending seemed to jangle on high alert. I called Clemmie's best friend Amber. She said she was arranging to fly out to New York as soon as possible. I got up and made a cup of tea because I didn't know what else to do. Being so far away made the helplessness even more acute. I drank my tea and then felt so sick I went to the toilet and threw up. Over the following hours, a fuller picture began to emerge. Clemmie had been at a work meeting when she suddenly found herself struggling to speak. Her words started slurring. Her thoughts were coming out as gobbledygook. Then the world went dark. It was an extraordinary piece of luck that she was with people who were able to call an ambulance immediately. Their swift response, and the subsequent surgery to stem the bleed – performed by Dr Christopher Kellner and his team at Mount Sinai West – saved her life.

Clemmie had suffered a massive brain haemorrhage caused by an arteriovenous malformation (AVM) – a tangle of abnormal blood vessels connecting arteries and veins. An AVM, which is rare, is something you're born with. Most people are oblivious to the condition, just as Clemmie had been. A bleed is even rarer: fewer than 2 to 4 per cent haemorrhage. In most cases, an AVM is only discovered through a severe rupture that can often be fatal. This was the battle that Clemmie was fighting. Not only did the medical experts not know if she would survive; they didn't know what damage the bleed had done and they warned her closest family to prepare for the worst. She was in a coma for seventeen days.

But Clemmie survived. In fact, she did more than that. Over the following weeks and months, she confounded every single medical expectation. The doctors had dealt with many other brains before but it seemed they hadn't ever encountered a brain quite like Clemmie's. Her neuro-plasticity – the brain's ability to adapt both structure and function in response to experience – was substantially helped by the fact that she had been playing the violin since the age of two. When I visited her, four weeks after her haemorrhage, she was already taking her first few shaky steps, with the aid of a vast contraption which hung from the roof of the hospital gym and slid on rollers along a ceiling track. Her beautiful head was concave where they had removed part of her skull to reduce the brain swelling and she was wearing a much-hated plastic helmet that was uncomfortable and affixed with Velcro (she later had a cranioplasty where her skull was artificially rebuilt and the helmet, thankfully, could be abandoned).

I had been anxious about seeing Clemmie again. I wasn't sure what I would find, nor was I sure how much help I would be. I doubted I was up to the task. I didn't know how changed she would seem. Then I walked into the hospital and there she was: in a wheelchair and that terrible helmet, thin and hollowed out, but still indisputably and overwhelmingly her. Her eyes flashed with recognition. She gave me one of her familiar, strong Clemmie hugs. And I realised how stupid I had been to worry. She was still completely herself. She couldn't speak much beyond single, short words but she could understand and remember everything and even without the language she was in the process of re-learning, she possessed an extraordinary capacity to communicate. I could mostly glean what she was trying to say, even when the words got lost in the space between her mind and her mouth. She had been diagnosed with complex language and speech disorders called aphasia and apraxia – a common feature in those recovering from brain trauma. Apraxia was a loss of her ability to execute or carry out movements, despite her desire to do so. I could see the struggle of this. One of the symptoms of aphasia, I learned, was a confusion of thoughts (as well as a difficulty in finding the words to express them).

And yet all of Clemmie's complex, nuanced, generous thoughts and memories were, as far as I could tell, fully intact.

'But,' I said to Amanda, the speech therapist, 'Clemmie doesn't have any confusion.'

'No,' Amanda agreed, grinning. 'She doesn't.'

Clemmie had always been brilliant at connecting, and here that skill was again, pressing itself back into use with such insistence that she rapidly became the favourite patient of everyone who worked in the hospital.

'Everyone's in love with her,' James said one night when I debriefed him on the day's events in hospital. He was right.

She was always asking everyone how they were – myself included. She wanted me to make the most of my time in New York and go sightseeing so that I wasn't just stuck in hospital.

I didn't want to be anywhere else, but it showed me how full of love she was. Stripped back to her purest essence, this was Clemmie. Not once did she express either complaint or bitterness. Yes, there were tears of anguish and frustration, but never did she ask why it had happened to her. Never once did she question the unfairness of it.

She explained that she had made a deliberate decision to choose life. Asking for a pen and paper one day in the family room, Clemmie told me the story of what had happened to her during her coma. Unable to use her right side, she wrote out single words with her non-writing left hand to communicate a certain point. She remembered seeing a bright light beaming in from the side of her head. Her mother's former partner, who had died some years previously, was there. Clemmie found his presence comforting. I made the following notes in the immediate aftermath of our exchange:

A voice was ushering her into the light, saying it was so calm and easy in the light; there was no pain, no stress and it would all be so much better if she just followed the light. When I asked Clemmie who she thought was speaking, she wrote on a piece of paper 'Angel'.

CLEMMIE

'And weirdly ...' Clemmie said, and then asked for the paper again. She wrote the name 'Kobe Bryant'.

'Was he there?' I asked.

He was, Clemmie said, and there was a sense that maybe some sort of choice was being made between the two of them, and that she too had a choice to make about whether to go left or right – into the calming light or back into the world.

The legendary LA Lakers basketball player, Kobe Bryant, had been tragically killed along with his daughter, Gianna, and seven others in a helicopter crash on 26 January 2020. At the time, Clemmie was lying in a coma on a ventilator in a hospital bed. Clemmie had no religious faith. Her vision was the most deeply spiritual encounter of her life. She recalled that the voice had offered her a choice: either to head towards the bliss of the light, or to choose to go back to her life, even though it would be fraught with pain and challenge and difficulty. Clemmie didn't even hesitate. She chose life. She would remain forever grateful that she was given that choice, when so many are not.

I later read *My Stroke of Insight*, written by the neuro-anatomist Jill Bolte Taylor. Bolte Taylor had endured an AVM bleed in the left side of her brain and a subsequent stroke in her late thirties, just as Clemmie had. She too experienced a state of what she describes as 'nirvana' and 'bliss' where she became searingly aware of how all life was connected and how beautiful this connection was. She too survived, defying medical expectation. Bolte Taylor is now sixty-three and her 2008 TED Talk became the second most viewed of all time.[75]

'I choose life' became a mantra for Clemmie. She kept returning to it, again and again, to get her through her most challenging days. Shortly after I left New York, the Coronavirus pandemic locked down entire cities and countries. Clemmie was the first patient in her hospital to contract it and endured long, awful, lonely days. The rehab sessions stopped, guests were banned and staff walked around in hazmat suits. It was desperate for her. But she got through it. On 10 April 2020, less than three months after the brain haemorrhage that almost killed her, she walked unaided out of the hospital wearing a T-shirt emblazoned with the words 'Choose Love'.

Although she chose life – and love – Clemmie's recovery was still in its early phases. The path ahead was one pitted with struggle. She experienced frequent seizures, which were frightening and undid many of the physical advances she had worked so hard to make. She had to navigate a labyrinthine and expensive American healthcare system to sort out her rehab. Her drugs were constantly under review as doctors tried to get the balance right. Her sleep was fractured. Her anxiety was high. Simple everyday tasks such as opening a jar of peanut butter for her children were still beyond her. She was exhausted a lot of the time – something that, in her past life, she had never had to contend with. Now, she spent afternoons in bed, protecting her precious energy reserves. Even a short car journey overstimulated her nervous system. She was constantly scanning her environment for threats to herself or her family. In everyday life, people are used to taking the risk that things are going to turn out more or less OK. We contend with the ever-present threat of danger in crossing the road or taking a flight or allowing our children to stay out late by saying, 'Well, what's the worst that could happen?' If we didn't, we wouldn't be able to live. We would be too hamstrung by panic to do anything other than cocoon ourselves in a small, safe room and lock the door.

But for Clemmie, one of the worst things *had* happened. And it had happened suddenly, without warning, out of the blue, blue sky of an otherwise unexceptional January morning. Now, her awareness of the fragile membrane between life and death made her frightened and lonely. Yes, she was grateful to be alive. Unbelievably so. She was grateful to have been given that choice. But it was a choice that came freighted with a fundamental shift in knowledge. Nothing could be taken for granted and everything could explode at any given moment – literally, in Clemmie's case, as her brain surgeon had not been able to remove the AVM entirely which meant it could still bleed again.

It was debilitating and depressing. And because she was inside her own body and her own mind, Clemmie could not see the gains that the rest of us still marvelled at. Her language continued to improve exponentially. By the time I was able to visit her again in January 2022, she had been writing pieces of journalism and presenting podcast episodes. Yes, it took an unfathomable amount of effort on her part and she was the first to point out that her speech was not as quick as it had once been, but it was still an exceptional achievement. The miracle of her survival had returned Clemmie to us and this meant a familiar lack of self-worth that co-existed with her undimmed passion for life and love for others. It was, in so many ways, a beautiful thing. Here she was again: our friend who didn't believe in her own wonder.

This was a special time for our friendship. During successive lockdowns, Clemmie and I spoke every day, sometimes for well over an hour. Afterwards I would take notes on our conversations at her request. I was convinced (and still am) that she would write a brilliant book about her experience and could draw on these notes for material. I got to know her even more intimately than I had before. I got to know her thoughts, her philosophies, the inner workings of her heart. I was perpetually astonished by her emotional resources. She was so strong, so determined and so full of grace, even in her lowest moments.

I felt lucky to have this friendship. So lucky. I still do. But one of the things that Clemmie had to confront during this time was a realisation – as she puts it – that she didn't have as many friends as she once thought she did. There were friends who had continued to show up for her in the long, slow process of her recovery and there were those who had fallen by the wayside, who had not been able to accommodate the change in circumstances. That had been an excruciatingly difficult thing for her to come to terms with, especially because there was seldom any explanation. I suppose – and this is my own view – it could have been because their lives were already too full to create space for such a shift, or it could have been that it is just too demanding or triggering for some to keep looking at mortality and illness and depression in the face.

I wanted to talk to Clemmie about friendship because it seemed to strike at the very root of what true companionship was. What happens to friendship when one of you goes through a life-altering trauma? And because Clemmie is a person perpetually interested in asking questions to unravel the mystery of life, she did me the honour of agreeing. We spoke over Zoom in May 2022. Clemmie was lying in bed on a Monday afternoon in her New York apartment. Her straight, fair hair had grown back much wavier than before and – to her surprised amusement – it had also turned a very dark brown. Clemmie went to the hairdresser for blonde highlights as soon as she felt up to it and, gradually, she had also begun to wear jewellery again. On that day, she was wearing a gold chain necklace, and rings on her long, elegant fingers. Her nails were painted neon coral. She looked great, but she never believed it when I told her so.

I asked her to begin by describing her attitude to friendship *before* the events of January 2020.

'Friendship has been a primary goal for me,' she said. 'I feel like other people are much more self-sufficient, whereas I have been, since I was tiny, *obsessed* with my friends and thinking that my friendships were the most important thing in my life.'

Her childhood was happy but in some ways not straight-forward: her father was not on the scene and she was raised by a single mother who had two sons from a previous relationship (with the man who had appeared to Clemmie in her near-death vision and who was a constant, kindly presence in her life). Clemmie loved her older brothers – they would go to Arsenal matches together and watch Australian TV soaps after school. But her friends performed a role that her siblings didn't.

She compared friendship to 'falling in love. I've always believed there is a real chemical reaction' and then went on to say that a disagreement or a break-up with a friend left her 'just as distraught as when a boyfriend dumped me'. Her friends offered her 'a sort of shorthand about life, whether it's values or what kind of person you are' and she had so many of them that she knew which friend to call on for specific occasions and contexts – which friend would love a classical music concert, which she could go clubbing with, and so on. Clemmie was adept at making connections. When she first had her stroke, there was an inundation of messages from concerned people who had, at some point in their lives, been drawn to her. She said her husband James, by contrast, 'literally has three friends'.

CLEMMIE: Of course he would say, 'Yeah, sure, I like lots of people.' But in terms of actual ride-or-die friends, he has basically one, but maybe two or three or four. And he doesn't need any more. He doesn't want any more whereas I was like, 'No, I need this person for this, this person for that …'

And maybe the lesson that I've learned through this nightmare has been like, 'Oh right, I've got two friends.' And that's what James has been talking about.

She said she separated her life into 'a before and after'. There were multiple phases along the way: motherhood, moving countries, the pandemic, but the biggest marker for Clemmie was her brain injury, which had made her 'really brave and clear-eyed about who is actually a proper friend now'. When she first had her stroke, there was a flurry of activity as she went through the early stages of rehab, but she noticed now that much of the attention had dissipated. Partly the pandemic put paid to international travel for two years so it was harder for friends back in the UK to visit, but it was – she sensed – more than that. She feared it was because she had so little left to offer as a friend, so the weight of obligation was skewed.

CLEMMIE: I don't want to give the sense that I'm being slighted or wronged, it's just that awful feeling when in life or love or friendship, there's an imbalance there. It's very rare to actually have total balance and alignment. When I was about sixteen, seventeen, I had a very, very, very close friendship with a boy and we would talk through the night. And he was talking one day about planets. Like, human relationships are like planetary beings. Most of the time you need the smaller planet to be in orbit. And the amazing thing that the smaller planet – the weaker one – has up their sleeve is that if they stop orbiting that bigger planet then it shifts on its axis ... I think there is something of that in most relationships, friendships. In my experience, it's very rare to have that total alignment. And most of the time it's fine because there's a dance that we go through. Sometimes you're the stronger planet and sometimes you're not. But if you're both aware and want to be in the relationship, you just decide that you're in this together.

ELIZABETH: I love that.

CLEMMIE: And it's not an abuse of power, it's just an imbalance of power sometimes.

ELIZABETH: So now since 2020 – this is such a huge question – but how have the planets realigned? How has your view of friendship evolved in that time?

CLEMMIE: The problem is because I have basically no independence and no agency, I get very paranoid. Like, even with the people who show up for me. I'm obviously not expecting unconditional love. But oh my God is it scary when you stop being able to do things for people! Just doing *anything*, like being a normal friend to go to a party or a dinner or whatever with. When I can't give anything back ... And people will always say, 'Yeah, but you are enough.' But it turns out I'm not enough because very few people show up for me.

It was painful hearing her talk in this way, so I spent some time reassuring her that all I had ever wanted in her as a friend was for Clemmie to be herself. And this she indisputably still was. Even in her lowest moments, her generosity was such that she would always ask how I was, sometimes sending me presents out of the blue – a miniskirt patterned with cats one day; a tote bag with 'I am carrying intense emotions' across one side the next (I love this bag and use it every week to carry my things to yoga).

She was also one of the few people who truly understood what it was to experience pregnancy loss. Clemmie had gone through three miscarriages in between the birth of her two children and she knew only too well the pain that went with wanting a baby you can't seem to have. She encouraged me to talk about my journey, insisting that it was one of the most difficult things to go through, even compared to her brain injury, and she always gave me a safe space to express my own emotions. I felt bad about this sometimes – weeping over FaceTime to someone who had endured such unimaginable pain. Who did I think I was? But Clemmie reassured me that when I admitted to sadness, I was actually doing her a service. I was making her feel as though she still had a purpose as my friend.

We continued chatting and I wondered if the distillation of her wide friendship group into one or two of her most trusted confidants reflected not just her own personal situation but a wider re-assessment that was taking place for many of us.

ELIZABETH: I've realised there's far fewer people than I might have thought who actually are there for me, who actually see me, who I actually want to spend time with. So maybe part of that is the age we're at and the pandemic and everything. But obviously this huge life shift that you've been through has massively accelerated that process.

CLEMMIE: That's so interesting and I think you're, as always, just incredibly astute. And it's interesting because our previous life courses looked quite similar, not necessarily completely the same but we were on the same sort of path. I think most people would have said, 'Oh yeah, we're in the same category ...' Whereas your star, if you want – which is a cliche but also useful shorthand – your star has been in the ascendant and so quickly and so steeply as mine has been the opposite: a total wane.

And so, because you are not a person who is superficial, you still see me how I was to you four years ago. And yet actually for other people – I'm not necessarily saying it's even conscious, it's not even that it's malicious or uncaring – but they don't see *me* any more. Which is even more hurtful.

CLEMMIE

Clemmie said that if it were blatantly obvious that an acquaintance was using her simply because of her contacts book and successful career, the break in communication after her stroke was easier to deal with. They could simply be labelled as 'bullshit humans' (her words) and she could move on. But she suspected some of the friends who had stopped calling didn't even realise they were doing it. This bothered her. It felt as though they wanted to believe she was back to full health without ever taking the trouble to check if this were actually the case. Partly this was because she had been able to take her first tentative steps back onto social media, posting the odd picture of incremental gains with a moving and eloquent caption. You could look at these photos and believe it was all going swimmingly for Clemmie. Her lyrical prose and facility with words was unchanged. What the image never showed was the agonising effort that went into ordering her thoughts, then typing them out painstakingly with her left thumb because she had lost so much feeling and movement in her right side. What the image never showed – not fully – was the unvarnished truth of what she was going through to get to this point. To know that, you had to be in regular touch with the human behind the Instagram account and not everyone took the time to do this.

ELIZABETH: And that must make you feel unseen on a whole other level.

CLEMMIE: Yeah.

ELIZABETH: The lack of interest or capacity to look beneath the surface of life at what's really important is perpetually astonishing. It's a bit like falling for a disappointing man. It's that thing like, 'Oh wow, *that's* who you are.'

CLEMMIE: Yeah, exactly. But, as you know, it still hurts. And it's not even their fault sometimes, the sense of betrayal. Where it gets really icky is the fact that you did that to yourself because you wanted them to be something that they could not have been.

It was all the more challenging because although Clemmie would not have described herself as a person of any religion before her stroke, her certain belief remains 'that human beings fall out of the sky and the chemistry is real and I've always believed in that and it's an article of faith to me that on any given day suddenly you could be enriched for the rest of your life by this random exchange'.

CLEMMIE: You know, I really believe in that. And in a way, as I said, I have been very lucky in that I've had so many incredible friends and incredible experiences that I don't think now will be available for me, probably ever again.

ELIZABETH: I think they will be, my darling, I do.

CLEMMIE: In a way I don't want any more bonds that could be jeopardised or broken. I really don't want that right now. It's just that it's another thing that ...

ELIZABETH: That you're mourning.

CLEMMIE: Yes, exactly.

Occasionally people would get in touch because they happened to be in New York and they would ask to see her, which was nice on one level and yet it also sometimes required Clemmie to put on a front.

CLEMMIE: I think to so many things there's a performative aspect. You have to put on a show, to be like, 'Can I give you a cup of tea?' But it's a bit like people perform grief. Suddenly you're having to get a cup of tea to make *them* feel better.

ELIZABETH: What do you think you've learned then, that constitutes a good friend? What are the qualities of that friendship for you?

CLEMMIE: I really think that the most important thing is being seen in totality and being expansive enough to tolerate a change in circumstance. I've been thinking about the idea of friendship vows and what I would say if they existed and how important it is to stay true to them.

There's nothing transactional to true friendship. I couldn't say how many times I have, since 2020, heard people say to me, 'I just didn't know how to broach it …' and I get it. What happened to me is a wild and out-of-the-blue thing and I understand it's very hard – what are you supposed to say? What are you supposed to do?

But to the people who say, 'I didn't want to bother you, or disturb you,' I want to reply: 'Well, by the way, I'm not doing literally fucking anything! I'm literally in my bed all day, all day, all day. Every day. All day.'

And yet a few real friends are willing to shoulder the discomfort and to broach the unbroachable. They're the ones who showed up, who continue to show up consistently.

For the rest of them, I feel like too much time has elapsed and it's not that I feel resentful or hurt exactly, it's just: how are we going to have that conversation now?

ELIZABETH: You can't bring everyone up to speed. There's a traumatic microaggression every single time you have to recount your history to someone who hasn't been there through it.

CLEMMIE: Yeah. Or for people having to say, 'How are you?' It's like, well you would know if we'd had a conversation in the last few months. Again, I want to emphasise I don't expect contact or judge the lack of it, but seeing who's there for me and who isn't has been a useful gauge for me.

CLEMMIE

It's a bit like now, after the brain injury, I have no sensation and no sense of my right side in space from the top of my head to the tips of my toes. But I've had to train my brain to know that it's there; that my right side is there even though I can't necessarily feel it or see it. With my true friends, I can also trust that they're there in space even if I don't see them. That is a beautiful thing.

It struck me that Clemmie's longing for feeling seen was simply another way of expressing the need for empathetic friendships: the ability to imagine multiple dimensions of an experience, rather than taking the two dimensions of a static social media picture or a brief WhatsApp message to be the whole truth. That was harder and more effortful to do when the friendship planets had dropped out of each other's orbits. Clemmie had gone through multiple shifts and realignments: the move to America was one transplantation. But then she had found herself crossing the borders into another country entirely – that of a brain injury survivor who cannot easily explain what this new, foreign territory is like and who feels stranded there, fervently wishing to travel back to the land she once knew.

ELIZABETH: That must be really isolating.

CLEMMIE: It's incredibly isolating. And lonely.

ELIZABETH: I think there are some ways that friends can't [always] be the friend that you need when you're going through infertility or miscarriage in the same way that I think – when there's a seismic life shift such as yours – other friends can't be there. Do you see any sort of comparison between those two states?

CLEMMIE: Yes. I hope that I am standing next to you – or walking, or hobbling – through this fertility nightmare just as you are accompanying me through the terrain of brain injury survival. The overarching thing is just empathy, support and love. But obviously empathy has very many grades.

When I'm feeling generous to other people that I feel quite let down by, I think, 'Oh yeah, why *should* anyone have any inkling about what this is like?' And you definitely don't have any inkling and yet I still feel totally supported and accompanied through this. And I hope that I can empathise with your pain – just a very small fraction of that pain, because I have two healthy children. I can't even imagine – I know that's the most annoying phrase – I don't even try to imagine the agony of what you're going through. But empathy isn't 'Oh, let me think of a commensurate thing that happened in my life'. You don't have to say, 'Oh, I know this feeling ...' or 'Oh, let me tell you about when my essential organ failed,' or 'Oh, let me tell you about my miscarriages,' or 'Let me tell you about when the war started in my village ...' Instead, it's about having the capaciousness in your

imagination to hold space for not even trying to
imagine.

It was such a profound definition of a different kind of
empathy. As Clemmie saw it, empathy wasn't always about
feeling or guessing exactly what someone else was going
through; it was about being brave enough to hold space for
the not knowing and the impossibility of resolution. This,
I think, is the key to ensuring friendships survive and thrive
through different life phases. You do not have to travel the
same path at the same time. But if you value your friend
enough, you can leave a room for their pain in the home of
your own imagination. You can make that room welcoming
and safe, available for them at any time they need it.
Sometimes it will go many months without being occupied. Sometimes it might stay empty for years. Sometimes
you will meet there and marvel at the love you share and
sometimes, it will be more difficult to make that connection. On other occasions, you will lie there on your own,
staring at the ceiling to let the sadness pass. But you will
never be fully alone. Because a true friend knows that the
silent space of understanding is often more important than
the words which fill our lack of it. And so the room exists,
with fresh sheets on the bed and flowers on the mantel-
piece, ready to welcome any feeling in.

For me, one piece of writing that beautifully expresses
this idea is 'The Guest House' by the thirteenth-century
Persian poet Rumi. In the poem, Rumi contemplates the
necessity of letting all feelings into our metaphorical homes

– the good and the bad, the positive and the negative –
because each one instructs us in some meaningful way
about life. Here it is:

> This being human is a guest house.
> Every morning a new arrival.
>
> A joy, a depression, a meanness,
> some momentary awareness comes
> as an unexpected visitor.
>
> Welcome and entertain them all!
> Even if they're a crowd of sorrows,
> who violently sweep your house
> empty of its furniture,
> still, treat each guest honourably.
> He may be clearing you out
> for some new delight.
>
> The dark thought, the shame, the malice,
> meet them at the door laughing,
> and invite them in.
>
> Be grateful for whoever comes,
> because each has been sent
> as a guide from beyond.[76]

He knew what he was talking about, did Rumi. And perhaps it should have come as no surprise that when I first mentioned 'The Guest House' to Clemmie, long before the shattering events of January 2020, and told her it was a poem I returned to again and again to help me through darker times, she replied: 'It's my favourite poem too.' Almost a decade before our planetary orbits had crossed at that wedding in Brooklyn, she had included it in the epigraph of her first novel.[77]

For those seventeen days she lay in a coma, Clemmie's friends were asked to send recordings of themselves in case she could hear us. I recited 'The Guest House' by Rumi and pressed send. It said everything that needed to be said. It still does.

The Friendship Tapes
SARA

Sara Gulamali, mid-20s, artist and co-founder
of the artistic collective, Muslim Sisterhood

'When I was fifteen, my mother passed away, and so my friendships at that time became a maternal family support, because I felt there were things that I couldn't talk to my family about. So my friends were my grounding point. If I had problems at home or I was going through puberty, they became a maternal group. That's what that friendship meant to me.

'Then, going to university and having to navigate those spaces, being a Muslim woman of colour in a very white space, Muslim Sisterhood really did become a sisterhood. It was more than a friendship; it was somewhere I talked about faith or about problems I was having ... I wouldn't have been able to get through some of the most difficult times of my life without my friends.

'I had no Muslim friends growing up, so I had to create a community of people who really understood what I'm going through. For example, if someone in my family was sick, I could reach out and say, "Hey, can everyone pray for them?", and that's a level of friendship that we wouldn't get with anyone else.

'My dad used to always say this phrase "Blood is thicker than water", and I never related to that. Because what I've gone through in my life, my friends have really kind of become my family and I haven't really seen it as any different. Obviously, friends come and go and your family are with you forever. But at the end of the day, they are the people who understand every aspect of your life; they don't have those kinds of preconceptions about who you need to be. You can just be yourself with them, and there's still that acceptance.'

11.
DOUBLE TAP TO LIKE

Friendships in the Online Age

Although social media was an imperfect way of under-standing exactly what Clemmie was going through, it was at least a means of staying in touch with her when she moved to a different country. When she first went to New York, those who followed her on Instagram could see what her apartment looked like, the books she was reading and the guests coming up on her new podcast series. It afforded a valuable window into her day-to-day existence that, even a few decades ago, would have been impossible.

When I went to live in South Africa for six months in 1998 as part of my gap year between school and university, I was packed off with airmail envelopes for the letters I would write my parents to let them know I was still alive. There were no mobile phones, let alone smartphones. I was dimly aware of something called 'the information super-highway' or 'cyberspace' (how quaint that terminology now seems) but the invention of email had only just impinged on my consciousness. I arrived in a terraced house in Mowbray, Cape Town, with little else apart from a stuffed rucksack bought from an outdoor activities shop that came with a lifetime guarantee. The rucksack had a zip-front rather than opening from the top, which meant I didn't have to stack all my clothes together and rootle through all of them to get to the one item I needed at the very bottom. This struck me as the acme of backpacking sophistication. Forget the internet – that's what *I* thought of as advances in technology.

I remember one of my housemates, James, introducing me to something called 'Hotmail' which, he explained to me patiently, was a way of sending an electronic letter that could *arrive almost immediately* on the other side of the world. He sweetly sat beside me at the shared computer on the upstairs landing and showed me how to set up an account. I chose my username and was given a hotmail. co.uk suffix, and both have stayed with me ever since, as if they came with the same lifetime guarantee as the front-opening rucksack. Of course Hotmail later evolved into something called Outlook, and most people were given .com addresses as a matter of course. It's generally only old-timers like me who hold onto their .co.uk domains with much the same passion as one might keep old vinyl, or vintage Biba dresses. I always get a frisson of delight when someone contacts me from a retro email address. I was once sent to interview a famous actor and we corresponded for some months after we met and it was sort-of-maybe-a-bit flirtatious. Now, looking back, I wonder how much of that attraction was simply because he had hotmail.co.uk attached to his name.

Although I didn't know it then, the year after I set up my first email account, a publishing site called LiveJournal was launched, enabling users to write down their thoughts, opinions and recipes for macaroni cheese and to publish them online. The opportunities this opened up were huge: for the first time, you could get your work out there without having to submit it to the conventional gatekeepers of newspaper, book or magazine editors. That became blogging.

At around the same time as the first blogs were making their way onto our screens, a woman called Julie Pankhurst who lived in Barnet, north London, became curious about what her old schoolfriends were up to. She and her husband Steve devised a website called Friends Reunited, which launched in 2000. A year later, they had 2.5 million users. The original site was designed to reconnect people who had been at the same school or university. When I entered the world of newspaper journalism in 2001, Friends Reunited was one of the most valuable tools at my disposal. I was often required to track down classmates of people who found themselves in the headlines, or to contact the newsworthy individual themselves. Friends Reunited was my first port of call, and frequently the people I got in touch with said yes to speaking with me.

In 2002, LinkedIn was launched as a networking site for career-minded professionals. Myspace followed in 2003, becoming the most visited website in the world within three years and kickstarting the careers of many musicians (including Lily Allen, Arctic Monkeys and Adele) who were able to share new music directly on their profile pages. But it wasn't until 4 February 2004 that social media really took off. That was the date when an unassuming nineteen-year-old sitting in his dorm room – Suite H33, Kirkland House, Harvard University – clicked on a button that would change the world and make him into a billionaire. The teenager was Mark Zuckerberg, the website was Facebook and the idea was simple: a communications tool for keeping track of your friends and informing them of what you were up to. Whereas other social networking sites such as Myspace and Friendster were difficult to use and enabled interaction predominantly with strangers, Facebook was about connecting with your real friends online. It could act as an electronic social diary and as a means of self-expression, but perhaps the most potent attraction for the four male college students in Suite H33 was that it could also be a way of flirting with your undergraduate crush from behind the relative safety of a computer screen. The site grew exponentially beyond this initial remit, and now has roughly 2.93 billion active monthly users.

Facebook paved the way for other social media platforms: Twitter came onto the scene in 2006, Instagram in 2010, Snapchat in 2011 and TikTok in 2016. As of January 2022, more than half the world's population uses social media – that's 4.62 billion people, with 42 million of them being new users who came online in the previous twelve months. We spend an average daily time of two hours and twenty-seven minutes on social media.[78]

So in the twenty-four years since I got myself a hotmail. co.uk address, the world has gone through a social media revolution. It is a revolution that has toppled regimes, caused an outbreak of fake news and changed the outcomes of elections. It is also a revolution that has dramatically changed our friendships.

At the time of writing this, I am on three main social media platforms: Instagram, Twitter and TikTok. I'm technically on Facebook, but I barely ever update my profile and remain active only because I can't be bothered to leave as I'd have to download all of my photographs first. I have a LinkedIn profile, but similarly I never check it because I possess neither the time nor the inclination to respond to Barry Goddard, self-employed director of Goddard Pest Extermination Services in Aberdeen, even if I do get daily reminders that his invitation is eagerly awaiting my response. My three main social media platforms have an accumulated total of 280,000 followers. I have 971 Facebook friends and almost 3,000 followers on my Facebook author page. All of which is to say: the sheer volume of interactions I have with people online is far, far beyond the number of my actual friendships. This serves its own purpose. The Stanford University sociologist Mark Granovetter has argued that weaker links in our social networks can be useful. It is through this widespread web of contacts that we find out about job vacancies and other opportunities.[79] And many of us now meet our romantic partners online, too. When I met Justin on Hinge in March 2018, it was still an app that relied on Facebook friend lists to facilitate connections (this has now changed).

Even though I first joined social media purely as a way of keeping in touch with people I *actually* knew, it rapidly became something different and bigger and more unwieldy. I now use platforms like Instagram to inform, entertain and connect with a community who are engaged with either the things I create (books, podcasts, radio and TV programmes) or who have like-minded interests. And of course I have real-life friends on there too – the ones who exist from the Before Times or the ones I like keeping in touch with on a regular basis, even if we aren't able to see each other as often as we might choose. With friends who have moved away, social media is a lovely means for me to touch base and see pictures of new babies and anniversary parties, tapping the 'like' button and commenting with celebratory emojis to let them know I still love them and think of them. My friends on social media encompass all sorts of outer circle acquaintances whom I like very much and want to have some kind of loose contact with, but who I can't commit to spending any kind of quality time with in person.

In fact, my very closest friends have minimal social media presence, if any. I realised this when, after lockdown restrictions started to lift in London and we were allowed to meet up in groups of six outside, I organised an al fresco dinner. To restrict the guest list to five people was an interesting challenge for a friendaholic like me, but in the end, I decided to suspend my anxiety that other people might be offended or expect to be invited, and I just opted for the group I most wanted to spend an evening with who I thought were most likely to get along with each other. It was only afterwards that I realised the one thing that linked them – other than knowing me – was that none of them had an active social media presence. And even though I am an enthusiastic user of social media myself, there was clearly some part of me that felt safe with them. I knew that they valued me for me, not for a version of me they could find online.

Of course, the clue's in the name: it's social, yes, but it's also media. As a journalist for much of my life, I got used to frequenting glamorous parties that I was invited to not as guest but spectator: those glitzy 'meejah' dos where people would air-kiss and tell each other how fabulous they looked, only to blank you the next time you met. My job would be to report on the evening's festivities, not to be an active participant. I was an observer of other people's lives.

Although, in my early journalism days, I nurtured a misguided need for everyone to like me, I realised pretty swiftly that most of the individuals I met were not going to be my friends, no matter how hard I tried. If I was sent to interview a celebrity and got on with them, the chances of striking up any kind of friendship in the outside world were minimal. The celebrity in question would often have far healthier boundaries than I did and they also had a team of publicists and managers and make-up artists who would be impossible to penetrate. Plus, they had media training, which meant they were equipped to be professionally charming without giving anything of themselves away.

All of this meant that, after a few years, there was a clear delineation in my mind between true friends and 'media' acquaintances. The older I get, the more I have developed an almost allergic distrust of 'media friends'. I can have friends who work in the media, but I realise now that we both have to earn each other's trust over time. But *social* media has mashed all the friendship genres together. We feel we know a famous person intimately through their Instagram profile, while forgetting that these pictures are only one part of their fully rounded lives; that we are still only observers rather than active participants in a two-way friendship. Taken to its extreme, this results in a 'parasocial interaction', where one person extends emotional energy, interest and time, while the focus of their attention remains completely unaware of the other's existence.[80] This term is mostly used with reference to celebrities, but I think it can be applied to non-famous acquaintances too. We are all capable of directing one-way emotional traffic and fixating on a friend who has little awareness of our fascination with them, often to the detriment of our own mental health. And many of us will know all too well the stomach-lurching sensation of discovering someone you thought was a friend has not just stopped liking your posts but has actively unfollowed you – the online equivalent of ghosting.

This is why I think the group-of-six dinner turned out to be – and I say this without exaggeration – one of the best nights of my life. We ended up sinking margaritas in the

garden, playing charades and eating late-night cheese toast-
ies. When I reflected on what had made it so special, I
realised that none of us had cared about documenting our
night online. It wasn't just that this meant we were more
present in the moment than we might otherwise have been;
it was the additionally delectable sensation of having a
secret kind of fun, in much the same way as I imagine
drinkers might have felt frequenting bootleg bars during
Prohibition. To have fun and not feel I had to post about it
on Instagram? How thrillingly *illicit*!

So what I've learned through many years of trial and
error is that, for me, social media is not a tool or a replacement for inner-circle friendship, but it does ensure the
healthy maintenance of my outer circle. And when it comes
to circles of friendship, it is almost impossible to write
anything without name-checking the eminent evolutionary
psychologist Robin Dunbar. Dunbar is the head of the
Social and Evolutionary Neuroscience Research Group in
the Department of Experimental Psychology at the
University of Oxford (try miming that during a margarita-
fuelled charades game). In 1992, Dunbar had a hunch that
there was a ratio between brain sizes and group sizes
through his studies of non-human primates. He mapped
out this ratio using neuroimaging and an observation of
time spent on the social behaviour of grooming. Dunbar
concluded that the size of the neocortex – that is, the part
of the brain associated with cognition and language – is
linked to the optimal size of a cohesive social group. The
ratio limits how much complexity a single social system can

handle. By using this same correlation for the human brain, Dunbar found that the natural upper limit for a group in which an individual knows each person – as well as knowing how they relate to everyone else in the cohort – was 150. This became known as Dunbar's Number and it turned out to be organically replicated again and again in human social organisation. It was the average size of an eleventh-century English village and remains the size of a basic military unit. The clothing manufacturer Gortex confines its operational units to 150 in order to avoid communication blockages. This is because, as the *New Scientist* summarised it, 150 is 'the cognitive limit on those with whom we can maintain a stable social relationship involving trust and obligation.'[81] Trust and obligation. These are two qualities that rely on equal reciprocality. You simply can't have them with everyone because there isn't enough time to nurture that level of emotional input. It's the idea of safety again: safety in limited numbers.

One hundred and fifty is also, interestingly, the size of an average Christmas card list.[82] This is one way in which social media is, in my opinion, an unalloyed force for good. I count myself very lucky to live in an era where I can keep in touch by pressing a 'like' button. In my parents' day, one of the only ways of doing something similar would be writing festive missives containing lengthy summaries of a year's worth of family life. I remain haunted by the mammoth seasonal task facing both my mother and grandmother every December as they diligently worked their way through writing hundreds of 'seasonal greetings' cards by hand. I remember the prospect of it hanging over the household like a thundercloud in the weeks running up to the last posting date before Christmas; the frantic dashes to buy more stamps; the stress of wondering whether so and so might have moved or whether the 1985 address still worked for them and so on. The experience marked me to such an extent that I resolutely refuse to write any Christmas cards myself, even if someone sends one to me. Luckily, I don't have to – because of social media (and because it's kinder to the planet).

As with anything that becomes too headline-grabbingly popular, Dunbar's Number inevitably got debunked by other scientists who argued that human brains couldn't be compared to primates', although I personally think the 150 figure withstands scrutiny.[83] Dunbar himself continued to test his own hypothesis. In his 2021 book, *Friends: Understanding the Power of Our Most Important Relationships*, Dunbar fine-tunes the original number and argues that it isn't so much an absolute numerical limit, as much as one of a series of concentric circles or layers. Each layer represents a qualitatively different kind of friendship. Each circle is three times the size of the one preceding it.

'The innermost layer of 1.5 is [the most intimate]; clearly that has to do with your romantic relationships,' Dunbar said in an interview with the *Atlantic*. 'The next layer of five is your shoulders-to-cry-on friendships. They are the ones who will drop everything to support us when our world falls apart. The 15 layer includes the previous five, and your core social partners. They are our main social companions, so they provide the context for having fun times. They also provide the main circle for exchange of child care. We trust them enough to leave our children with them. The next layer up, at 50, is your big-weekend-barbecue people. And the 150 layer is your weddings and funerals group who would come to your once-in-a-lifetime event.'[84]

The layers continue to expand, like a thrown pebble causing outward moving ripples in a lake. Our social media circle, for many of us, would be somewhere between the seventh (1,500) and eighth layers (5,000). These are what Dunbar terms 'known faces' – we might recognise them in a crowd, but we don't intimately understand who they are because the time we have to invest in interaction is not, and can never be, infinite.

A study by Jeffrey Hall from the University of Kansas found that it required 200 hours of investment in the space of a few months to make a stranger into a good friend.[85] Baldly stated, this means that we simply don't have enough time to maintain all the friendships we might like or encounter during a lifetime, and it also accounts for why, as Dunbar puts in his book 'falling in love will cost you two friendships'. When we fall in love, we understandably put a lot of time and effort and attention into our romantic partner – and that means space has to be made in one's innermost circle or we risk sacrificing the stability of our attachments.

The first time I read that fact, it felt as though someone had lobbed a grenade into the neatly picket-fenced landscape of my mind. I'd never fully understood before that the capacity to maintain friendships was not inexhaustible.

Writing that down, it sounds stupid. But I truly felt that I should be able to maintain every single friendship I'd ever made. I think it's because so much of the cultural discussion around friendship – especially female friendship – is that it must be prioritised above all else, and that if you don't continue to nurture your friendships in exactly the same way as you always have, whatever else life throws your way, then *you* are the one who is failing. You are the *bad* friend. You are the one who is choosing something or someone else over your nearest and dearest. The consistency of friendship should be pre-eminent, standing entirely separately from life's shifting circumstance – a fortified island castle, unshakeable amidst the ocean's changing tides. But the reality is different, of course it is. We meet people and fall in love, we move cities and countries, we have children or we don't, we endure illness or the sickness of those close to us, we experience success and failure, we go to weddings and funerals, we are bashed around by life while at the same time understanding more about its terrible beauty. When a friendship falls by the wayside, it does not necessarily mean it has failed or is not in some way 'good'. It simply means it no longer fits. Or it means that you have both been taught what you needed to know, and can move on with love. Or that friendship wasn't one that was important enough for either of you to make the effort to preserve it. The end of a friendship does not automatically make you a bad friend.

All that time I'd been worried that was the case. All that time I'd spent accumulating friendships in case I ended up alone, and I had been completely unaware that not only was I undermining the quality of my most meaningful friendships in favour of quantity, but also that there was no way in which this approach could ever be sustainable *for anyone*. It didn't matter if I had a 'gift' for friendship or not. It was a question of time, investment and cold, hard scientific fact. Yes, friendship takes work but that work should be focused primarily on my inner circle. No wonder I was exhausted. There literally were not enough hours in a day for me to ensure every single one of my friends was getting what they deserved.

It's all very well for me to have had this singular revelation, but not everyone has read the same research papers. That can be an issue. I know there are some friends of mine who now exist on the outer edges of the Christmas card circle, either because circumstances have changed or because one of us has realised we're maybe not quite as close as we thought, who remain confused as to why I might not have as much time for them as before, when my life appears to be lived so publicly on Instagram. The difficulty with social media is that it gives an implication of intimacy, even if the intimacy itself has ceased to exist in real life, and that causes an imbalance.

I have one particular friend – let's call her India – who consistently made jabs at how 'busy' I seemed on social media, yet I appeared to have so little time for her. India and I had been close during our first year at university. She wore repurposed army jackets and tied her hair up in vintage silk scarves and smoked clove cigarettes her father brought her back from his home in Bali, all of which impressed me. I was surprised she wanted to be my friend but, looking back, I realise it served her well to have me next to her as a mousy counterpoint to her superior glamour. India was always far nicer to me when it was just the two of us than when we found ourselves in company, when she would frequently make me the butt of the joke, claiming it as evidence of her affection. She needed, above all, to be adored by men. Once, on a night out, I kissed our friend Jacques, who I had secretly really liked for months. India hated it, claiming it would 'ruin our friendship group', and put such pressure on the poor bloke that he ended things with me after forty-eight hours.

'I don't want to risk losing my friendship with India,' Jacques said, looking at me regretfully through the loose Backstreet-Boys-inspired curtains of his hair. 'I fancy you, but it's not worth it, is it?' We hugged and although I was disproportionately heartbroken, I definitely thought it was the right decision. Chicks before dicks, I reminded myself. *Friendship* was the most important thing. After graduation, India met a man on holiday and promptly married him. Shortly after the wedding they moved out of London to take over running his family business and India popped out four children in quick succession.

Over the years, India and I had kept up a kind of closeness predicated on retrospective loyalty. I remembered the times she had been nice to me and put any past discomfort down to our youthful cluelessness. We didn't know any better, I reasoned. And besides, hadn't she been right? Our friendship had survived and neither of us kept in touch with Jacques any more. He had drifted out of our lives after university, never to return. Sometimes we would laugh about him, with India saying 'I can't believe you liked him *like that!*' And I would giggle and agree, even though deep down I actually had liked him a lot and had seen a future, however brief.

India was always holding out half-promises to me about how I would be a bridesmaid at her wedding (I wasn't) and how I would be godmother to one of her children (it didn't happen) and how she simply *had* to come and see me when she was next down in London (she never did). Instead, she kept asking me to visit her. On a few occasions, I did, schlepping across the country on unreliable weekend trains, hauling my weekend bag onto rail replacement bus services and waiting in sheeting rain for a local minicab to take me the final leg. When I walked through the door, I would often be confronted by a harassed India giving me a baby to hold and bottle-feed while she attended to another child's bathtime. India talked a lot about the stresses of motherhood. She appeared to dislike being a mother while simultaneously urging me to get pregnant at the nearest available opportunity, and I wondered if she was truly happy. I tried, several times, to ask her how she was really feeling, but on each occasion she laughed off my enquiry as if I were being absurd.

Over dinner, she and her husband would ask me questions about my career as if sending verbal telegrams across a vast distance to a foreign country. They were intrigued by the more ludicrous aspects of my work (a story about the time I'd interviewed a roadkill chef and eaten badger stew was frequently wheeled out).[86] It was as if they saw my career as an indulgence, when I could be settling down to the important business of having a family like theirs. In short: they were smug.

My friendship with India had always been predicated on my being the junior partner, pliant and willing to submit to her influence. She was cool and worldly while I was not. At university, when I was unsure of myself and happy to trail along in her shadow, I wasn't a threat but someone who could benefit from her largesse, in much the same way as poor little Fanny Price gets taken in by her richer relatives, the Bertrams, in Jane Austen's *Mansfield Park*.

The dynamic lasted for a time after graduation. But as we grew older, her contact lagged and I found that I was relieved by this. I would still get in touch to invite her and her husband to parties and group events (and they would still attend) but I no longer made the effort to sacrifice my weekends in order to travel to her. When I met Justin, the communication became more infrequent still, although I would occasionally receive a frantic flurry of texts insisting I absolutely must come for Sunday lunch in order 'to see the children. They'd love it. They've grown so much you won't recognise them! We never see you any more!'

On the face of it, you might think: well, that's a nice offer, isn't it? How kind of her to invite me to a family Sunday lunch. But there was always a tone that made me feel guilty, as though I'd done something wrong by not being present enough. I would sense check them with Emma, who was more straightforward.

'With all due respect, her kids don't give a fuck about seeing you,' she said.

It was Emma who pointed out to me that, in one way, India was correct in her assumption that I *did* have less time for her. I was, by this stage, a woman in her late thirties who wanted to forge a happy relationship with a man who had children of his own, while also pursuing an increasingly busy career that I'd worked hard for. Perhaps it was OK to re-prioritise according to a change in circumstances, in the same way that India and her husband had done when they'd had children. Not only was it acceptable to use my time in more nourishing ways than maintaining draining friendships; it was necessary.

So I gradually dialled down the contact with India. I wasn't rude. I would reply, but less frequently than before. As my public profile grew a little bit, so did my social media following. India initially claimed she found Instagram 'tacky' and 'basic' and looked at my presence there with wry amusement. But the more followers I got, the more I noticed she was tracking my every move. I would see her looking at my Instagram Stories every day, even though she never actually liked or commented on any of my posts.

She fell into a pattern of texting me after she'd seen my news on Instagram, but the messages would never be supportive and I could often sense a latent anger behind them.

'Wow! A new book! I don't know where you find the time.'

'Another trip abroad? Nice work if you can get it!'

And so it went on. For months.

'Hello stranger! Having fun with your new friends? Looks like you've been busy!' she WhatsApped me the day after I posted a picture of me at my publishers' summer party. The party was full of famous authors, and I could feel the disdainful jealousy dripping off every syllable.

'Ugh,' I said, flinging my phone down on the table. I felt a familiar surge of shame and guilt. I was having dinner with my friend Francesca and when she asked what was going on, she introduced me to the concept of appearing 'happy and stupid' in response to any manipulative behaviour. In other words, you had to take everything at face value and channel the breezy nonchalance of a perpetually happy person, content to exist at an entirely superficial level and never looking for deeper meaning in anything. I did just this when I replied, 'It was great, thanks!'

India answered within seconds.

'Would be nice to see you one of these days. If you can find the time for the little people like me!'

It was a classic of the genre. The non-specific nature of 'one of these days', which meant that it was up to me to come up with a window in my 'busy' schedule and that we'd probably be exchanging dates until the sun burned out and chronology itself ended in the second Big Bang. The passive-aggressive 'if you can find the time'. The labelling of herself as one of the 'little people' who doubtless was beneath my concern now that I went to publishing parties with Nigel Slater (love you, Nigel).[87] And then the pièce de résistance – the repressed hysteria of the exclamation mark, intended to emphasise the fact that no insult should be taken too seriously and to retain the ultimate defence, if pressed, that 'it was just a joke!'

Once again, I played happy and stupid and replied that 'work was hectic' just now but I'd be back in touch 'when I resurfaced' (thank you, Joan).

Three dots, disappearing and reappearing. India was typing. Then – ping! – another text.

'Shall we get a date in the diary now for a few months' time so that you don't get too booked up again?'

At this point, I'm ashamed to say, I left her on read and returned to my dinner with Francesca. There was a part of me that felt I'd stated my position and I didn't owe her anything more than what I had already given. Not all boundaries have to be verbalised. When there is no socially accepted language of friendship, it can be difficult and awkward to manage those intersecting layers identified by Dunbar. What can you say? 'You used to be in one of my inner circles, but now a change in our life circumstances plus the clarity of vision that comes with age means I've realised you'd be better in an outer circle' doesn't sound all that appealing. The problem is further exacerbated by social media, because platforms like Instagram can make it seem as if one person's capacity for friendship is endless, when in truth I am only giving limited glimpses of myself. These glimpses are true and authentic in and of themselves, but they cannot possibly make up the whole story. And sometimes it's easier to post your news in a place where lots of people can see it simultaneously, rather than keep updating every single individual who exists on the periphery of the 150 (especially the resentful ones like India). It's like spreading your chips across a roulette table, rather than feeding individual tokens into a broken arcade machine.

When I started doing How to Fail live shows, the sensation was similar: here was an auditorium of people with whom I could connect in a single evening. By doing this, I wasn't taking away from my other friendships but I was seeking to spread meaningful reciprocity at scale. I'm often asked how I can consider myself an introvert, yet go on stage and speak in front of an audience. There are two reasons: the first is that I've spent a lot of time practising – I used to be on a debating team at secondary school and although public speaking terrified me (especially when I had to think on my feet), I learned how to manage this terror and to appear outwardly confident. Every time I get on stage, I still feel heart-poundingly anxious, but I also have faith that I will be able to do it because I've done it several times before. Secondly, my specific kind of introversion means that I often find it far more draining to have one-on-one interactions with people than a big group. If I'm talking to one person, I will seek to establish connection and to ensure that they feel comfortable and that there are no awkward silences and so on. On stage or on a podcast or online, I can say or post one thing to many and do not have to take on their individual emotional energy in quite the same way.

Social media is similar. I am generally in charge of whether or not I read or respond to private messages and unless someone tags me in a negative book review or trolls me in the comments, I can believe that I'm in a large group of friends and can communicate with them on that basis. There is a specific kind of beauty to this, I think, which often gets ignored in the rush to condemn social media for all its undoubted disadvantages. We can create our own communities online and the amount of effort it takes to sustain those communities is comparatively low key when you compare it to real-life friendships. Social media has also made marginalised parts of society more visible: a gay teen-ager who wasn't out to their family or friends in the 1980s would find themselves in a very lonely place. These days, those teenagers can connect with others online. That's not a complete solution to inward torment, but it helps. As does the fact that, when we scroll through Instagram or Twitter or TikTok on our phones, we are shown so many different and diverse ways of being. That's not to say social media will ever replace real-life friendship, and nor should it, but it can be a complementary adjunct. It can also be a gateway to it – my friend Jo met a good mate via Instagram because they shared an obsession with K-pop.

Of course, the focus of the chapter has been on adult friendships in an online age because that's my specific sphere of reference given that daily internet use didn't really exist until I was in my twenties. The influence of social media on the awful reality of cyber-bullying among teenagers is beyond the scope of this book, although I count myself extremely lucky to have grown up in an age when bullies stopped at the school gates. According to research conducted by the Office of National Statistics in the UK, around one in five children aged ten to fifteen in England and Wales experienced at least one type of online bullying behaviour in the year ending March 2020.[88] But social media is also widely acknowledged to be a positive force for friendship among both adolescents and adults.

The first major survey to examine the intersection between people's lives on and offline was conducted in 2011 for the Pew Research Centre. The survey of 2,255 respondents found that more active social media users had stronger relationships across the board (although, this being 2011, Instagram was still in its infancy and most of the data focused on Facebook). According to this study, Facebook users received more social support – advice, companionship, help when ill, and so on – than those without an account. The researchers stated: 'Someone who uses Facebook multiple times per day gets about half the boost in total support that someone receives from being married or living with a partner.'[89]

A later study of 387 adolescents in 2021 found that those who used Instagram most frequently 'experienced the highest levels of friendship closeness in their daily lives'. The constancy and frequency of online communication actually cemented their real-life friendships.[90] Or, as Lydia Denworth, the author of *Friendship: The Evolution, Biology and Extraordinary Power of Life's Fundamental Bond,* puts it: 'The more media we use to maintain a relationship, the stronger that bond is likely to be.'[91]

As I was writing this book, my two teenage stepsons, aged eighteen and sixteen, were discussing whether to plan a trip to Amsterdam to meet their friends. The friends in question had been made online, while playing video games. The sixteen-year-old told me he saw no distinction between friendships formed through a screen and ones pursued at school. In truth, he said, in some ways he probably knew them better: they'd already spent hours together in pursuit of a shared interest. They'd also FaceTimed outside the parameters of the game itself (which reassured me that they weren't being catfished). For many teenagers who feel socially anxious, online friendships can offer a welcome respite from the pressure of a real-life interaction. A 2020 study into social support in the gaming network system bears this out: it found that members of the same gaming network 'may be filling an IRL social support deficit with friends they have met online. Additionally, members who reported more depressive symptoms may be seeking help from informal online connections through online gaming.'[92]

By contrast, my thirteen-year-old stepdaughter has a lively and expansive friendship group which relies on a combination of real-life meet-ups and online communication. I can see, first-hand, how the friendships in question are embedded with a vast amount of intimate knowledge – far more so than I would have had about my friends at the same age. That can be both a good and a bad thing, but her online presence definitely enables her to keep in touch with more people, from different schools, for more time than I ever had access to in the days of ringing up a landline and asking 'Mrs so-and-so' whether it would be possible to speak to her daughter. Plus, keeping in touch online has one major benefit over phone calls: it's free. If, like me, you're a Generation X-er (or a geriatric millennial ... I lose track), you'll have been familiar with the horror of the itemised phone bill, which could be checked by an attentive parent to see exactly how much money you'd cost them in any given month by nattering endlessly with friends you'd only just seen at school. Teenagers with access to the internet no longer have the same limitations, other than the cost of their smartphone data.

And, as a forty-something woman, neither do I. My most frequent means of communication with friends is arguably over WhatsApp – an instant messaging system created in 2009. It is exceedingly rare that I will have a day without sending at least one missive on WhatsApp, either via text or voice note. WhatsApp has a breezy irreverence to its aesthetic that makes it feel less serious than sending a conventional text. A WhatsApp can be dashed off or considered – the choice is yours. You can send illustrative gifs, pictures, videos and emojis in order to ensure the intent of your message isn't lost. And you can also mute and archive chats so that you no longer have to see the evidence of your doomed relationships writ large on the screen.

But I think the main reason I like WhatsApp is because of its group function. I have never had a large group of interconnected friends, and have always looked rather wistfully at those acquaintances of mine who have held on to their school or university cohorts. Members of friendship groups get to do all their socialising at once rather than having to find different dates to accommodate separately befriended individuals. That can sometimes be stultifying – I know of one university friendship group that only ever socialised with itself. In the fullness of time, several of the members ended up marrying each other. The ones who didn't find a partner were cast out like unsuccessful players in a game of musical chairs. The married couples, many of whom had once dated someone else's spouse in the same group, now go on holidays together with their young children, who are also destined to be friends with each other. If a couple strays to book a holiday outside this remit, this is interpreted as a slight by the other members. The result is that they feel no need to evolve beyond where they were at eighteen. On the one hand, this must be a gloriously accepting space to exist in – if you're still loved for being that drunken, naive first year, the chances are you always will be. But when I see them, they're rather like those celebrities who remain in a state of suspended development at the age they were when they became famous and feel no need to challenge the groupthink of their collective worldview. Although there have been no divorces yet, I wonder what impact a breakdown in one relationship could have on the finely balanced structure of the group as a whole.

I've never been a friendship group person – in fact, the largest friendship groups in my life consist of three people.

In real life, groups of three can be tricky to navigate, as it often feels as though the triangulation of attention means no one gets the one-on-one quality time they need and everyone leaves feeling a bit dissatisfied. But for me, the perfect WhatsApp group consists of three – or, at a pinch, four – people. I have a handful of WhatsApp groups that I am in regular contact with. Within those groups, we share news stories that interest us, songs we love, updates on our personal lives, frustrations about work, support through the tougher times and jokes. Lots and lots of jokes. One of my WhatsApp groups will regularly reduce me to howls of laughter. Another was a way of keeping in touch with a friend whose mother had just died, without her having to update us all individually. The number three means that there is never a weak link – a troublesome person we know slightly less well than the others who might digress into an anti-vaccine rant when we least expect it. I've been in bigger WhatsApp groups after communal events such as weddings and weekends away and they never, ever work in quite the same way. After the first flush of shared experience and hilarious photos, most of us realise we don't know each other well enough to sustain the chat beyond the end of the week. Instead our inboxes become jammed with inane trivia about the chief bridesmaid's broken boiler and questions like *Hey guys, can anyone recommend a gripping summer read?*

A WhatsApp threesome ensures that we all feel safe enough to reveal our deepest, darkest thoughts and secrets (when I asked one of my WhatsApp group friends why he felt the format worked for us, he replied, 'Because there are no safe spaces nowadays. Nowhere you can truly share your horrible opinions without consequences.' He was half joking. But only half).

A WhatsApp group performs a similar function to a small, protected social media network: we can keep in touch every day across various time zones and life phases, without having to go to the arduous bother of syncing diaries to meet up in person with the same regularity. When we do meet, we already know most of what is going on in each other's lives, so there is none of the excruciating 'No but how *are* you?' chat that can hamper so many White Wine Wednesdays. And similarly, there is no pressure to reply to every single message – a group means someone else will probably step in to answer so you don't have to if you're feeling less sociable than usual. My friend Mia, who I was introduced to on WhatsApp by a mutual friend who correctly suspected we'd get on, will sometimes disappear from our group chat for weeks because there is other stuff going on in her life. On these occasions, I will text her individually, away from the group platform, to check in on her. There is a tacit understanding that our group (as magnificent as it is) isn't always the right place to share everything about a challenging personal situation. And because we're all introverts who find the one-step remove of WhatsApp a relief, we get this without it having to be explained.

In her 2016 book, *Connecting in College: How Friendship Networks Matter for Academic and Social Success*, the sociologist Janice McCabe identified three main categories of friend among university students: tight-knitters, compartmentalisers and samplers. McCabe explained it like this: 'Tight-knitters have one densely woven friendship group in which nearly all their friends are friends with one another. Compartmentalizers' friends form two to four clusters, where friends know each other within clusters but rarely across them. And samplers make a friend or two from a variety of places, but the friends remain unconnected to each other.'[93]

Tight-knitters are the university peers of mine who holidayed together and married each other. I am a sampler. But WhatsApp gives me the capacity to be a compartmentaliser, something I valued even more during the pandemic and especially as a freelancer who doesn't have the built-in daily interactions of a friendly office environment.

My hunch that WhatsApp is a force for good in friendships turned out to be supported by some of the science. A 2019 study of 200 WhatsApp users conducted by Dr Linda Kaye, a senior lecturer in Psychology at Edge Hill University along with Dr Sally Quinn from the University of York, found that the messaging service 'has a positive impact on psychological wellbeing'.[94]

'The more time people spent on WhatsApp, the more this related to them feeling close to their friends and family and they perceived these relationships to be good quality,' said Dr Kaye. 'As well as this, the more closely bonded these friendships were and the more people felt affiliated with their WhatsApp groups, the more this was related positively to their self-esteem and social competence. Group affiliation also meant that WhatsApp users were less lonely. It seems that using WhatsApp to connect with our close friends is favourable for aspects of our wellbeing.'[95]

It's frequently said that online friendships cannot be a replacement for real-life interaction. I don't think this is true. Every friendship has its own internal balance and its own evolutionary cycle. Some friends require a physical presence, but not all of them do. A bond can be formed in multiple different ways, according to the situations we find ourselves in at any given moment in our lives. True friendship is about growth and acceptance rather than stasis and fear. Part of that growth is understanding all the tools we now have at our disposal to nurture those relationships in all their varied complexity, rather than being stuck in a singular, inherited mindset of what a friendship 'should' be. Some relationships will be best served via Instagram or WhatsApp or Snapchat or a hotmail.co.uk email address. Others will bring you most joy by meeting in person. A friendship shouldn't *have* to be anything other than the thing that best serves all parties. And if I have any further thoughts on this, I'll probably send you a ten-minute WhatsApp voice note.

The Friendship Tapes
SALLY

Sally Al-Roubaie, 30, accounts executive

'As an introvert with autism, I don't usually like to go to parties or socialise too much because I find it very exhausting. I can shut down and not talk, and then people can see I don't have a good time and then they won't ask me to come again.

'I've always felt like I've had to try and mask as much as I can – and oftentimes, it fails. That's when people slowly drift away. When you recognise that as an autistic person, you feel like it's your fault.

'Ever since I got my autism diagnosis at the age of twenty-four, the light in my head that was always switched off has been turned back on. I was blaming myself for everything: the way I was, the fact that I didn't have many friends, and didn't get on with people very easily. Before [my diagnosis], I never had any rational explanation to back things up, I could never really stand up for myself and say, "No, I'm not unreasonable. Other people are being unreasonable, they're choosing to judge rather than understanding."

'A few months after I started a new job, my brother asked if I'd made friends, and I didn't really know. I thought "friends" was a bit ambiguous. I asked him: "When you say, 'make friends', does that mean taking down someone's phone number and meeting up with them outside of work? Or does it just mean going into work and having conversations with people?" In my mind I couldn't tell.

'Because I'm not really good at reading signs, I don't necessarily know who really wants to be friends, and who doesn't want to be friends. And even if I know that I'm not the problem, and the problem is something that they have, you still keep thinking that you've done something wrong.

'The weird thing about autism is that you have this part of you that wants to have friends and to hang out with people but then at the same time, you also want to have your own space, and you want to call your own shots ... When I'm on my own, I feel like I can think straight and I can come up with ideas.

'For some reason – I don't know why – in this country, people get so disturbed by a quiet person, to the point of being hostile, almost like it's a disease. That was always strange to me because if I was around Iraqi people, no one would care if you were quiet or if you were loud! They just love having you in the group; there is no condition for being included.'

12.
EMMA

Best Friends

Throughout the course of this book, I've been examining what friendship means to me and studiously avoiding the flip side of that coin, which is what I bring into the equation as a friend. I've partly been ignoring the issue because, well, it's hard, isn't it? I know that there are elements to my past behaviour as a friend that are neither honourable nor loving. I know I've acted in ways that cover me in shame rather than glory. So it's easier to look outwards, to blame others for one's own conspicuous lack. That makes it a one-sided story, made even more so by the fact that I'm telling it. Although I strive for honesty, I'm aware that my own blind spots – be they borne of privilege, faulty memory, a fear of doing things badly or a combination of all the above – have made me incapable of giving a fully accurate account. But any conversation about friendship can't just involve one person talking. That's why I've tried to include as many different voices as possible, to round out my own necessarily narrow perceptions. And yet there is still a missing link to this exchange, which is a clear-eyed dialogue with myself.

So. Here goes.

Am I a good friend?

Like any self-respecting A-level History student, I'd first like to challenge the premise of the question. The term 'good' is a specific one. When used as an adjective, as it is here, the *Oxford English Dictionary* defines it as '1. To be desired of or approved of. 2. Having the required qualities; of a high standard.' When used as a noun, good means '1. That which is morally right; righteousness. 2. Benefit or advantage to someone or something.'

'Good' carries within it both an implicit sense of upright virtuosity and a belief that its value is determined either by someone else's opinion (to be desired or approved of) or an invisible metric (having the required qualities). So if you end a dysfunctional friendship, are you a 'bad' friend? Or are you, in fact, making a clear-sighted and compassionate decision about wanting to be better for the friends who *do* reciprocate your love? And who is setting the standard for friendship? It's certainly not some bureaucratic committee appointed by the World Health Organisation, meeting regularly to discuss the International Friendship Consortium. There is no formalised, universally accepted agreement of what friendship is, so it's almost impossible to live up to the standards that 'good' implies.

I think a better term is 'true'. True implies loyalty, truthfulness, authenticity, acceptance and clarity, without the necessarily subjective moral overlay. Am I, then, a true friend?

In the minus column, I list the following:

I struggle to say what I think if I believe it will trigger conflict. This makes me cowardly. It means I let people down, because I allow them to believe everything is fine rather than being honest about the things that hurt me.

I haven't always been honest about how a friend has made me feel, allowing grudges to fester and lead to resentment.

I am not good at navigating endings and sometimes fall silently out of people's lives in order to avoid a showdown. Yes, I've ghosted friends too and I feel enormous shame for this but I'm too scared to get back in touch with them and say sorry.

Being a 'true' friend necessarily involves truthfulness and I know I haven't always been that. I've lied instead of clearly addressing a potentially contentious issue head-on.

Wow. Writing that makes me sound awful. It's a miracle anyone wants to be friends with me, given my flaws. But before I add 'wallowing in self-pity' to my minus column, let's also consider that being a 'true' friend must incorporate authenticity. And on this front, I think I'm doing a bit better. The root of 'authentic' is from the Ancient Greek for 'original, primary'. It is the same root for 'author' and 'authority', which implies we cannot be an authority in our own life without first knowing ourselves. More than that: we can only write the narrative of our existence if we inhabit that authenticity. Being authentic is not just about being 'real'; it's about claiming one's own power to tell the story of our lives. Being inauthentic means other people will project their version of who you are onto the blank page you provide.

So in the plus column, I would write:

I'm loyal.

I'm accepting – sometimes to an extreme, which is at least part of the reason I stay in dysfunctional relationships for too long and then feel guilt over them ending.

I've started being more authentic, and have dabbled in straightforward truth-telling.

In summary: I'm a work in progress.

Ironically, given that I'm not even sure I want to be categorised as a good friend, I have absolutely no qualms about defining myself in the superlative as a *best* friend. Where 'good' can be a sliding scale, viewed subjectively in several different lights according to what one person considers their most valued friendship qualities, 'best' is pre-eminent. For me, it is also singular. I have one best friend in my life, and you know her already because she's been liberally sprinkled all over this book like a dusting of platonic confetti. Her name is Emma.

The advantage of calling her 'best' is that when you're investing in a friendship with one other person who holds such value in your life, it's easier to be clear about what you both want from your alliance. You've already put a label on each other and said 'Yes, you. You're the one I want.' The significance is clearly delineated – both for the best friends themselves, and for their wider group of acquaintance. In this respect, a 'best friend' is arguably the closest we get to a socially recognised contract of affectionate love between non-romantic partners.

Emma and I built our best friendship over time. Recollections of how we met vary. For years, I claimed I had walked into our college bar during freshers' week to find a gorgeous blonde woman surrounded by a gaggle of men laughing riotously at her every joke, and that I noticed she was wearing a slogan T-shirt emblazoned with 'One For The Rogue'. She seemed so confident, so funny and so sure of herself. *Ugh*, I thought as Emma delivered another punchline with perfectly executed comic timing and her circle of acolytes erupted into another fit of wild laughter, *whoever she is, we are so not going to get on.*

But one of the laughing men was someone I knew a bit, and he beckoned me to join them. I was nervous and yet intrigued by this woman who seemed to represent all the things I was not – so extroverted, so self-assured, so *blonde*. As soon as I walked over, Emma was interested in me and what I had to say. She didn't seem to care if the boys were there or not. I've never had such a rapidly overturned first impression. I had got her totally wrong. Much later, I would find out that the show of overt confidence and extroversion in our college bar had been her way of masking her own insecurity and feelings of unease. And her natural hair colour was dark brunette – just like mine.

I have told this story many times over the years – to friends, family and to her two kids, who call me 'Auntie Liz'. I wrote about it in an earlier book.[96] I even dedicated my third novel to her, with the words 'Here's one for the rogue'. It was only over the pandemic, during one of our Zoom margarita sessions with our husbands, that she told me I'd remembered it wrongly. She hadn't been wearing that T-shirt. She knew that for a fact because she had only bought it in December that year when she went to a Robbie Williams concert in Paris (before meeting her husband, Robbie Williams was Emma's ideal man) and freshers' week had been in September.

'*What?!*' I gasped. Suddenly this seminal memory, which had seemed so clearly etched in my mind's eye became pixellated and warped. I had learned over the decades that Emma's powers of recall were those of a wartime spy (I asked her once whether she ever got to the end of a sentence and couldn't think of the word she needed to complete it. 'No,' she said, as if this were a curious question. 'Why – do you?' I looked at her, dumbfounded. 'All the bloody time, are you *serious*?')

So I had to admit that I'd misremembered a key detail of our meeting. Not only that, but I'd enshrined it again and again in the many versions of the story I'd told and Emma had never once said anything. All this time, she had known and stayed quiet so as not to make me feel bad. Perhaps what she was really saying is that the individual facts didn't matter as much as the overall feeling.

In truth, neither of us can accurately recall which of her many slogan T-shirts she was wearing that night. Emma thinks it would either have been a market stall rip-off of Tommy Hilfiger reading 'Totty Highflier' or 'Bed Taker' written in the style of the Ted Baker logo. In our defence, it was 1998 and slogan T-shirts were the last word in cool. Shortly after meeting Emma, I bought a long-sleeved version which had the Evian logo reversed across the front to read 'Naive'. I know. *So* edgy.

Although our connection was almost immediate, it took us longer to label ourselves as each other's best friends. In some ways, our friendship journey mirrored a modern-day dating process where we started off by liking each other in a group, then spent more time together one on one before mutually deciding to be exclusive, eventually pairing off and giving our friendship a label.

In popular culture, there's a misguided sense that the most magical kinds of love are ones that start with a *coup de foudre* – that lightning bolt of instant recognition which tells us we've met our soulmates and must instantly give in to our passion and run away to Rio together where we will remain inseparable and high on our mutual love, quoting poetry to each other until the end of days. I certainly used to think this was the case in my romantic relationships, and it took me until the age of thirty-nine to realise that actually the kind of love I value the most is the slow-burning variety: the one that starts with a spark, but that builds gradually over time and makes me feel safe in its steady accumulation of feeling. I don't want fireworks that bang loudly then fizzle out into darkness. I want a methodically built and well-tended bonfire that keeps us warm for longer.

I realise now that I trust the same thing in friendships. I have often lost sight of this, in the friendaholic excitement of wanting to bond, only to discover several months down the line that the friend in question is not who I thought they were or that they have vastly different expectations of our friendship than I do. By then, it's always awkward to extract yourself.

Mine and Emma's best friendship was built slowly. By the final year of university, we were living together but our closeness became deeper after graduating, when we faced the challenges of adult life – work, money, boyfriends, break-ups, house moves and the fact we finally had to pay taxes.

It included necessary moments of rupture, where we (unconsciously or otherwise) tested the strength of our union. I decided not to live with her when we first moved to London, but instead became part of a house-share with three other graduates. My reasoning at the time was that I didn't want to risk the preciousness of what Emma was to me by polluting it with everyday stresses like who would buy the toilet roll, how will we split the rent and by-the-way-that-was-my-hummus-in-the-fridge. But it hurt Emma, who felt overlooked and excluded and as though she was losing me, and I was too immature back then to know how to heal that hurt. When I spoke to Emma for this chapter, she brought up this moment as one of her key memories in the progression of our friendship.

EMMA: I did feel less secure in our friendship because I wasn't being true to myself. And I think that's fundamentally what creates our insecurities. There was a point at which, at the end of university, I felt like I wanted to pull away from the world and just be with you. I think that was really tough because you, on the receiving end, weren't in that space. And you were growing a circle of friends that met lots of different needs for you. I remember that point as 'I need to make a decision here as to whether I'm going to push my tolerance for someone having multiple relationships and be able to be OK with that.'

I would have preferred if I could have just enlisted you to retreat with me. And that wasn't where you were at. You were moving back to London and expanding. I think I really needed that experience because even though I know it was difficult at the time for me to process – and I know you processed this reciprocally – that feeling of actually: 'What do I want? I want to grow myself and I want Liz to be her fullest self.' And at that point I didn't even see that this was you, in a way, working through your own stuff and that you were going to come out the other end of that with your own understanding that was going to be quite different. So I'm really glad that it happened because I felt that leap of faith for both of us. I have become more secure in our relationship because I didn't cling on to you in that space and I think I have also become more secure in our relationship because I've seen you then come back to a place where actually you no longer want that kind of large group relationship.

Emma was right: the house-share wasn't exactly what I'd thought it would be, and I came out of it knowing I wanted to spend more one-on-one time with her because that was what nourished and sustained me the most. I'm also glad I had that experience, even if I wish I'd handled it differently at the time, because it made it much clearer to me how highly I valued her.

Up until this point, I had deliberately circumvented any putative tension or disagreement in my friendships because I was too scared of losing them. This was one of the first occasions I discovered that, in the right relationships, rupture can not only be withstood but repaired. Emma was honest with me about how she felt, and it meant that we could both explain our motivations. That salutary experience made us closer: one more brick slotted into the solid foundation of our friendship.

After the house-share, I moved into my own rented flat. Emma sewed me blinds and a patchwork blanket. The landlord had left me a folded futon chair and often she would come and sleep over. One night, walking back home from work, I got mugged on the street by four men. They stole my laptop, but I managed to cling on to my handbag despite one of them thumping me in the face. The police later told me they'd had a knife – the bottom of a plastic bag of groceries I'd been carrying had been cleanly slashed across – and that I'd been very lucky.

Shaken and unsure of myself, I did the one thing that I knew would make me feel safe. I moved around the corner from Emma. There just so happened to be a flat for sale a two-minute walk from her front door. And, this being the mid-2000s, I was able to get an interest-only mortgage with a deposit that essentially consisted of some scraped-together pennies found down the back of a sofa.

I spent four blissful years in that flat. This was one of the happiest, most fulfilling phases of our best friendship. We had got as close as we feasibly could to the improbably idyllic lifestyle on display in *Friends* (although Emma's apartment was above a grotty tattoo parlour and the nearest equivalent of a neighbourhood cafe was McDonald's in the Southside Centre, Wandsworth).

I remember laughing a lot. There was the time when, trying to impress a work colleague she fancied, Emma had danced energetically in high-heeled boots on a bar table. In attempting to execute an ambitious can-can kick, she had fallen over and badly sprained some essential leg muscle. Determined not to embarrass herself further in front of the man in question, she immediately got up, dusted herself down, numbed the pain with booze and carried on dancing. I don't know how, but she managed to get herself home despite barely being able to walk. The next day, she called me saying she couldn't get out of bed and please could I come over and tend to her?[97] This I did.

Then there was the Christmas Eve we spent together when we played a game of 'name the song from the first few chords of music' and she correctly guessed everything from 'Agadoo' to Craig David's '7 Days' after about two seconds.

There was the evening we went for dinner at Carluccio's (RIP) and she took an unflattering photo of me that sent me into a spiral of despond.

'Is that what I really look like?'

'No, it's just bad angles and lighting. Look, I'll show you …'

We spent the next half-hour deliberately taking the worst possible photos we could of each other in order to demonstrate the untrustworthiness of phone cameras. By the end of it, we were in hysterics. To this day, I will occasionally take an intentionally terrible selfie and WhatsApp it to Emma with no explanation.

Outside our friendship, our twenties were a confusing and high-pressure decade. We were both trying to forge our identities and careers while also pretending to have a rollicking good time at the weekend going out clubbing with big groups and knocking back Cosmopolitans, just like *Sex and the City* told us we should. The thing was, it was never *that* much fun. We preferred hanging out as a twosome and being silly. We found safety in each other's company, where we knew we could let the pretence drop. One of our favourite things to do was to sit companionably next to each other watching a film in the cinema, neither of us having to talk while we embraced the quiet joy of a shared experience. Not a Cosmopolitan in sight. Our attachment to each other deepened.

In her work as a therapist, Emma often uses attachment theory with her clients. The theory, developed by the British psychologist John Bowlby, focuses on relationships between humans, especially the one between a baby and a primary caregiver.[98] It has four stages: secure attachment, where infants show distress when separated from their caregiver but are easily comforted when the parent returns; anxious-resistant attachment, where an infant seeks comfort while also attempting to punish the parent for their absence; avoidant attachment, whereby a baby shows no stress on separation and either ignores or actively avoids the care-givers when they come back; and finally, disorganised-disoriented attachment, where children have no predictable pattern of behaviour.

Whether or not it's informed by our early childhood experiences, most of us will identify with one form of those attachment styles. I'm anxious and insecure, which means if someone shows me affection or the promise of love, I want to keep their attention by continuing to gain their approval. I fear rejection above all else, because I'm worried it will end the attachment altogether (although, as I'm learning, sometimes an ending can be a good thing).

In my thirties, I began to understand this shaped my attitude to romantic love but it's taken me until now to realise it might also have considerable bearing on my friendships. Emma explains attachment theory like this:

EMMA: Say you were a child in a playground, what you need is for your parent or your caregiver to pick a spot, put their blanket down, sit there and preferably attune to you. If a parent does that, you as the child – and this is metaphorical but also literal – are going to be able to come and go as you please. You're going to be able to experiment and explore and discover and develop and grow. You're going to be able to try all the different things in the park and the playground, and every time you look around they're going to be exactly where you left them. And that's what's going to help you go as far as you want to go, safe in the knowledge that whenever you come back, they're still there. If they're not there – because actually they're moving around, or they're looking at something else, or every time you look back they've changed position or they're facing a different direction or they've left the park altogether – you're not going to be able to do that. You're going to have to circle them, stay in their orbit, only ever going so far away from them because you're the one that's responsible for keeping that connection – they're not taking that responsibility. They're not sharing that responsibility.

Emma's attachment style is avoidant, which means she has a tendency to remove herself from risk altogether, for fear of being let down. That's why she wanted to live with me – and only me – after university. According to her, this ultimately makes us well-matched friends.

EMMA: If you're in a friendship and you have this insecure ambivalent attachment style – Elizabeth – what's going to really help you is if you have someone who stays still – Emma – which doesn't mean that they can't be fully experiencing their own life and having their own journey and their own discoveries, but that they are rock solid. Every time you turn back, they're the same, they're exactly where you left them. I think that's why, actually, having a more avoidant best friend helps if you have a more ambivalent insecure attachment style. The flip side of that – what you give to me – is that for someone who often only feels safe if she sits still, who doesn't necessarily feel that the world is going to take care of her if she emerges or reaches out, you're always reaching back and taking my hand and saying, 'Come on, let's try this. Let's go over here. What about that? What about this?' You're always challenging me to have hope and belief and take huge emotional risks. And that's something that you regularly teach me about.

I reminded Emma that it took me years (literally) to gain her trust enough for her to allow me to hug her. And then several more years until I felt her relax into my embrace, rather than merely tolerating it. Now we hug all the time. Sometimes she even enjoys it.

The security of that metaphorical picnic blanket has meant that when I make bad life choices, Emma knows that the wisest, most loving course is to be supportive of me while also gently probing the decisions I'm making. She has often patiently waited for these bad choices to play them- selves out, rightly understanding that the time needed to be right for me to learn the lesson contained within them.

At around the time we were living around the corner from each other, I got into a relationship with a man whom Bowlby might have put in the 'disorganised-disoriented' attachment category. In colloquial parlance, he was a bit of a fuckboy. Predictably, I was hypnotised by his charm and his good looks and the fact that he was so … *tall*. I couldn't believe he was interested in me, but he was.

This man carried a packet of wet wipes around with him in order to ensure his white trainers remained box-fresh, whipping one out as soon as his pristine pair of Stan Smiths made contact with the tiniest speck of dirt, dropping to his knees and rubbing aggressively to ensure the leather wouldn't be stained while muttering swear words under his breath. It's a sign of my delusion that I thought this was a loveable character quirk.

It took him ages to agree to meet Emma – another sign he was a wrong 'un – and when we did go over to hers for dinner, I was at pains to smooth over any gaps in conversation in order to ensure that Emma found him as handsome and funny as I did. She was polite and nice and chatty. My boyfriend deployed his usual charisma with military-grade precision, and his trainers were as spotless as ever. Afterwards, she didn't say much about him. I told myself this was because Emma was never one for overly demonstrative shows of affection. Deep down, I could probably sense something was awry but I chose to ignore it. Looking back, I realise she never actually said one qualitative thing about him.

The relationship dragged on for far longer than it should have done. I remember calling her once, about six months in, when my boyfriend had refused to come to a thirtieth birthday party with me.

'He says that having too many plans in his diary makes him feel stressed,' I told Emma over the phone. 'Which I completely understand,' I added, launching into a long defence of his excuses.

Emma replied saying that it was fair enough I felt rejected and then added: 'He's not a bad person, but this is his immaturity showing itself. He's acting in a way that's just ...' she searched for the appropriate psychotherapeutic terminology '... a bit shit. It's not that he doesn't love you, it's that he's ...'

'A bit shit?'

'Yes.'

Weirdly, this made me feel better. Someone could be 'a bit shit' and I didn't have to take it personally. The boyfriend never came to the party. Instead, I took Emma as my plus one and had a much better time than I would have done otherwise. I dated this man for over a year, after which he broke up with me out of the blue, saying he wasn't 'ready' (although, in a classic fuckboy manoeuvre, he failed to specify exactly what he wasn't ready *for*). Only then did Emma tell me what she really thought of him. In summary: she called him 'a micro-twat-baby'. She had known that speaking her mind earlier, when I was in the full flush of love, would have pushed me away and made me less likely to confide in her. It would also have made me feel rejected by the most important person in my life – not the micro-twat-baby, but Emma.

After being dumped, I went over to Emma's to sleep over. The next day, she toasted me crumpets for breakfast and slathered them with butter and Marmite. She let me weep and took me to the cinema where we shared a big bucket of popcorn. Then we traipsed to Nando's where, as a mark of my distressed state of mind, I somehow ordered the quinoa salad. It was revolting because, as everyone knows, you should only ever order chicken at Nando's.

After a few days of Emma's tender, loving care, I felt stronger. I didn't need to explain anything to her. She knew how sad I was and that the best thing she could do was ensure I always had a picnic blanket to retreat to.

Emma also got into a relationship in her twenties with a man who started out nice enough but, after a few months, turned possessive and jealous. Their partnership was occasionally tempestuous. They broke up and got back together a handful of times before they ended up living together. Emma could see the good in this person, and understood that he had been damaged by his past. Repeatedly, she tried to help him get back to his true self, but it never worked.

I told Emma I didn't think the relationship was sustainable, and she replied that it wasn't my business. It was the closest we've ever come to a falling-out, and I still hate thinking about it. But she was right – it wasn't my place to intervene or judge. It was my place to do what she had done for me – to support *her*, and to help her through her thinking process, rather than feeling I had to support everything about their relationship.

When they did break up – permanently this time – she asked me to be there when he moved out of her flat and I sat on the sofa, making sure she was OK as he packed up his CDs and his PlayStation in silent anger.

EMMA: I think that if we hadn't had those experiences, we wouldn't have the same security in our relationship now. We'd have one based on faith and optimism but not based on lived experience. I look back at that now and I don't recognise myself because I can see now how I dug into that avoidant part of me to go onto autopilot through some decisions that I felt I *should* make as opposed to wanted to make …

I think every time I've done that, it's come from a slightly inauthentic place. And that was what you were noticing: that I, in order to do it, had to be a bit inauthentic and be dismissive of what you were actually noticing which was that I was behaving in a way that you weren't recognising and that was uncomfortable to be around and represented distance. And I think I was doing that in order to coast through some patterns of behaviour that weren't healthy for me at all, particularly that relationship. Why? Because …

ELIZABETH: Because you wanted to save him.

EMMA: Yes.

During the decades-long course of my own bad decision-making, there has only ever been one occasion that Emma felt she had to step in and actively intervene. I was in an abusive romantic relationship and Emma feared I was unsafe. Both of us remember this as a seminal point in our friendship. It was brave of Emma to take the gamble that I might react badly and it was also exactly what I needed to hear at a time when I felt too scared to do anything on my own. We refer to this moment as 'the Perspex screen'.

EMMA: I remember that event as a focus point. I'd experienced you get quieter and quieter and quieter for months – psychologically quieter, and more and more blurry. We had a conversation and I felt that there was an AI version of you sitting across from me at the table and that your truest self had shrunk to something almost imperceptible. I remember saying to you it felt like knocking on a Perspex screen because we were talking about the realities of how you were feeling and how psychologically unsafe you were. And that tiny part of you was slipping away. That's how I experienced it.

It was a point at which I just felt, 'We have to call this now.' And then what came out of that was several conversations about what was really happening. [Before] I might have let things play out when I saw them, but this was the point at which I wasn't going to let it play out any more …

I felt like I was taking a slightly out-of-character dive into your life and, with no judgement, putting across some quite confronting opinions about what I felt needed to happen – in a way that I *never* want to do with you because I always want to give you the space and support to feel your way through.

ELIZABETH: But I needed it.

EMMA: You fucking did.

ELIZABETH: I know, because I'd lost myself so deeply. I needed someone.

EMMA: The scarier moments were before that, in terms of my experiencing actual fear. They were the moments where I would be on the phone with you, for one of these rare phone calls that we would psyche ourselves up for, and I would hear your ex walk through the front door and you would go from talking to me in your normal tone of voice to something that felt like the voice of a seven-year-old suddenly shifting her full attention to this authority that had entered her environment. This self-deprecating, self-dismissing, revering voice. That was scary.

It was Emma who gave me the strength to leave that relationship, who helped me put a timeframe to my departure and who reassured me I was doing the right thing in the panicked aftermath of uncertainty and confusion. When I spent months in a state of nervous self-doubt, she remained rock solid. She never judged me for having fallen into such a toxic dynamic or for having stayed too long or for being the failure I thought I was. Instead, she told me she loved me more for my realness. She helped me break through that Perspex screen and watched, relieved, as I returned to myself again.

EMMA: Similarly, I know there is nothing I could do, there is no decision I could make, no choice, that I couldn't come to you and say, 'I've decided this', that you wouldn't go, 'OK. Let's talk about that and see how we make that work and maybe what that's about. But sure.' No question of going, 'I don't think you should do that.'

ELIZABETH: Unless your choice was: 'I'm interviewing for a new best friend'. Then I'd shut that shit down.

I was joking, of course. But, as we've seen, a getting-to-know-you process isn't a wholly terrible idea, given that one of the most important aspects to a successful – and best – friendship is an evaluation of what your friendship metric might be. For some people, their metric will be time: the more hours they spend with you, the more they will feel your friendship is healthy. For others it is shared interest: you belong to the same book club or pre-natal class or you go to the gym together. For some it is attention, which is slightly different from time in that it can be given in focused bursts filled with compliments and reassurances, even if those bursts only happen once or twice a year. My metric is reciprocal generosity. Not in the physical sense of someone lending me money or baking me cakes (although if you're asking, it'll be a lemon drizzle) but in spirit. I need my friends to think generously of me, to give me the benefit of the doubt, to feel goodwill towards me. I, in turn, will do the same. We don't have to meet up. We don't have to speak on the phone. We don't have to remember each other's birthdays. But every time I think of you, I will feel warm and safe in the knowledge that you love me and that when we do see each other, it is nourishing and kind and we can pick up from wherever we left off. The picnic blanket is still there. We do not make each other feel guilty. We never start a text with 'Hello stranger'. We never imagine the other person doesn't care. We allow each other to be our true selves, and we value that more than anything else. We are happy for our successes and empathetic for our sadness. We are there in whatever capacity we can be during a life crisis. Sometimes we will simply ask, 'What do you need from me?' and we will listen – really listen – to the answer.

My friend Haylie lives in Perth, Australia. Her daughter, Uma, is my godchild. I am absolutely appalling at keeping in touch with any regularity. I have been a terrible godmother because it's actually really difficult to find suitable birthday and Christmas gifts from stores which ship to the Antipodes and I somehow never manage to make it to the post office in time. But Uma once said to me during a trip to England when she must have been about five years old: 'I don't care about presents, I care about love.' And so it has proven. Now, instead of stressing about a present, Uma and I record each other video messages. I recently sent a voice note to Haylie that was months overdue. I apologised for its tardiness. She replied saying it didn't matter how frequently we were in touch, but that she always thought of me as one of her 'favourite friends'. She continued: 'Time and space is folded, like origami! So I know when the paper is folded back on itself, you'll be there like ten years hasn't passed.' She's right: when the paper is folded back, it will be even more joyful to see her because of the absence of expectation or guilt.

Another friend of mine, Daisy, is the same. There is never any pressure from either of us to be or act a certain way or, indeed, to see each other with routine frequency. The knock-on effect is that when we do meet up, it's because we genuinely want to. When we went on holiday to Mallorca together, leaving our partners back home, we spent time sunbathing companionably in silence side by side. We booked separate hotel rooms. One night, we each ordered room service, independently happy that we were doing our own thing and would catch up over breakfast the next day.

But for someone whose primary metric of friendship is time, they might experience separation as rejection. Maggie, my neighbour who wanted to meet up for long lunches and invite herself to stay over, is arguably one of those. India, too, valued time above all other considerations – including whether or not I had any of it to dispose of. We never had the conversation about how we measured friendship and we never gave ourselves the space to discover that about each other before we became friends. Perhaps we should have done, because the ease that I have with Daisy or Haylie or Emma means we don't have to perform togetherness in order to feel close. In truth, our closeness is even more pronounced because physical proximity is not a prerequisite. That, for me, is a precious form of generosity.

Although Emma and I value our time together, neither of us believes it's the most important factor. Both of us are capable of hitting what Emma calls 'relational depth' fairly quickly. We don't need small talk. And we're both really busy with our own careers and families. So we've learned to make our periods of togetherness short but effective. We make the most of what time we do have, rather than mourning the time we don't.

According to a 2020 poll of 2,000 Americans, it takes four years of knowing someone before they can be considered a 'best' friend and the friendship itself needs to be tested: 32 per cent said they needed to have been supported through a romantic break-up before someone could become their best friend.[99]

In order to think generously of each other, we have to start from a place of no judgement. Being unthinkingly judgemental often stems from ignorance (of why someone might act the way they do) or fear (believing their life choices are a threat to your own). In friendships you get less judgemental the more you know each other and the more you're able to talk about what's going on. Those early experiences of rupture and then repair had served me and Emma well: we now understood we could withstand disagreement.

EMMA: I always know that there will be a really good reason for you doing or saying whatever you do or say. And you always have the benefit of that doubt with me. And it doesn't mean that I won't also then have concern, care, and will make myself available at the other end of that if it doesn't go the way you hoped. I never look to control you, which I guess is what judgement is. I never look to pull you into line or I never look for you to reinforce my own narrative and make me feel better about my choices.

ELIZABETH: [laughing] I *do* look to you for that. I'm like, 'Em, am I doing the right thing?'

EMMA: And yet you ask me directly. What you don't do is decide a course of action and then shame me for not following the same course of action in an unspoken, ulterior way that would make you feel validated. That's what you don't do.

ELIZABETH: Yes, we don't play games with each other. And there are shitloads of friendship games.

EMMA: There are … My daughter Elsa will say someone said something or did something and she felt hurt or she felt overlooked or she didn't understand why. And, as an eight-year-old, she's looking for how to act on that information and I quite often say to her, 'There are times that I say things to Auntie Liz that I'm sure don't sound right, maybe I send a text message and the tone's off, or maybe she doesn't reply to a text message to me.' And actually what we both gift the other is this complete, positive, generous, warm interpretation of all our actions that there's no harm intended, that everyone can have off days or be busy or be unavailable because they're having their own process somewhere else that day and that that's not a reflection on our relationship. That feels so unique to me, that if I don't text you back you know that it's because something is happening for me.

ELIZABETH: Ditto. Ditto. I mean, what a gift. It's one of the great gifts.

To have no judgement while giving each other the benefit of the doubt. To see your friend with love when they struggle to see themselves. That, for both of us, is the truest friendship.

EMMA: Friendship is fundamentally not the same as being *friendly*. I feel really strongly that just because I'm friendly to someone, it doesn't mean that I want their friendship. That's because of how highly I prize the integrity of friendship and its purpose. And I think sometimes we're hoodwinked into believing that if we are not friends with someone, we're *unfriendly*. And I can be friendly and meet you at a party (not that I would be at a party) and I would say, 'Really nice to meet you, I had a lovely time this evening. All the best.' As opposed to: 'We have to do this again!' And let's kind of create something romantic about this one moonlit night we've shared.

ELIZABETH: But then if someone is constantly in touch with you, having met you once and says, 'Oh, we've got to do lunch', how do you deal with that? Are you like, 'I'm afraid I don't have space in my life for friends, all the best'? Or, do you just ignore the texts?

EMMA: I think I would use non-verbal boundaries in that way. So I would act congruently. And my congruent action at that point would be to say either nothing or 'I'm not in that place right now', or 'I'm not looking for lunch'. I might literally say, 'That sounds lovely, I think you're looking for something that I haven't got.'

ELIZABETH: Wow.

EMMA: I suppose I think of myself more as a friendship freelancer, in that if the work is there and the terms work for both of us, then that's my relationship. I don't want to be on the payroll. I don't want to be a salaried friend with a twelve-month notice period and where I have to find my replacement before I can leave. I don't want that responsibility.

ELIZABETH: So how do you define real friendship and what do you think its purpose is?

EMMA: What it brings me is a sense of unconditional love and a space where I feel completely welcome and known in ways that I don't yet know myself. It brings me both higher highs and a sense that there's a safety net for my lowest lows. It contains a part of me when I feel out of control. It celebrates me in a way that historically I haven't given myself permission to celebrate.

I feel like the purpose of it is probably more general than that, which is something about meeting all of those unmet needs that we maybe brought with us from childhood and may have greater or lesser awareness of. But it doesn't reinforce the harm; it heals. And fundamentally, the purpose of friendship, for me, is healing. And I now understand that difference. As soon as it feels harmful it has already ended. It's just going to be a matter of time before I unclip that relationship and let it fall away and I recognise that it's already ended or that maybe it never began or that maybe it was there to show up the personal work that I needed to do on myself. But it's only healing for me. Friendship can only be something where I can be my absolute truest self.

I loved that. Sathnam had told me a friend is someone who can help. Here, Emma was saying something similar. A true friendship will help heal past disappointments and present wrongs. A true friendship is a raft in the ever-changing waters of life. When pressed on what she thought my approach to friendship might be, Emma went a step further.

EMMA: A friendship is about two parties who voluntarily want to experience each other's connection for all those positive purposes. Anything other than that is a re-enactment of trauma from our early lives. So in answer to the question: what do I think about you and friendship? I think you are really learning the difference between those two things.

She'd nailed it. All those years that I'd been frenetically gathering people around me; all that time I'd spent fretting over whether someone liked me; all those evenings I'd lain anxiously in bed worrying that I hadn't been a good enough friend because I hadn't been able to say yes to whatever they wanted of me – all of this was a re-enactment of my past feelings of loneliness and fear when I was a child who was *friendless*. And because that feeling was so well known to me, it became my default. It became the one I reached for again and again when a friendship went awry: I was the *bad* one; the one who had failed; the one who had led them on because I didn't know what I wanted; the one who didn't deserve them. I was the one who, in order to avoid turning my gaze inwards, would have to keep making more and more friends to feel less alone and avoid rejection at all costs. And so it continued: a vicious cycle that didn't serve anyone caught up in it, until the pandemic hit and I was forced into a necessary re-evaluation.

I'd been on this long journey to find answers by writing this book and here I was, 100,000 words later, and it turned out all I had to do was ask my best friend what she thought. Dammit.

Hearing Emma say this made even clearer to me the importance of having a select group of inner confidantes – what the essayist Samantha Irby calls 'capital F' friends – who understand you, accept you and in whom you invest the bulk of your time and emotional energy.[100] These are the friendships that, for me, build gradually over time so that both parties feel safe. These are the friends who never judge but rather offer wise, compassionate counsel when it's needed. Of course, as Dunbar's interlinked layers demonstrate, we can't pursue more than a handful of them because this would undermine their integrity. And it's why, for me at least, the label of 'best friend' is important. It might sound childish or simplistic, but it's a shorthand for telling the rest of the world what we are to one another.

Is there any objective value to having a 'best' friend? Or is the notion twee and retrograde? In 2017, a team of researchers investigating childhood development found that having a best friend when we're younger can play a significant role in our future mental wellbeing. The study tracked 169 adolescents at three ages: fifteen, sixteen and twenty-five. By the age of twenty-five, those who had close friendships (defined by the study as a 'high degree of attachment, intimate exchange and support') tended to have lower social anxiety, an increased sense of self-worth and fewer symptoms of depression.[101] The respondents were chosen from various different backgrounds that were socioeconomically, racially and ethnically diverse. The label of 'best friend' did not have to be mutual to both parties and nor did participants have to name the same person at different stages. Crucially, it seemed to be quality not quantity that had the most impact. In fact, the teenagers who preferred to socialise in bigger networks rather than focusing on a few close friends turned out to have more social anxiety in their twenties. They were, according to Rachel Narr, one of the doctoral students who conducted the study, prioritising being popular instead of forming deep connections.

'The phrase "feeling alone in a crowd" comes to mind when thinking about those kids and their heightened social anxiety later,' she said.[102]

To say this struck a chord with me would be something of an understatement. When I first read this piece of research, it seemed as though an entire orchestral string section was swelling in synchronised crescendo. As I've previously described, I poured most of my energies throughout my teenage years into acquiring a big group of friends, believing that a degree of popularity equated to safety. But did this make me feel accepted and more confident? No. Quite the opposite. In order to keep in with as many of my peers as possible, I had become a social chameleon. I had first sussed out what *they* wanted in a friend and then tailored my own personality accordingly. I never had a best friend who accepted me wholesale for who I really was. The knock-on effect was that I didn't really know myself until much later. I wonder how different I might have been had I met Emma as a child.

The effects of a childhood best friend are not purely psychological. A study of 103 ten- and eleven-year-olds published by the University of Nebraska, Omaha, in 2011 found that those with a best friend had lower levels of the primary stress hormone cortisol when dealing with a negative experience.[103]

I remember really wanting a best friend when I was younger. I would read about them all the time in books, and think how wonderful it must be to have someone who understood you completely. One of my favourite novels as a ten-year-old (precisely the age of those University of Nebraska respondents) was *Anne of Green Gables* by L. M. Montgomery. Anne Shirley, the red-haired orphan who arrived at the doorstep of her adoptive family with nothing but a carpet bag to her name, was passionately convinced of the need for a best friend – or, in her words, 'a kindred spirit'. Although it was never explicitly stated that Anne's desire for this kind of companionship was a result of her lack of biological family, Montgomery implied that a young girl whose parents had died of fever when Anne was a baby and who had been passed from pillar to post before being sent to an orphanage and then on to the Cuthberts, would surely seek out companions who could give her that longed-for acceptance. Even Marilla Cuthbert was initially disappointed by Anne's arrival, having originally asked the orphanage for a boy to help with work on the farm but Anne, with her irresistible spirit, won her over.

I loved Anne Shirley. I loved her for her feistiness, her humour, her imagination, her obsession with puffed sleeves and her ability to stand up for herself – when Gilbert Blythe teased her in the schoolroom, pulling her 'long red braid' and calling her 'Carrots', she refused to play the role of passive victim. No, she hit him over the head with a slate 'and cracked it – slate not head – clear across.'[104]

And I loved Anne Shirley for her determination to find her kindred spirit. We learn in the early chapters of *Anne of Green Gables* that she has resourcefully leaned on imaginary friends to endure the loneliness and drudgery of her life until this point. I, too, had an imaginary friend at primary school, although my friend was formless and had no name – it was more of a reassuring, understanding presence to whom I would sometimes address my innermost thoughts.

By the time Anne meets the pretty, raven-haired Diana Barry, the daughter of a neighbouring family, she has firmly made up her mind that this will be her long-anticipated best friend. And so it turns out. Before long, the two are swearing allegiances to each other in the garden, solemnly promising to be each other's bosom friend 'as long as the sun and moon shall endure'. Later that day, Matthew Cuthbert gives Anne a box of chocolates, and she asks straight away if she can give Diana half of them the next time they see each other because: "'The other half will taste twice as sweet to me if I give some to her. It's delightful to think I have something to give her.'"[105]

Reading that back now, I realise how intuitively wise Anne was about friendship. Here she is identifying the need for generous reciprocity while also understanding that a friend adds incalculably to the pleasure of life by sharing the same experiences. It's also notable that Diana, although a kindred spirit, is different from Anne – not just physically, but in outlook and character. In Anne Shirley's eyes, a kindred spirit is a friend with whom you share a fellow feeling and an agreement of minds. You don't have to be the same, you simply have to understand how your friend might be thinking. It's the Aristotelian concept of *philia*, as seen through the eyes of a fictional eleven-year-old.

What about best friendship in adulthood? The 2019 Snapchat Friendship report, which surveyed over 10,000 people across the world, found that the average age for meeting a best friend was twenty-one. The cultural perception of what a best friend was, and how many one should have, varied across countries. In India, the Middle East and Southeast Asia, people reported having three times the number of best friends as those in Australia, Europe and the US. Saudi Arabians had the highest average number of best friends at 6.6, while Britons had the lowest at 2.6. Americans are most likely to report having only one best friend. Fourteen per cent had no best friend at all.

According to the report, the idea of best friendship in many Asian countries, including India, is built on an understanding that a relationship is about exchange as well as equality – a sense of 'if I do this for you, I hope you will return the favour'. A bigger network therefore makes sense. The respondents in India and the United Arab Emirates also stated that the quality they were most likely to value in a best friend was being 'cultured and intelligent' and their most frequent friendship activity was visiting museums and galleries. In the UK, however, only 16 per cent were interested in a best friend being cultured or intelligent. We're more likely to go to a bar or club with our friends, with 43 per cent saying it was their favoured activity, compared with 25 per cent for the rest of the world. And if you've ever been to Newcastle on a Saturday night, you'll know this to be deadly accurate.[106]

A best friend has even been shown to boost productivity – a 2010 Gallup poll of 15 million people revealed that the 30 per cent of employees who have a best friend at work are seven times more likely to be engaged in their jobs, produce higher quality work and are less likely to get injured on the job than their counterparts without a close colleague.[107]

So having a 'best' friend is not, in fact, a desire that should be confined to the playground. It contributes in myriad ways to our health, wellbeing and self-assurance. And because, as previously stated, friendship is such a diffuse and all-encompassing term, there is something worthwhile about having a specified category that is respected by all parties involved, and also by wider society.

EMMA: Over time, it has become more and more important and special to me that 'best friend' is a recognised role that you play in my life and me in yours. It's a little bit like a marriage, isn't it? There is something about the safety that provides that I need. It takes a lot for me to attach and to feel safe and contained. That label of 'best friend' means I can just level up my vulnerability in a way that matters to me hugely if I'm going to get all those things I said I was going to get and have the purpose that I said I wanted to have in a friendship.

Elsa, my eight-year-old, was asked at dinner last night by her grandparents, 'Do you have a best friend?' and she said, 'I think so.' And then she shared who her best friend was. They said, 'Oh, is she nice?' and she said, 'She's really nice. The tricky thing is, she's so nice that lots of people consider her their best friend.' And I thought, yeah, I really know that feeling of having to compete for that position.

She really does. Imagine being best friends with a friendaholic. Maybe you already are and maybe you, too, can relate to what both Emma and her daughter described. As I widened my friendship groups, stretching every opportunity for connection to the point of a snapped elastic, Emma remained resolutely someone who had maybe three or four close friends. I got used to throwing big parties – book launches and birthdays – and Emma not being there. She told me, with the loving clarity that is foundational to our friendship, that she didn't particularly enjoy parties, nor did she like having to share me with other people who only got a one-dimensional version of me. It frustrated her to be in a crowd of people, unable to have the relational depth with me she most valued. For years I would invite her to parties with the preface 'I know you won't want to come, but ...' Emma did actually attend my last book launch – but she came early to see me on my own and then got the 9.30 p.m. train home, and it was a compromise that left both of us feeling seen and cherished. I think it's because, in our forties, we know ourselves better and we know beyond doubt that no one could supplant either of us in each other's lives.

EMMA: That's what our best friendship removes. There's no competition, there's no one that could usurp you in my life and we are really vocal about that. What it frees up is a level of connection that I personally couldn't get to without feeling 1,000 per cent secure. I suppose it is a bit like family. You are 'Auntie Liz' in my household. And when our family is listed, you are always in the list. If one could go and sign some deed poll type document to add a family member, that's what I'd be doing with you, because it has that permanence and it's just something that feels so secure.

I know that it's seen as naff by some and I think: fair enough, if that doesn't matter to you, that's totally cool. You do you. And also, if it's not something you've experienced, it might seem naff. And also if you're not on the right side of it, it will seem excluding and I've totally been on the wrong side of it plenty of times in my life and been part of a group of three. And now you and I know that a group setting does not work for us. But I think for people who *are* in a best friendship, there's something that is really special about that.

All of this was true. It *is* really special. In many ways, although I've loved writing this chapter because it's made me feel so close to Emma and so lucky to have her in my life, I've also found it hard. I've tried to put into words something that lies beyond mere syllables. What makes our best friendship the extraordinary, life-affirming, healing thing that it is will remain, in some fundamental sense, intangible. We can't pin it down. It just is. Emma is my Totty Highflier, my Bed Taker, my One For The Rogue, my reluctant party-goer, my avoidant hug-refusenik, my rock, my unpaid therapist, my kindred spirit, my laugh-until-I-cry dinner companion, my quinoa-salad-ordering witness, my companion, my safe harbour, my life-raft, my unmoving picnic blanket forever. She is, in short, the very best of best friends.

The Friendship Tapes
WILKIE

Wilkie Bobin, 10, Year 6
primary school student

'I think it's important to have friends. I think life would be hard without them. For example, if you want somebody to get a packet of crisps because you can't be bothered and if you don't have anyone to call, that wouldn't be much help. But if you have a friend, you can go with them. Also, I think if you're really depressed, if you have friends then hopefully they can comfort you.

'I am good friends with my brother and sister, but you know they're always going to be there. They can't just run away (and if they did run away, you'd go with them) but with friends, they could move away or not like you any more – things like that – so you have to put more effort in.

'My definition of a friend is someone that I look forward to seeing and someone that invites me over to their house and I invite them over to my house. Having a friend is different from being friendly because you can be friendly to someone you don't like, but you can't be friends with someone you don't like.

'I'm quite a *person* person. At school, there are fifty-six in my year and maybe fifteen to twenty of them are my friends. Out of school, I probably have about ten. My parents have lots of friends, so I don't have much choice but to be friends with their kids. I have probably about twenty adult friends. I like to stay in contact because if you lose contact, you can't really see them any more. I prefer seeing them in person or on FaceTime.

'My friends all have strengths and weaknesses. I know which friend to go to if I'm depressed, or feeling active or chatty.

'I don't have a best friend because saying things like that often makes your other friends upset. I have five best friends, and then ten I would say "mid-friends" who I'm not in the same class as, so I can only see them at break-time and home-time.

'Quite a lot of people get very jealous. I think I'm unique because I'm not jealous. I don't really mind if somebody starts not hanging out with me.

'I think girls and boys respond to friendship differently. In my opinion – and I'm trying not to be sexist – if boys fall out, they just shove each other and say, "No you did it!" "No *you* did!" "No you did it!" until one of them says, "Yeah, OK, I did it." And the other one goes, "Told you so." Then that's it.

'The girls in my school spend most of their break-time and lunchtime talking about friendship problems when they could just say "Soz" and move on.

'The five most important qualities I look for in a friend are kindness; the ability to be fine with me not playing with them, which I suppose is being chill; not being too stubborn and being quite open with ideas; being interesting because it would be boring being friends with a boring person; and being active. I would say an added bonus would be respect and a sense of humour.'

13.
ENDINGS

Break-ups are monstrous. Even when the person in question wet wipes his trainers. Even when you know it's the right thing, and the sadness is accompanied by a healthy dose of relief, the process of telling another human being you were once close to that you no longer want to be with them in the same way as before is an emotional assault – both for the person being broken up with and, in a different way, for the person doing the breaking up. With romantic relationships, there is, as we've already noted, a culturally accepted way of doing it – stock phrases that have become almost cliched in their overuse: 'It's not you, it's me,' or 'I still love you, I'm just not *in* love with you,' or 'The person I've chosen to couple up with is …' (OK, so that last one is solely for *Love Island* contestants.) With friendships, there is no socially sanctioned way of doing the same. We expect our friendships to be lifelong, rather than finite. The idea of a friendship lasting for a specific stage of our lives – a contained experience with its own beginning, middle and end – is anathema to many of us. As Anne Shirley swore to Diana Barry, we are taught to believe they should last 'forever and ever'. That is perceived as 'good' friendship.

The reality is that it's as unrealistic to believe all friendships will last a lifetime as it is to believe that all marriages will. Endings do not automatically equate with failure. Endings are inevitable. A well-managed one can actually add to the richness of the shared experience that preceded it.

But the twenty-first century is scared of endings. We're living longer than we did before – the average global life expectancy in 1950 was just 45. In 2022, it's risen to 72 (well, 72.98 to be specific).[108] In the Western world, death of any sort is a source of terror. We inject botulism into our foreheads to look younger; we invest in new workouts and diets to ensure we stay alive for longer; we even seek to control the afterlife by cryogenically freezing our bodies. In an era where we have acquired so much knowledge, made so many medical advances and where so many outcomes can be controlled, we dislike the idea of something being beyond our power. We dislike, in essence, the thought of something being done *to* us. We want everything to last as long as it possibly can, wrongly believing that relentless permanence is the key to success.

This is also because endings are particularly difficult to navigate in an age saturated by communication. There are far fewer excuses for not keeping in touch with anyone, no matter the geographical location or life phase. Even if you no longer want to see your friend, the chances are they still have ways of reaching you. More than that, they will – if you have any social media accounts – be able to track your movements, your life progress and your interaction with other friends. They will wonder why they weren't invited to your daughter's bat mitzvah or why you're on holiday with your mutual acquaintance or why you're not replying to that text you sent weeks ago. In 2022, it is vanishingly difficult to vanish.

But Emma has managed it. She hasn't vanished, exactly, but she has moved to Southsea (that's no shade to Southsea, incidentally – I love it there). Her circle has always been small, and in order to keep it that way, she knows that some friendships will have to end. Emma has broken up with three friends in her lifetime. She has done so with such compassionate clarity that she's become my own kind of break-up guru. If I need to communicate something uncomfortable to a loved one or a work colleague, I will almost always sense check it with Emma first. She has been known to draft texts and emails for me, which I then read through and, horrified by their candour, re-write with appropriate emotional puffery before sending.

'You'll need to Liz this up a bit,' she'll say when she gives me a draft.

I've always admired her directness, and her ability to stay true to herself. It's an enlightened way to be because there's never any scope for fuzziness or miscommunication. If you act with integrity, you don't need to take on someone else's guilt.

With her own friendship break-ups, Emma noticed a common theme. She says in each case, it got to a stage where her friend's values no longer aligned with hers. They were making decisions for which they sought her approval, but which she was unable to support. When I asked her how she managed the endings, Emma said she was a big believer in 'the non-verbal boundary'. In one instance, she simply didn't invite the former friend to her wedding and the message was clear.

EMMA: I think the misconception is that friendships are permanent until otherwise. That they are a given unless we have a good reason for interrupting their course. I think *that's* the myth.

Let's just accept that friendships have a lifespan. When people don't believe that, they end up with these sprawling accumulations of associates that they can't possibly sustain and they're bound to let down and they feel this huge pressure to keep juggling more and more friendship balls in the air. My personal view is that your friendship is not the default. You create, grow and maintain a friendship for as long as it feels right to both parties and then you stop, you cease, it changes. And that doesn't have to be brutal.

This all sounded eminently reasonable. But afterwards, I wondered what the difference was between non-verbal boundaries and ghosting? Perhaps there isn't one. Perhaps, in some instances, ghosting is an acceptable way to end an unsustainable relationship, however difficult it is to be on the receiving end. With some friendships, there is a mutual – if unspoken – awareness that they are no longer working (in Emma's framework, they are no longer healing but harmful) and so the ghosting goes both ways. With Becca,

I had no idea at all that she felt aggrieved until our friend-ship ended with shocking abruptness. Maybe if there had been a more gradual dwindling of communication, it would have been easier to accept. It's not that I expected a face-to-face explanation of everything she was feeling. It's more that the suddenness of the silence, after years of close communication, was hurtful.

I have my own guilt on this front. Although I don't think I've ever ghosted a friend in the way Becca did, I have left longer and longer gaps between texts and calls. I have with-drawn – imperceptibly at first and then more noticeably. And I have felt so bad about it, that only once (with Ella) have I explained why. As Emma identified, I have always believed I need to give a reason – a valid, cogently argued piece of evidence that can be understood by both parties. But maybe it's enough to feel that a friendship is no longer the nourishing force you need it to be. Maybe, just like a romantic relationship, it's OK to not be in love any more. Love – and the end of love – is not always explicable. It just is. And maybe, like a romantic relationship, you need to be clear in yourself that you have tried your hardest to keep a friendship alive, while accepting that occasionally it will fizzle out in spite of your best efforts because you've grown into different people, with different needs and wants and hopes and desires. Maybe that means you can live with less regret. Maybe a break-up doesn't mean our version of friendship is any better or worse or more morally 'good' than another person's; it simply means there was a disso-nance in what we each needed that friendship to offer.

Because, in truth, I'm not sure there *is* a healthy way to break up with a friend. If you fail to give an explanation, that can be heartless. At the same time, if you take the trouble to tell them why you're doing it, that can be unnecessarily cruel. My friend Bonnie, now in her seventies, still recalls a letter she was sent by a close friend twenty-five years ago, in which every single one of her alleged character flaws was listed with brutal clarity as an excuse for ending their relationship.

The far healthier approach, I think, is a broader acceptance in society that friendships, like seasons, will go through their cycles. Some friendships will keep regenerating. And some of them will come to a natural close, but their impact on you is forever felt. *That's* the permanent bit. Not the friendship itself, but the way it has left its mark on you. We will always be shaped by the phases of life we walked through together, hand in hand. A past friendship will inform our future friendships because of what it taught us, because of who we were and who we now are.

If generosity of spirit is my key metric of friendship, it also means I need to apply that to the friends who belong to my past. Thinking generously of people I was once close to – understanding that they were going through their own difficulties and that life is complicated and that everyone bears personal suffering we can't possibly have access to – this is my way of continuing to respect what we once had. And simply because a friendship ends, it does not mean that our interaction with that person stops. We still have an interplay with a memory of it and so, in a way, the friendship itself still exists – even if, like a volcano that has forever altered the landscape that surrounds it, it now lies dormant.

This is not to say that break-ups always need to be permanent. Many of the older people I have spoken to for this book have said that friendships can resurface in later years. Those volcanos have become active again. A few years ago, Bonnie reached out to that woman who had sent her the break-up letter, to wish her a happy Christmas. She didn't expect anything in return, but enough time had elapsed for her to feel more at peace with what had happened and to realise that she didn't want to carry that negative energy any longer. The friend got back in touch, apologising for what she'd written and explaining she had been going through a particularly tough time when she lashed out. The friendship has resumed.

At the same time as accepting that friendships end or pause, we also have to look honestly at how we might have co-created untenable situations. With India, for instance, I unwittingly put forward a version of myself that would constantly strive to meet her demands and travel to her (both metaphorically and physically) at her request. With Ella, I had given the false impression that I was always going to be the fun one, my personality forever suspended in party mode. With Becca, I had slotted willingly into the position of junior partner, relying on her for advice and mentorship on everything from divorce to ear piercings, not realising she found it 'suffocating'.

Yet the common thread in all these situations is me: I helped to construct a friendship built on half-truths and unfulfillable promises about who I was and what I could offer and what I desired in return. I tried to be who they wanted in a friend without realising that this isn't how the best friendships work. There has to be reciprocity rather than co-dependency – and by reciprocity I don't mean a total mirroring of interests and obligations, simply traffic that goes both ways.

The danger with co-creating dysfunction is that some friends will be angry when the supply is turned off. When you break up with them and remove yourself from the dynamic, you risk their righteous fury. Emma compares this to the parasitic rage she learned about when she was treating her kids' headlice. She told me that at the point the headlice were facing extinction following her judicious application of medicated shampoo, the symptoms got worse as the lice tried to cling on before being eradicated. When she told me this I had an immediate image of those tantrum-throwing male leaders who refuse to cede power when it is no longer theirs, preferring instead to claim elections were stolen and holing up in official residences until they are forcefully turfed out. They know the end is coming, yet they dig in deeper because their entitlement is at risk. But just because someone is angry or refuses to accept an ending, it doesn't mean you've done the wrong thing. Often, it can mean quite the opposite. No one has the automatic right to rule over your life. Friendship, like power, can be corrupted.

How might it have turned out with Ella, Becca and India if I'd been honest from the beginning? If we'd all taken the risk of proffering our friendship CVs and saying, 'Actually, I hate big groups' or 'No, I don't like playing tennis' or 'Yes, I love going out to dinner' or 'You know, I'd prefer the cinema to a bar' or 'I really like you, but I don't have a lot of time right now' or 'I dislike the phone, but I'm great in person, does that suit you?' Or simply: 'I can't do lunch.' And what if we allowed other potential friends to say the same thing back to us? Might that not be the route to better friendships? Not 'good' or 'bad' friendships, but ones that allow us to be ourselves in all our flawed reality, and ones that meet varied needs. We rightly talk a lot about body diversity and the need for diversity of representation. Perhaps we also need to start introducing the idea of friendship diversity: the concept that some friendships will be deeper than others; others will be valued according to different metrics and not every one of them requires the same amount of attention. We don't all have to be each other's closest friends. We can be friends from a distance or school-gate friends or friends who see each other twice every decade and each one of these can be appreciated for its intrinsic nature and for what they offer rather than the things they don't. I no longer believe that every acquaintanceship is a stepping stone to a bigger friendship if only we put in enough time. Some friendships will only ever remain in our outer circles, but that's not demeaning. They are a crucial part of a bigger ecosystem: those smaller planets that Clemmie referred to.

The existential philosopher Friedrich Nietzsche had a bit to say about this. In his 1882 book, *The Gay Science*, he wrote about the idea that dormant friendships still had their part to play in our lives, and that we should not mourn their ending but embrace their continued resonance as we take our separate paths through life. He coins the term 'star friendship' to denote both their dazzling nature and their different courses – some of them shooting and bursting with rapidity towards the horizon; others solidly twinkling over the decades in the same corner of the night sky. I quote the passage here at length because it's so good:

'We were friends and have become estranged. But this was right, and we do not want to conceal and obscure it from ourselves as if we had reason to feel ashamed ... But then the almighty force of our tasks drove us apart again into different seas and sunny zones, and perhaps we shall never see one another again, perhaps we shall meet again but fail to recognise each other: our exposure to different seas and suns has changed us! ... And thus the memory of our former friendship should become more sacred! There is probably a tremendous but invisible stellar orbit in which our very different ways and goals may be included as small parts of this path – let us rise up to this thought!'[109]

What Nietzsche is saying is that we change through the living of life, and the accumulation of our specific and unique experience. We evolve and we grow and sometimes we move away from the things and the people we once relied upon. But this is as it should be. This is us confronting 'the almighty force of our tasks' as we weather both storms and sunshine.

Some friendships, however, are cut short before anyone is ready to let them go. Some endings are merciless in their finality. Sometimes, our beloved friends die. This is a loss of such magnitude that I cannot write about it without feeling immediately emotional. It is one of my worst fears.

Other than my ex-boyfriend Rich, I have experienced the death of two friends. The first was a work colleague: not one of my inner-circle kindred spirits, but a man who was kind and funny and made me laugh. He struggled with addiction and was found dead by police at home after concerned friends raised the alarm. He never saw his fortieth birthday. I kept his number in my phone for years afterwards. I didn't want to delete this final trace of his presence. I refused.

The other friend was called Camilla, known by her family nickname of Moo. She was the kind of person you were always, *always* happy to see. She possessed an infectious energy and a wild, throaty laugh and an emotional intelligence that meant I would occasionally catch her looking at me and know she knew what I was feeling. Plus she was so cheerful. One of my core memories is of the time we both handed out leaflets at the Oval cricket ground to earn some extra cash as students. Dealing with red-trousered drunken blokes with wandering hands wasn't the best job in the world, but all I can remember was how much we laughed and how unflagging Moo's optimism was.

When she was twenty-seven, Moo was diagnosed with lymphoma. After four years of treatment and remission and then further treatment, the cancer returned. Moo died at the age of thirty-one.

Her funeral was shockingly beautiful: a Catholic service with a full choir and a church bursting at the seams with her family and friends. We were told not to wear black, but to turn up in a blaze of colour. At the wake, I remember a lot of cake.

I want to tell you about Moo, but first I want to tell you about her best friend, Alice. I met Alice at around the same time as I met Emma. All three of us were at the same college and hung around together. I shared rooms with Alice in my second year. During the summer holidays, the two of us backpacked round Mexico, knocking back cheap tequila shots and climbing up Inca ziggurats. To this day, she is one of my absolute favourite people. Our friendship has grown throughout the years in a way that is profoundly meaningful to me. Alice allows space for change while remaining consistent in her love and kind in her understanding. She's also really bloody wise and recently retrained as a child therapist. I don't know what it says about me that my two closest friends are now both therapists, but there we go. Anyway, the innermost layer identified by Dunbar? Alice is part of it.

After graduating, Alice invited me to join her family on holiday in France and Moo was there. We were all in our early twenties. The two of them had known each other since birth – in fact, their fathers had been best friends since their schooldays and Moo and Alice were born within a fortnight of each other. There was an in-built serendipity to their friendship, as if it were destined to be.

ELIZABETH: What was she like as a best friend?

ALICE: She was so funny and silly, and really playful. We were always laughing. And she was devoted. The most loyal and loving human in the world. She knew everything about me. She had the most extraordinary memory and remembered everything that ever happened. I never remember anything, so when she died it felt like half of my life died with her.

In writing this book, I knew it wouldn't be complete without addressing what happens when a friend dies. What happens when you lose someone you know intimately, whom you love fully and have shared so much with but are not related to, and there is no formally acknowledged status to represent your closeness. Where does *that* grief go and how can it be processed? When society at large does not place a friend on the same footing as a spouse or a family member, does it make the subsequent loss harder to bear because of the lack of recognition? Is grief more crushing when it is sidelined? And what do you do with that silence – with the pain of it? So I asked Alice if she'd talk to me about Moo, and about what the label of 'best friend' meant to her.

ALICE: I need the world to know that she was my best friend because it somehow helps to explain the importance of who she was. Do you know what I mean? It's not a competition, but that feeling, for myself, of acknowledging how important she was – how best she was – is necessary in order to honour her and how much she meant to me. And also to help me understand why losing her feels so big. It's because she was so special.

ELIZABETH: I think that it's one of those losses that society as a whole doesn't acknowledge in the way it possibly should do. It can be marginalised.

ALICE: Exactly that. I don't talk about it that much because it feels too hard to explain. But when I do, language doesn't feel enough. I say 'my bestest, bestest friend', but she was more than that, so I say 'she was like a sister' but that doesn't feel right either. She was part of me. And there isn't really the word for that or a way to acknowledge how big that is.

When Alice asked Moo's mother how she would describe their friendship, she used the word 'soulmates'. Again, we only have the romantic equivalent to explain something so precious. Perhaps, like Nietzsche, we need to reach for the heavens for appropriate terminology. Maybe Alice and Moo had a planetary friendship – an extraordinarily lucky alignment of an entire solar system, in which each orbit was integral to the whole. When Moo's planet dropped into the blackness of space, Alice's universe was forever altered.

Even in the grip of this incalculable loss, Alice found things to be grateful for. She was grateful for the time they had shared between diagnosis and death, which meant they were able to say the things that needed to be said.

When death comes suddenly, without warning, there is a desperate and lingering sense of all that was left unspoken; the mundane torture of unanswered questions. Did they know how much I loved them? Were they happy? Were they in pain? Did they think of me? Do they know how much I miss them? Was that bird flying past my window a sign, a message from beyond? And: dear goodness, how do I live knowing what I now know? How do we carry on placing our hopeful chips on this reckless gamble of life? How?

With Moo, there was a chance for Alice to speak, to share, to be. It wasn't enough time, of course it wasn't. But it was something.

ALICE: When she got ill I was with her as much as I possibly could be. I spent days with her, watching old episodes of *Dawson's Creek* and holding hands on the sofa. I tried to help her wonderful mummy, Sue, as much as I could. I used to go to chemo with her at the Royal Marsden and just try to keep things jolly. I definitely felt a bit panicked all the time: is it enough, am I doing enough, am I here enough? Am I spending enough time with her?

ELIZABETH: Do you feel, on reflection, that if her dying had to be one way, you're glad it was that way?

ALICE: Yeah, I do. We said it all. So it feels simple. It just feels like I want her here and I love her and I miss everything about her. But it doesn't feel complicated. I don't have regrets, nothing was left unsaid. It just feels like she should be here. And I think that makes such a difference in how we heal. It's just love. It hurts so much but … I know she knows.

Against the backdrop of this slow-motion trauma, there were also patches of unexpected joy and laughter. In a twist of fate that is either beautiful or tragic depending on how you look at it (maybe it can be both), Alice was pregnant with her first son when Moo was diagnosed. When Moo died, Alice was pregnant with her second.

ALICE: She'd asked me to shave her head because the chemo was making her hair fall out and it was upsetting her. So I borrowed my fiancé's clippers and sat at her dad's kitchen table and buzzed her head. She looked beautiful. We went out for a walk and she was like, 'Yes! This feels amazing.' I was pregnant and fat and tired. She was bald. And as we walked down the street, these builders whistled at us. 'All right, darlings!' they called out. And she just smiled at them and said '*Really?* I've got cancer and she's eight months pregnant!' She was amazing.

ELIZABETH: [laughing] Did they say anything back?

ALICE: They looked so mortified and horrified. It was so funny. That was her. She was so, so full of life. She loved dancing. She loved music. She danced with her eyes closed because she was so free. And every time she laughed, she would cry. You remember, don't you?

ELIZABETH: Yes.

ALICE: Tears would stream down her cheeks. She was just full of life.

When, shortly afterwards, Alice got married, Moo rearranged her chemotherapy to ensure that she was at the wedding.

ALICE: She had this amazing gold turban made and she wore this turquoise dress. She was just so brave. And I don't mean that in a 'She was *really brave*' way; she was ... bold – maybe that's the word I mean. And spectacular. In the midst of all of that fear she must have had – and terror, probably – and feeling so awful, she made space for me to be special. That was her, completely.

On 10 February 2011, Moo died. What Alice remembers most of those early days of grief is the exhaustion. The dragging, heavy weight of it all. The funeral helped a little. But now, over a decade later, Alice finds that the single thing that helps most of all is being with the people who loved Moo as much as she did.

ALICE: Spending time with her family helps me so much. But it can also feel quite painful. One of her nephews is so like her. And it actually breaks my heart when I see him. I get used to it, but the first time I see him after a while I gasp because his little face is so like her. But being with her mum helps a lot. And being with her dad really helps because he laughs like her. It's, like, getting little tiny bits of her, you know?

Because it's not just that I feel really angry that she didn't get to do life properly, to do all the things that she would have loved and getting to do them with her. But it's also just that I miss so many things about her. So many things. My life would be so much more fun and rich if she was still here. And it is lots of fun and still rich, but, you know, it's like … She would just be so beautiful with my children. They would love her so much.

ELIZABETH: Does talking about her help? Do you talk to your sons about her?

ALICE: Yeah, we talk about her all the time. We have pictures of her everywhere. It does help.

ELIZABETH: But is it also painful?

ALICE: No. I don't find anything about her painful. But I find seeing other best friends be best friend-y really painful. Not many films or TV shows get it right, but when they do ... Like, when I watched *Girls* [the comedy drama created by and starring Lena Dunham] I found it excruciating because I just felt that the intimacy – the level of intimacy between them as friends – was what I didn't have any more. I find that really painful. Sometimes – and I've never told you this before – but sometimes, seeing you and Emma – I find it a little painful.

ELIZABETH: I'm really glad that we're talking about it because I'm so aware of that. And I love you so much in a completely different way from how I love Emma and how Moo loved you and how you loved Moo, that exists with its own beautiful integrity. And I'm so aware of that and I just ... I want you to know that I feel it.

ALICE: You know, it's beautiful to have it [a best friendship] and not everyone is that lucky and I feel so joyful that you and Em have that. So it's not ... I don't think it's jealousy. I just miss her.

ELIZABETH: Also, there's nothing anyone can do to make that not painful because what you're saying so eloquently is that it's the absence. It's that you miss *her*. There's nothing that can take that away or lessen that missing.

ALICE: Yeah. There's just a space which will always be there, I guess. I find my birthday hard … When I was about to turn forty, I was really resisting marking it or doing anything. I couldn't work out why. And maybe it was because it all feels wrapped up in celebrating her birthday too … I don't know. I don't know what helps really.

When a loved one dies and their death is, in some way, unforeseen, it shakes your faith in any certainty you might once have had. It is as if the normal rules no longer apply, and the world has been tipped on its axis. This surreal, topsy-turvy strangeness co-exists with grief and makes the future seem scary, full of unanticipated dangers.

ALICE: Now, if I'm not well, the first thing I think of is cancer. When I get a sore lip, I'm like, 'Oh, well clearly I have got lip cancer' … I'm sure there's some stuff that still needs to work its way out. There's a lot there that I still haven't processed. And I think it comes out as a kind of fear.

There's that famous quote about grief being the price we pay for love – often wrongly attributed to a whole host of self-help gurus when, in fact, it was popularised by the late Queen Elizabeth II, who spoke the words in the aftermath of the 11 September 2001 terrorist attacks on the Twin Towers in New York. The longer, original quote comes from the psychiatrist Dr Colin Murray Parkes, who wrote that: 'The pain of grief is just as much part of life as the joy of love: it is perhaps the price we pay for love, the cost of commitment.'[110]

But perhaps there's another price to pay for love. Perhaps our fear is part of the debt too. We have to make ourselves vulnerable to love another person and to trust them with our hearts, and with that comes the frightening prospect of being hurt. It's why we find these endings so difficult – because where once there was togetherness, there is now an absence that means we make less sense to ourselves. The memories that two people made can't be shared by one person. So our experience of life itself diminishes. And perhaps the only way to cope with that is to understand how lucky we were to love and to be loved with such fullness that it now causes us the equivalent pain of emptiness. The pain is a corollary to our love. Nothing can fully assuage it, just as no person can ever take the place of the friend who is no longer here to walk through life with us and to dance with their eyes closed.

14.

WHAT I'VE LEARNED ABOUT FRIENDSHIP

My name is Elizabeth Day and I am a recovering friendaholic.

I have many friends, some of whom you've met in these pages, but I have fewer than before, which is as it should be. We grow and we change and we live through different phases of existence and it stands to reason that not every single human relationship will survive the distances that open between us. I have learned that one of the secrets to fulfilment is to understand friendship as circles, layers or planetary systems. There are a handful of closest confidants who exist in our immediate orbit; further out there are dear friends whose less frequent gravitational pull is still necessary for our happiness; then there are those fondly felt acquaintances whose trajectory will occasionally cross our own in a meaningful way; and further out still, there are Nietzsche's star friendships, those past platonic loves we no longer interact with but whose imprint still exists in our shared galaxy. The existence of the all is necessary to the equilibrium of the whole. And, in turn, every planet or star in our solar system will be at the centre of their own. No friend is either 'good' or 'bad'. They all have their part to play in our understanding of the world, in the fundamental balance of it.

I have learned that we have different metrics of friend-ship, and sometimes these will be complementary to another person and sometimes they will not. My metric is reciprocal generosity of spirit: the idea that our starting point is always to think the best of each other. My metric is not physical togetherness or shared hobbies or phone calls or quantity of time. What I value most is magnanimous love, a hospitable nature in both parties that says, 'I see you for all your qualities and all your flaws and I accept you wholeheartedly,' and which enables us to be curious about life together. My metric is not having all the answers; it is having someone with whom to ask the questions. A friend is someone who helps, who heals, who hears. A true friend will never make you feel guilty (even if, occasionally, you might make *yourself* feel this). A true friendship, for me, is one that embraces Joan's wisdom, Sharmaine's clarity, Sathnam's non-romantic companionship, Clemmie's loyalty and Emma's generosity. And laughter. A lot of that.

And no, friendship is absolutely not about numerical density. That's where I had been going wrong all these years. I had to learn that it was OK to let some friendships go. Not just OK, in fact, but necessary. I couldn't hope to be the friend I wanted to be to the ones who mattered the most if I kept spreading myself too thinly in a futile quest to prove I was, in some fundamental way, loveable. I was never going to be able to convince those school bullies retrospectively. It was pointless – unless I first befriended myself.

I have learned that I do not always live up to my own friendship standards. I avoid conflict. I tend to withdraw rather than to verbalise my hurt. I still have a tendency to get carried away and give the wrong impression of the kind of friend I could realistically be in that first rush of connection. I still panic that I have unwittingly offended someone; that they are silently hating me; that I have no worth unless absolutely everyone likes me. But on those days, I remind myself that we are all just doing the best we can. We are all travelling through our individual solar systems and as we spin through the sky, we can be reassured that the rest of the universe is vast. It is filled with endless possibility.

In the end, this is what the truest friendship does. It offers the promise of understanding, of transformation, of planetary realignment. It gives us that most essential quality: it gives us hope.

ENDNOTES

1. 'You're not alone: the quality of the UK's social relationships', David Marjoribanks, Relate research report, March 2017.
2. 'Social Relationships and Mortality Risk: A Meta-analytic Review', Julianne Holt-Lunstad, Timothy B. Smith, J. Bradley Layton, *PLOS Medicine*, July 2010.
3. 'Too Many Friends: Social Integration, Network Cohesion and Adolescent Depressive Symptoms', Christina D. Falci & Clea McNeely, University of Nebraska – Lincoln, June 2009.
4. 'Can having too many friends affect your mental health?', Ziggi Ivan Santini, Paul E. Jose, Robin Dunbar, Vibeke Jenny Koushede, *The Conversation*, October 2020.
5. 'The Friend Number Paradox', Si, Kao, Dai, Xianchi, & Wyer Jr., Robert S., *Journal of Personality and Social Psychology*, 2021.
6. 'The cultural grounding of personal relationship: Friendship in North American and West African worlds', Glenn Adams, Victoria C. Plaut, *Personal Relationships*, August 2003.
7. 'A Cross-Cultural Perspective on Friendship Research', Monika Keller, Max Planck Institute for Human Development, October 2014.
8. The Friendship Report, Snapchat, 2019.
9. *Book of Words* (pp. 31–40), Abai Qunanbaiuly (1845–1904).
10. *Bihar al-Anwar* is a comprehensive collection of traditions (*ahadith*) compiled by 17th-century Shia scholar

Mohammad-Baqer Majlesi, also known as Allama Majlisi, between 1106 AH (1694 AD) and 1110 AH (1698 AD). As a hadith collection, it is second only to the four books.

11. Luke 6:31; Matthew 7:12, The New Testament, Authorised King James Version.

12. John 15:13, The New Testament, Authorised King James Version.

13. Upaddha Sutta: Half (of the Holy Life) translated by Thanissaro Bhikkhu, 1997.

14. The Friendship Report, Snapchat, 2019.

15. Hinge, if you're interested.

16. Please don't get annoyed by the fact I'm mentioning a big chain. I adore my local independent cafes too – shout out to District in Nine Elms. Still, you have to trust me when I tell you that Starbucks does the best tea on the high street. Years ago, when I gave up coffee on the advice of a fertility specialist, I spent many months researching this topic. I needed a green tea that would give me a pleasant buzz but that didn't taste like metallic fish. The Starbucks jasmine pearls meets both these requirements with aplomb.

17. *Big Friendship*, Aminatou Sow and Ann Friedman, Simon & Schuster, 2020.

18. *How to Be a Friend: An Ancient Guide to True Friendship*, Marcus Tullius Cicero, translated by Philip Freeman, Princeton University Press, 2018.

19. 'The Rapid Rise and Spectacular Fall of London's Greatest Bonesetter', Eric Grundhauser, *Atlas Obscura*, 28 November 2017.

20. 'Stimulus-value-role: A theory of marital choice', Bernard I. Murstein, *Journal of Marriage and Family*, Vol. 32, August 1970, 465–81.

21. *Social Penetration: The Development of Interpersonal Relationships*, Irwin Altman and Dalmas A. Taylor, Holst, Rinehart and Winston, 1973.

22. 'A social psychological perspective on marital dissolution', George Levinger, *Journal of Social Issues* 32 (1), 1976, 21–47.

23. *Man the Hunter*, Richard Borshay Lee and Irven DeVore, Routledge, 1968.

24. https://metro.co.uk/2020/11/05/9000-year-old-female-hunter-gatherer-shows-men-didnt-do-all-the-work-13541236/

25. https://www.theguardian.com/world/2004/jan/23/gender.uk

26. https://www.sciencedaily.com/releases/2010/07/100727174909.htm

27. *Malory Towers* was a series of six novels by English children's author Enid Blyton. The books were based on a girls' boarding school that Blyton's daughter attended, Benenden School.

28. Patrick Radden Keefe's *Say Nothing* (William Collins, 2018) is a brilliant analysis of the province's turbulent political history.

29. 'Why people make friends: The nature of friendship', Menelaos Apostolou, Despoina Keramari, Antonios Kagialis and Mark J. M. Sullman, University of Nicosia, October 2020.

30. https://www.spinalinjury101.org/details/levels-of-injury

31. According to accessibility.com, crip time is 'used by some disability theorists and advocates to describe disabled individuals' unique relationship to time. Crip time indicates the complexity of disabled experience in a world with many barriers to accessibility. In this sense, the term denotes the extra time – and need for time accommodations – a person might need to perform any variety of tasks. Crip time also notifies a conflict with normative time, the seemingly normal apportioning or segmenting of time in daily life.'

32. *Cassell's Household Guide*, Cassell, Petter and Galpin, 1869.

33. *Dictionary of Phrase and Fable*, E. Cobham Brewer, Cassell and Company, 1898.

34. 'The Cut Direct' from *Etiquette*, Emily Post, Funk & Wagnalls, 1922.

35. 'Ghosting and destiny: Implicit theories of relationships predict beliefs about ghosting', Gili Freedman, Darcey N. Powell, Kipling D. Williams, Benjamin Le, *Journal of Social and Personal Relationships*, January 2018.

36. https://www.theatlantic.com/family/archive/2019/08/why-do-people-want-stay-friends-after-breakup/596170/

37. 'Staying friends with ex-romantic partners: Predictors, reasons, and outcomes', Rebecca L. Griffith, Omri Gillath, Xian Zhao, Richard Martinez, *Personal Relationships*, September 2017.

38. *We Need to Hang Out: A Memoir of Making Friends*, Billy Baker, Simon & Schuster, 2021.

39. https://www.moscasdecolores.com/en/lgbt-glossary/bromance/

40. *We Need to Hang Out: A Memoir of Making Friends*, Billy Baker, Simon & Schuster, 2021.

41. *How to Be a Friend: An Ancient Guide to True Friendship*, Marcus Tullius Cicero, translated by Philip Freeman, Princeton University Press, 2018.

42. https://www.dailymail.co.uk/news/article-7488709/One-five-men-no-friends-loneliness-epidemic-leaves-thousands-living-isolation.html

43. https://www.americansurveycenter.org/research/the-state-of-american-friendship-change-challenges-and-loss/

44. Reader, I never did. But the outfits were fantastic.

45. *Nicomachean Ethics*, Aristotle.

46. 'Assessment of fight outcome is needed to activate socially driven transcriptional changes in the zebrafish brain', Rui F. Oliveira, José Miguel Simões, Magda C Teles, Catarina R. Oliveira, Jörg Dieter Becker, Joao S. Lopes, *Proceeedings of the National Academy of Sciences*, January 2016.

47. 'FRIENDSHIP: What is it and why do we need it now more than ever?' An episode from the *We Can Do Hard Things*

podcast, 25 January 2022. https://podcasts.apple.com/au/podcast/we-can-do-hard-things-with-glennon-doyle/id1564530722

48. *The Wisdom of the Body*, Walter Cannon, W. W. Norton & Co., 1963.

49. In 2009, the sociologist Gerald Mollenhorst of Utrecht University in the Netherlands conducted a survey of 1,007 people aged 18–65. Seven years later, he re-interviewed 604 from the original group. He asked them questions such as 'Who do you talk with, regarding personal issues?', 'Who helps you with DIY in your home?', 'Who do you pop by to see?', 'Where did you get to know that person?', 'And where do you meet that person now?' His findings showed that although the social network size remained stable, only about 48 per cent of the original cohort were still part of it.

50. Breonna Taylor, a Black medical worker, was shot and killed by Louisville police officers in March 2020 during a botched raid on her apartment. No officers were indicted for her death.

51. Ahmaud Arbery was a twenty-five-year-old Black man, chased and shot dead by white residents of a South Georgia neighbourhood in February 2020. They were found guilty on murder charges and sentenced to life in prison.

52. *Big Friendship*, Aminatou Sow and Ann Friedman, Simon & Schuster, 2020.

53. http://grantland.com/features/dumber-than-your-average-bear/

54. *Dementia Praecox: Or the Group of Schizophrenias*, Eugen Bleuler, Franz Deuticke, 1911.

55. https://www.accessonline.com/articles/gwyneth-paltrow-reveals-battle-with-past-frenemy-70037

56. https://berlinpolicyjournal.com/editorial-a-world-of-frenemies/

57. *Poison Penmanship: The Gentle Art of Muckraking*, Jessica Mitford, *The New York Review of Books*,1979.

58. *My Brilliant Friend*, Elena Ferrante, Europa Editions, 2012, chapter 7.

59. Ibid, chapter 42.

60. *The Story of the Lost Child*, Elena Ferrante, Europa Editions, 2015.

61. 'Social relationships and ambulatory blood pressure: structural and qualitative predictors of cardiovascular function during everyday social interactions', Julianne Holt-Lunstad, Bert N. Uchino, Timothy W. Smith, Chrisana Olson-Cerny, Jill B. Nealey-Moore, *Health Psychology*, July 2003.

62. 'Social stressors and cardiovascular response: Influence of ambivalent relationships and behavioral ambivalence', Julianne Holt-Lunstad, Benjamin D. Clark, *International Journal of Psychology*, September 2014.

63. Holt-Lunstad et al., 2007 'On the Importance of Relationship Quality: The Impact of Ambivalence in Friendships on Cardiovascular Functioning', Julianne Holt-Lunstad, Bert Uchino, Timothy W. Smith, Angela M. Hicks, *Annals of Behavioral Medicine*, June 2007.

64. 'Social Relationships and Health: Is Feeling Positive, Negative, or Both (Ambivalent) about your Social Ties Related to Telomeres?' Bert N. Ucino, Richard M. Cawthon, Timothy W. Smith, Kathleen C. Light, Justin McKenzie, McKenzie Carlisle, Heather Gunn, Wendy Birmingham, Kimberly Bowen, *Health Psychology*, November 2012.

65. *How to Fail: Everything I've Ever Learned From Things Going Wrong* by Elizabeth Day (HarperCollins, 2019) includes a chapter on 'How to Fail at Babies'.

66. https://extendfertility.com/extend-fertility-research-egg-freezing-success-rates-one-cycle/#:~:text=Number%20of%20eggs%20frozen%20per%20cycle&text=Our%20analysis%20demonstrated%20that%20a,freeze%20half%20that%2C%20or%20less

67. https://theconversation.com/ancient-greece-has-
    something-to-say-about-the-three-person-baby-debate-
    37121

68. Brené Brown speaking to Oprah Winfrey on *Super Soul
    Sunday*, August 2013.

69. https://www.you.co.uk/elizabeth-day-what-not-to-say-about-
    my-miscarriage/

70. *Motherhood*, Sheila Heti, Vintage, 2018.

71. https://www.thecourier.co.uk/fp/politics/scottish-politics/
    1658545/the-politicization-of-mumsnet-never-mind-the-
    biscuits/

72. https://www.stephenongpin.com/artist/237018/ludolf-
    bakhuizen

73. https://rkd.nl/en/explore/artists/3414

74. https://www.sothebys.com/en/articles/for-the-love-of-art-
    alain-de-botton-on-art-as-therapy

75. *My Stroke of Insight*, Jill Bolte Taylor, Hodder & Stoughton,
    2009.

76. *Selected Poems*, Rumi, translated by Coleman Barks, Penguin
    Classics, 2004.

77. *The Other Side of the Stars*, Clemency Burton-Hill, Headline,
    2007.

78. https://datareportal.com/reports/digital-2022-global-
    overview-report

79. 'The Strength of Weak Ties', Mark S. Granovetter, *American
    Journal of Sociology*, May 1973.

80. https://www.findapsychologist.org/parasocial-relationships-
    the-nature-of-celebrity-fascinations/#:~:text=Parasocial%20
    relationships%20are%20one%2Dsided,sports%20
    teams)%20or%20television%20stars

81. https://www.newscientist.com/definition/dunbars-
    number/#:~:text=The%20rule%20of%20150&text=This%20
    is%20what%20is%20known,basic%20military%20
    unit%2C%20the%20company

82. https://www.ft.com/content/29881680-7b3d-11e4-87d4-00144feabdc0

83. https://bigthink.com/neuropsych/dunbars-number/

84. https://www.theatlantic.com/family/archive/2021/05/robin-dunbar-explains-circles-friendship-dunbars-number/618931/

85. 'How Many Hours Does It Take To Make A Friend?' by Jeffrey A. Hall, *Journal of Social and Personal Relationships*, March 2018.

86. I go into this anecdote in more excruciating detail in my previous book, *How to Fail: Everything I've Ever Learned From Things Going Wrong* (HarperCollins, 2019).

87. Intriguingly, when Nigel Slater came on my podcast, *How to Fail*, in 2019, one of his three chosen failures was that he was 'a terrible friend'. He said: 'I think friendship, good friendship, it should be more about giving than receiving. And I think I receive a lot more than I give. My friends are so wonderful I cannot tell you. They are the most important things in my life and I suspect that they would probably do anything for me. Now, I like to think I would do that for them. So if somebody phones up and says, "We need to talk. I've got to talk to you about something." I'm there. I'm a good listener. If somebody says, "Shall we go out for dinner?" Yes, absolutely, I'm there in a heartbeat. But if they ask me to do something that I actually didn't want to do ... So, for instance, the words from hell: "I'm having a dinner party, would you like to come? Please come." "Oh, please come to my wedding." "I'm throwing a party, you've got to come, you're a big part of my life." No I don't. I will not do anything I don't want to do.' The straightforward way in which he stated this was so liberating. I would now count Nigel as one of my friends, but we barely ever see each other, and this doesn't detract from our mutual affection so much as add to it by the bucketload. (It was actually a miracle he was even at that summer party, given his dislike of big groups of people).

88. https://www.ons.gov.uk/peoplepopulationandcommunity/ crimeandjustice/bulletins/onlinebullyinginenglandandwales/ yearendingmarch2020

89. 'Social networking sites and our lives', Keith N. Hampton, Lauren Sessions Goulet, Lee Rainie, Kristen Purcell, *Pew Research Center*, June 2011.

90. 'Social media use and friendship closeness in adolescents' daily lives: An experience sampling study', J. Loes Pouwels, Patti M. Valkenburg, Ine Beyens, Irene I. van Driel, Loes Keijsers, *Developmental Psychology*, February 2021.

91. https://forge.medium.com/social-media-can-have-a-positive-effect-on-friendship-2c675c8ef2d0

92. 'Social support, depressive symptoms, and online gaming network communication' Tyler Prochnow, Megan S. Patterson, Logan Hartnell, *Mental Health and Social Inclusion*, January 2020.

93. *Connecting in College: How Friendship Networks Matter for Academic and Social Success*, Janice M. McCabe, The University of Chicago Press, 2016.

94. 'Psychosocial Outcomes Associated with Engagement with Online Chat Systems', Linda K. Kaye, Sally Quinn, *International Journal of Human–Computer Interaction*, May 2019.

95. https://metro.co.uk/2019/07/03/whatsapp-can-powerful-effect-mental-health-doctors-say-10109149/

96. *Paradise City*, Elizabeth Day, Bloomsbury, 2015.

97. Reader, the man in question is now her husband.

98. https://www.verywellmind.com/what-is-attachment-theory-2795337

99. https://nypost.com/2020/03/09/this-is-how-long-most-people-know-someone-before-they-consider-them-a-best-friend/

100. 'How to Survive This Absurd Life with Samantha Irby' An episode from the *We Can Do Hard Things* podcast, 30 June

2022 https://podcasts.apple.com/us/podcast/how-to-survive-this-absurd-life-with-samantha-irby/id1564530722?i=1000568222443

101. 'Close Friendship Strength and Broader Peer Group Desirability as Differential Predictors of Adult Mental Health', Rachel K. Narr, Joseph P. Allen, Joseph S. Tan, Emily L. Loeb, *Child Development*, August 2017.

102. https://www.thecut.com/2017/09/why-having-a-best-friend-is-good-for-your-health.html

103. 'The Presence of a Best Friend Buffers the Effects of Negative Experiences', Ryan E. Adams, Jonathan Bruce Santo, William M. Bukowski, *Developmental Psychology*, September 2011.

104. *Anne of Green Gables*, L. M. Montgomery, L. C. Page & Co., 1908, chapter 15.

105. Ibid, chapter 128.

106. The Friendship Report, Snapchat, 2019.

107. https://news.gallup.com/businessjournal/127043/friends-social-wellbeing.aspx

108. https://www.macrotrends.net/countries/WLD/world/life-expectancy

109. *The Gay Science*, Friedrich Nietzsche, translated by Walter Kaufmann, Vintage, 1974.

110. *Bereavement: Studies of Grief in Adult Life*, Dr Colin Murray Parkes, Penguin, 1972.

ACKNOWLEDGEMENTS

The first and most obvious thank you has to go to my friends. As identified in the previous pages, I am lucky enough to have many wonderful, kind, loyal people in my life but to name you all individually would require another book. I hope you know who you are, and I hope you know how grateful I am for your presence in my life. I'd also like to thank the friends with whom I'm no longer in touch, for whatever reason: you taught me a lot and I think of you with fondness.

Thank you to my agent Nelle Andrew for drawing this idea out of me. It was Nelle who took me for a lockdown walk one day and asked me what I was passionate about. After saying 'cats', I landed on 'friendship' and that was the start of it all. Nelle, thank you for always having my back, for your tireless work ethic and your exceptional accessorising.

Thank you to Michelle Kane. You are an editor of extraordinary insight and talent. I feel so hashtag blessed that our paths crossed, and that we are walking this journey together – in books and in life. Here's to many years ahead of falling in the gutter after too many margaritas.

ACKNOWLEDGEMENTS

Naomi Mantin: you are the best publicist I have ever worked with but so much more than that too. Thank you for always seeing me and for being so indescribably lovely, even when I send a 10-minute ranting voice note. Liv Marsden, digital supremo, thank you for your creative ideas and for indulging my TikTok obsessions.

Thank you to everyone at 4th Estate who has been involved in bringing *Friendaholic* into the world. I am incredibly fortunate to be published by you. Thank you specifically to Katy Archer, Amber Burlinson, Paul Erdpresser, Bethan Moore and Petra Moll. For the fun nights out and the tall man hugs, a special thank you to David Roth-Ey and Charlie Redmayne. The exceptional cover design is by the brilliant Jo Thomson.

Thank you to Beatrice Kight, Alex Fane, Serena Brett and Jacob Beecham for keeping my life (and me) together.

Thank you to Emma Reed-Turrell: meeting you was – and continues to be – utterly life-changing in all the best ways. Thank you for showing me what friendship really means.

Thank you to everyone who spoke to me while writing this book, especially Joan Harrison, Sathnam Sanghera, Sharmaine Lovegrove, Clemency Burton-Hill, Francesca Segal and Alice Patten. Sathnam, I know you hate sentimentality so just look away now: I love you all so much.

Thank you to Daisy Harrison and Raymond Gilmore for having me to stay at Bloodyburn when I needed to finish the manuscript – what a special time that was.

Thank you to Rosie Beaumont-Thomas for your fantastic research skills and to Andrew Lumsden, Kyla Harris,

Libby Hall, Mark Ford, Paula Akpan, Ray Winder, Sally Al-Roubaie, Sara Gulamali, Danielle Bayard Jackson and my honorary godson Wilkie Bobin for trusting me with your stories.

Thank you to my parents, Tom and Christine, for letting me rave about Cicero over FaceTime and for countless other acts of generosity and love.

Finally, thank you to Justin Basini. Being married to a friendaholic isn't always easy but I love you for understanding why I am this way. Thank you for your consistent love, support and thoughtfulness. Thank you for being my husband – but also for being my friend.